The Whitby and Pickering ~~gh~~ Railway

from

Early Victorian Guides

And the Lives and Times of the People who Designed, Built, and Travelled on the Line until 1865.

Edited by

Gordon Bell

BLACKTHORN PRESS

Blackthorn Press, Blackthorn House
Middleton Rd, Pickering YO18 8AL
United Kingdom

www.blackthornpress.com

ISBN 978 0 9546300 4 1

Printed and bound by CPI Antony Rowe, Eastbourne

For the benefactors, members and volunteers, past and present, of the Whitby Literary and Philosophical Society and the North York Moors Historical Railway Trust.

 also by Gordon Bell

Theakston's (1841) Illustrated Guide to Scarborough. Blackthorn Press 2002

H B Carter & Sons: Victorian Watercolour Drawing and the Art of Illustration. Blackthorn Press 2006

Whitby
From a Drawing by Geo. Weatherill, 1843

CONTENTS

FOREWORD

HE AIM OF THIS BOOK HAS BEEN TO delve into the story of how the Whitby and Pickering Railway came into being. It tries to trace the people and personalities that made it happen and assemble some reminders of the world they lived in.

The story centres on the early years when Whitby largely depended on shipbuilding and whaling, timber and stone, and Pickering was mainly a town of farmers, their families, and their workers. It tries to reveal some clues as to how these towns got a railway at a time when many other places did not. It explores the days when horses worked the line and tries to uncover what it was like when George Stephenson, Robert Stephenson, and George "The Railway King" Hudson got involved.

Recapturing the past means trying to hear the voices of those who have left some trace of their thoughts and feelings. This is why those who lived at the time inform the various parts of the unfolding picture. There is the voice of an anonymous "Townsman" who addresses his fellow citizens as they discussed building a rail-road. There are the thoughts of the solicitor who steered his way through the competing claims of landowners, investors, and engineers. There are the ideas of a travelling doctor who passed by and tells us about the medical benefits of journeys on railways. We share the observations of the writer who saw the line being built and who tells us about what happened on the day it was opened. We hear about an excursion in the opposite direction, travelling from Scarborough to Whitby and we meet the artist who drew the scenery on the line in the summer of 1835. These will be our early Victorian guides.

Meeting the artist of the line, George Haydock Dodgson, and hearing about his life through the letters and family papers of his direct descendant, will take us into the world of railway artists, engravers, and their publishers. These are the people who made the woodcuts and engravings that illustrate the various chapters that follow, showing us how the early railways looked when first built. Through the books they illustrated, we can find out about what was happening in other parts of the country as the idea of "travelling engines" and railways spread and help us to probe the exploits of George Hudson in Whitby and Pickering as he brought steam locomotives to link these towns with Scarborough and York.

Our story ends where Stephenson's machine for overcoming the steepest part of the line is by-passed, enabling the first steam locomotive to travel directly to Whitby from Pickering.....but, not quite. A brief history of what happened next brings us up to the present day pleasures of the North Yorkshire Moors railway.

ACKNOWLEDGEMENTS

I have been greatly assisted by numerous people, especially the historians and authors of the various sources listed in the final pages. I particularly wish to thank Alan Avery, Alan Hinton, Anne Dennier, Arthur Credland, Christiane Kroebel, Edna Hinton, Hugh Dodgson, Ian Beckett, Jill Dalladay, Joe Robinson, John Rushton, Mark Edwards, Mary Patterson, Roger Dalladay, Rosemary Bowman and the staff of Buckinghamshire Military Museum, the North Yorkshire Libraries at Whitby, Pickering, and Scarborough, Whitby Literary and Philosophical Society, Pannett Art Gallery, Ken Hoole Study Centre, Paul Mellon Centre for British Art, North Yorkshire Moors Railway, and the National Railway Museum.

Gordon Bell
Thornton-Le-Dale
North Yorkshire
April 2008

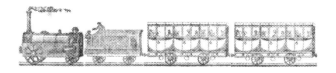

CHAPTER 1

BY RAIL FROM WHITBY TO PICKERING

A "New-Fangled Road" from Whitby into the Interior

HERE WERE MANY PLACES IN BRITAIN that did not get a railway as quickly as Whitby and Pickering. Why therefore were these two small and isolated towns, one on the Yorkshire coast and the other over twenty miles inland, able to create one of the first passenger lines in the country? And when we consider that so many other railways have not survived, the fact that the Whitby and Pickering railway still flourishes today carries with it the seeds of its own beginnings and the keys to its past.

To unravel this story, we need to enter the worlds of the people most closely involved. Who were they? How did they make this remarkable achievement possible? To do this, we shall encounter some first hand accounts of those who were living at the time and some reminders of the everyday life and times of those who seized the opportunities and took the risks.

The period we are entering, are the years following the wars with France. These were the years that launched a single track, horse-drawn rail-road that transformed itself into the steam railway that is our legacy today. Our particular journey, however, ends when Whitby bade farewell to some of the greatest railway pioneers of the Victorian age, marked in 1859 by the death of the town's M P, Robert Stephenson.

Our story begins at the turn of the nineteenth century. Pickering, and to a lesser extent Whitby, were having great difficulties in transporting goods and people to the main centres of population. Meanwhile, new towns and cities were mushrooming through opportunities for employment and improved access by roads and canals. Between 1801 and 1821, the population of Britain rose from approximately ten to fourteen million. Much of this growth took place in the newly industrialised towns and cities.

The need for change became obvious and urgent. George Stephenson's experiments to use steam power for moving coal and improving travel generally offered a tempting solution. He showed how just one "iron or steam horse" could do the work of many horses or oxen. It could by-pass roads (and their tolls) that in the winter became yet more dangerous, crowded and slow, and offered a speedy alternative to hauling heavy goods by carts. A radical re-organisation of trade beckoned by making a rail-road from Whitby to Pickering.

The prime movers in creating one of the oldest passenger lines in the country were investors in the locality and entrepreneurs from outside. Both groups came together at a decisive time. Who were these people and how did they meet?

The key players were engineers like George Stephenson who masterminded the famous Stockton and Darlington Railway nearby, his son Robert, and Henry Belcher, an enlightened local solicitor who championed the project. Financial expertise came from the Chapman banking family who also provided the first elected Whitby M P, and from the Campions, including Margaret Campion who can lay claim to being one of the first women bankers. Her son, Robert, erected the landmark monument to Captain Cook on the Cleveland Hills, to mention but one of his many literary and social activities. Both Robert Campion and his son John became directors of the Whitby and Pickering Railway.

The Challenge of Change

The main thrust finally came from members of the newly formed Whitby Literary and Philosophical Society. Fourteen of the twenty-five promoters of the Company that launched the line were also members of the Society. This venerable institution played a crucial role in the railway's development and still flourishes today with an unbroken history from its foundation in January 1823.

The Society was part of a movement already established in the region at Newcastle, Leeds, Hull, and York. Its main aims were to seek improvement through learning and to form a museum which;

> "will furnish the youth of Whitby and the vicinity with some pleasing subjects for study, and sources of amusement; it will prove a valuable repository, where interesting objects in nature and art, which might otherwise be lost, may be preserved to future generations: it will benefit the town by becoming an object of attraction for strangers, particularly literary characters, whose enquiries into the nature of our rocks and petrifactions it will greatly facilitate: and it will thus add to the respectability of Whitby, and make it rank higher among the Towns which promote literature and the arts"

2

To the modern eye, some of the early exhibits offer a disconcerting glimpse of the cultural values of their day. Amongst items in the "Department of Miscellaneous Curiosities" were;

"a piece of granite from the Great Pyramid...elephant's tail from Africa.... fragments of a knitting needle shivered to pieces by lightning.... ball of hair from the stomach of a calf...models of a Chinese lady's leg and foot, with a shoe,...and a New Zealand chief's head, beautifully tattooed." (The latter was returned in the early 20th century.)

However, the real influence of the Society was the opportunity it provided for discussion and debate. It created a melting pot of commercial and intellectual interests for its overwhelmingly male well-to-do members. Membership grew from forty-six founders in 1823 to one hundred and twenty eight in 1850. The Society hosted a particularly significant debate in March 1831 when its members discussed alternative routes for a proposed railway.

Several of the Society's members were also associated with a rich array of monthly periodicals appearing from 1825 onwards. These publications offered an outlet for railway supporters and opponents to air their views. A contribution to *The Whitby Repository, and Monthly Miscellany: Religious, Sentimental, Literary, and Scientific* – to give it its fulsome title, provides us with a flavour of the debate that finally launched the scheme for a railway from Whitby to Pickering. (see below)

The Idea of a Rail-road: Pros and Cons

Writing under a nom-de-plume in the *Whitby Repository*, "The Hermit of Eskdaleside" declares;

"a few searching questions, each pregnant with a negative and affirmative, will be offered to the consideration of those who are alive to the progress of moral, intellectual and physical improvement.... Of that isolated territory of which Whitby, socially speaking, is the centre and the capital.... Those who fail to observe how comparatively far behind Whitby is in literature, science, art, philosophy, and those pursuits and acquirements which adorn a country, refine its inhabitants, and indicate a high state of civilization, must possess limited visions, or be hoodwinked by local prejudices and affections."

Overleaf is a selection from the original list of fifty questions. They not only open up a window on the citizens of Whitby as they debated building a railway but also provide some interesting echoes for our own times.

3

"1. Is the population of Whitby more favourable or adverse to intellectual improvement?

2. Do the poor of Whitby consider it degrading to depend on parish relief, or manifest a disposition to seek it?

3. Are the farms in the district of Whitby managed according to the best methods of cultivation?

4. Would it be more beneficial or injurious to abolish the tolls on the turnpike between Whitby and Pickering?

5. Are parents at Whitby more alive or indifferent to the benefits derivable by children by education? ....

9. Has the education of the lower class at Whitby been perceptibly beneficial?

11. Is there reason to conclude that the population of Whitby is less depraved now than at a former period? ....

13. Have the interests of the town of Whitby been more promoted by strangers than by natives? ....

17. Does the deficient demand for labour at Whitby arise more from want of trade or want of public enterprise? ......

20. Have the maritime boroughs of England heretofore sent members to Parliament adequately qualified to represent their interests?

21. Is it probable that the dues derivable from a railway, between Whitby and the interior, would be sufficient to pay the interest of capital required for its construction? ......

23. Would the diffusion of scientific knowledge among the labouring class at Whitby, tend to advance their welfare?

25. Would commercial enterprise be more generally favourable to the prosperity of Whitby than mere navigational pursuits? .....

37. Would a canal from Whitby to Pickering, for craft of 120 tons burthen, now cost £66,447, as estimated in the year 1794?

44. Would the establishment of parish libraries for the diffusion of useful knowledge be more beneficial than injurious? .....

(The Whitby Repository, Vol. 1 No 5 1831 pp 15-20)

A variety of authors produced occasional publications in addition to periodicals and these were widely circulated. These pamphlets offer us insights into local opinion at a critical time for the formation of a railway. A particularly engaging one written by *"The Townsman"* addressed some of the questions posed above and his thoughts about a "Rail-road into the Interior" appear in the next chapter.

Whitby in the Early 19th Century

The main reasons for developing a railway were to do with boosting the local economy. Both Whitby and Pickering were under-developed and lacking support in different ways. Whitby was in decline because of its reliance on sea-faring activities. At its height, it occupied sixth position in a table of ship-owning ports but was by now gradually losing its trade and influence. At Pickering, there was a shortage of investment and a diversity of trades.

Here is a contemporary description of Whitby from *Pigot's Directory* c.1829,

"Whitby, a market-town and sea-port, in a parish of its name, and in the liberty of Whitby strand, north riding is 244 miles from London, 113 from Manchester, 47 from York, and twenty from Pickering and Scarborough....... The present town is situated on the German Ocean, near the mouth of the River Esk, over which there is a draw bridge, the ruins of Whitby Abbey forming an interesting object on the east bank of the river........During the time of the war, Whitby was a place of very great trade, principally with the Baltic and Mediterranean. The manufacture of alum in this neighbourhood is carried on extensively, and in the town are manufactured sail cloths: ship and boat building yards and roperies are here established on a large scale, and it once derived considerable importance from the Greenland fishery, but this has of late declined, and only four ships from this place are now in trade...Colonel George Cholmley is lord of the manor, and holds a court leet annually after Michaelmas, and a court of pleas for the recovery of small debts every third Monday; these courts are held in the town hall. The government of the town is in a bench of magistrates or justices for the north riding, who hold their sittings every Tuesday and Saturday at their office in Flowergate. The parish church is situated on the cliff, on the east bank of the Esk; the living is a perpetual curacy in the gift of the Archbishop of York...(there are)...six chapels belonging to the various sects of dissenters, besides one for the Roman Catholics, and a friend's meeting house. The charities in Whitby are numerous, and worthy of those surrounded by a considerable population, many of whom must look up for assistance to the benevolent and affluent; they consist principally of a seamen's hospital, which took its rise in 1676; many free schools for children of the poor, alms houses, and hospitals; several charitable societies, instituted and supported by the ladies of the town. Religious, scientific, and philosophical institutions have also taken root in this respectable town, and are supported with high credit to the founders and members. There are also newsrooms, a public library, a theatre, public baths, and a well-stored museum. The hills near Whitby to the south and west are wild and unfavourable, but the vale of Esk & the dales that open into it are fertile & pleasant, as is the country immediately adjacent to the town. The coast is bold and dramatic, and much picturesque scenery occurs in the neighbourhood."

John Hugill, bailiff to the lord of the manor and prominent member of the Whitby Literary and Philosophical Society, wrote a seventy page *Address to the Inhabitants of Whitby* in 1830. In his address, he laments the poor state of shipbuilding as its main industry, the closure of alum works in the district, the "unprecedently distressed" situation for agriculture, and the "appalling condition of the whale–fishery".

In Hugill's day, when four or five whales had been landed, the whalers of Whitby were considered "well-fished". At their most successful, such vessels were averaging catches of fifteen whales. However, with the advent of gaslight instead of whale oil and increased use of soft stays for garments instead of whalebone, trade dramatically declined. A similar reduction in shipbuilding from a peak of around twenty ships annually occurred due mainly to the ending of the Napoleonic wars in 1815.

Alum quarries processing local shales, arguably Britain's first chemical industry, had been developed in the Whitby area since Elizabethan times. Alum, extensively used in fixing dyes and preparing leather, was shipped in large quantities from Whitby (together with its by-product Epsom salt) and from many nearby staithes and landing points on the coast. The alum industries employed around 600 people as part-time workers with one of the largest sites being just three miles away at Sandsend. Urine, used in processing alum, arrived at the alum works in barrels collected from Whitby streets.

However, with new and more efficient means of production elsewhere, the price per ton of alum halved from £20 to £10 between 1816 and 1839. From the time of the first thoughts of a railway into the "interior", this industry went into a decline from which it never recovered.

Whitby Shops and Businesses c.1823

A more detailed overview of life in Whitby can be found in *Baines Directory* of 1823. The Directory records 88 "gentry" – around half of which were women. Its listing of trades and services provides a revealing picture of the town on the brink of building its railway. A selection is shown below together with the total number of each of the main groups.

" 17 Academies, 6 Attorneys, 3 Bacon and Ham factors, 16 Bakers, Bread, and Ship Biscuits &c., 5 Banks, 3 Block, Mast and Pump Makers, 3 Boat Builders, 25 Boot and Shoemakers, 3 Brass and Iron Founders, 8 Braziers and Tinsmiths, 14 Butchers, 16 Cabinet Makers and Upholsterers, 15 House and Ship Carpenters, 2 Carvers and Gilders, 4 Clog and Pattern Makers, 4 Coopers, 4 Corn Millers and Factors, 3 Curriers and Leather Cutters, 10 Fire & Life Insurance Office Agents, 9 Flax Dressers, 37 Grocers and Tea Dealers, 7 Hat Manufacturers and Dealers, 49 Hotels, Inns and Taverns, 4 Lightermen, 37 Master Mariners, 12 Milliners and Dress Makers," etc.

Whitby from the Mount showing the railway station and West Cliff developments c. 1860

An engraving from Thomas Roscoe's "London and Birmingham Railway" c.1839 heralding the demise of the stage-coach industry through railway competition.

Three stage-coaches provided services to York, Sunderland, and Scarborough. Vessels left for Newcastle, London, and Hull and eventually a Steam Packet plied between Edinburgh and London. "Land Carriages" regularly served many local towns and villages including Pickering and York - in a fashion. The main road into "the interior" was subject to tolls and identified in the case presented to Parliament for a railway in 1833 as a major obstacle. Referring to the proposed railway as "an undertaking of great general utility", the case in support went on to outline Whitby's potential for trade; "these natural and important advantages are in great measure lost for want of good inland communication…..the present… (turnpike road)…has long been justly reprobated….(as)… precipitous ….and much dreaded."

All of these Whitby trades, services, and businesses served a population of around 10,600 people in 1823. In the following year, Rev. George Young (1777-1848) published the first edition of his *"Picture of Whitby"*. His account of the "Streets of Whitby" provides a vivid portrait of their appearance. He notes that, "the first sash window was put up in 1725 and both town and country gazed at it as a prodigy". He goes on to comment on more "modern improvements";

With all these improvements, the streets of Whitby are still inferior to those of many other towns. Most of the lower and older streets are so deficient in breadth, as not to admit any foot-paths on the sides and the streets, though generally well paved, are not always well swept; an evil which is the more felt as we have no street lamps……The crowded state of almost all the older parts of the town, may be considered as another blemish. Not only are the streets narrow, but all the garths and back-yards, the tofts and half tofts of former ages, are crammed with houses, having only narrow yards or openings communicating with the street……The houses in Whitby are generally well built, especially the front houses; but as they are almost all constructed with brick and covered with red tiles, the town, when viewed as a whole, has that glaring appearance which is not conducive to beauty. The taste of the public in this respect appears to be altering for the better, several houses lately being built of stone and covered with slate.

Rev. G Young. *Picture of Whitby.* 1824.

Pickering in the Early 19th Century

By contrast, Pickering had about a quarter of Whitby's population. The main difference in the *Baines Directory* for Pickering when compared with Whitby for the same year (1823), is its largely agricultural character with thirty "farmers" listed. At the foot of the town, close to the railway station, William Marshall (1745-1818) planned England's first Agricultural College at Beck Isle. Most appropriately, it is now a noted museum of rural life in Ryedale.

Pickering's twelve "shopkeepers" can be compared with thirty-five at Whitby. In similar proportion were 7:37 "Grocers and Tea Dealers", 12:49 "Hotels, Inns and Taverns", and 3:9 "Surgeons". At the top of the marketplace were the town's shambles prominently placed below the steps leading to the Norman church. Here, the six butchers of the town slaughtered three bullocks a week. The town stocks stood on the north side. Each of these features provided a stark reminder of the material and spiritual character of everyday life.

Pigot's Directory c.1828 has this to say about Pickering;

"Pickering, an ancient market-town….. in the north riding, is 222 miles from London, 92 from Manchester, 26 from York, 8 from New Malton, and about 6 from Kirkby Moorside. This town is recorded to be of great antiquity, being said to have been built by Peridurus, a king of the Britons, 270 years before the birth of Christ, and to have derived its name from the circumstances of that prince losing his ring, when washing in the River Costa, which was afterwards found in the belly of a pike. It is situated on the verge of the mountainous regions of Blake or Black Moors, and crossed at the bottom by a small river or brook called Pickering Beck which in addition to the other romantic beauties that Pickering possesses, gives a great degree of pleasing and picturesque beauty to the town. The remains of Pickering castle are still to be seen standing, on the brow of a hill, at the end of the town, not far from the church………in this castle Richard II, was confined for some time previous to being sent to Pontefract, where he was murdered. A large square tower is now remaining, called Queen Elizabeth's tower, from a tradition that she was confined here during the reign of Queen Mary. Pickering was formerly the principal town in the district, and Scarborough, though now of much more importance was in its wapentake. It formerly sent a member to Parliament, which privilege it is said to have lost, from failing to pay its representatives their expenses, which in those days were allowed them. A court leet is held in the castle on Mondays after Lady-day and Michaelmas, in which small debts are sued for. The government of the town is vested in a constable and magistrate, appointed at the quarter sessions for the north riding. The parish church, which is dedicated to St Peter, is an ancient and spacious building with a fine lofty spire; the benefice of the Dean of York......... Here are besides a chapel each for the Wesleyan, Independent and primitive Methodists and Quakers have a meeting house. Great quantities of brooms are made in the town and neighbourhood, the materials for the manufacture of the article being obtained from the contiguous moors. Upon the River Costa (which rises at Kildhead) are two large flour mills, and upon the Old Beck stream are three others, all within a mile of the town."

The high point of the year in agricultural districts like Pickering, were the annual hirings fairs. Lasting for upwards of a week, the fairs provided the chief means of seeking work. At a peak in 1851, it was estimated that there were 1,284,000 male farm workers and over 199,000 females working in agriculture in England. An arable farm, for example would typically employ between six and twenty ploughboys together with other farm servants either living in the farmhouse or in tied cottages.

At the hirings, those with particular skills would stand in lines with distinguishing items, waggoners with whipcord around their hats, shepherds holding crooks, thatchers with fragments of straw etc. In nearby Malton, the hirings fair in 1867 attracted an estimated 10.000 men and 3,500 women seeking employment.

This traditional means of hiring agricultural workers, dating back to the 16th century, was a source of irritation and concern for the moral improvers. Agitation by clergy of the Church of England assisted in influencing their eventual regulation. The most important "Martinmas" hirings were held each November - at Pickering on the Monday before November 22nd. Clergyman, Rev. M. Morris writing in 1892 describes East and North Ridings hirings as follows;

" this institution was one of the curses of the country.........they take place at the worst possible time of the year. St Martin's Day is on November 23rd, and the days are then about at their shortest and darkest, and the roads at their dirtiest.... St Martin may be considered to be the patron saint of East Yorkshire farm-servants; but it is to be feared they lightly regard his name...(it)...was the season for the lads and lasses to change their 'spots' as they called their situations, and it was the occasion for a general holiday and merry-making.... It would be hard *to describe a hiring day ...... such scenes of riot and disorder were they .... A kind of slave market .... (with) ... entertainments .... Cheap Jacks and quacks carried on a brisk trade: shooting-galleries and Punch and Judy were attractions to not a few, and shows of fat women, wild beasts, one eyed and six legged monsters, and all manner of horrors were literally besieged by uproarious crowds of claimants for admission, till the places fairly reeked .... The public houses were also unfortunately also crammed almost to suffocation....(it was).. a sad sight. boys and girls, lads and lasses, men and women were crowded together in the parlours and passages of the inns in a state of wild excitement, uproar, and confusion. Music, if such it could be called, and dancing went on merrily; coarse jests were freely indulged in; and songs of every description were bawled out in solo and chorus, and shouts of approval rent the air .... There is no class so difficult to deal with as the farm-servants engaged under the Martinmas system."*

A Timeline of Local Events

c.1747	James Cook trained as a seaman at Whitby
c.1753-1837	Whitby actively involved in Greenland Whale Fishery
1748-1822	Fishburn and Broderick, Whitby Shipbuilders of Cook's *Endeavour*
1753	Francis Nicholson, watercolour artist born in Pickering
1760	Turnpike Toll Road opened from Pickering to Whitby
1781-1861	Improvements to Whitby Harbour
1785	Simpson and Chapman Bank opened at Whitby
1789-1857	William Scoresby Jr, arctic mariner and scientist born at Cropton
1802	Whitby's first lifeboat
1803	George Chambers, marine painter born in Whitby
1810	George Weatherill, Whitby and Pickering Railway clerk and Whitby watercolour artist born
1818	William Marshall , agricultural researcher and writer died at Pickering
1819	Whitby Parish Church enlarged
1823	Whitby Literary and Philosophical Society founded; Rev.George Young, local historian and Hon. Secretary (1823-1848)
1830	Collapse of tower at Whitby Abbey
1833-5	New Whitby harbour bridge
1836	Railway opened to Pickering
c.1843	Hudson's proposals for development of the West Cliff, Whitby
1845	New railway station at Pickering; line extended to Scarborough and York
1845	Institute of Popular Science and Literature founded at Whitby
c. 1850	John Dobson's Royal Crescent, Whitby
1853	Frank Meadow Sutcliffe, pioneer photographer of Whitby, born in Leeds
1871	Launch of last wooden sailing vessel at Turnbull's yard and launch of first screw steamer
c.1871	Closure of Alum works at Sandsend

The State of England

Before looking in more detail at the building of the railway and some of its personalities and politics, it may be useful to consider the broader background. What was going on in the country at large at this time? If we think about the period around fifty years before the line was built and around thirty years afterwards, what was happening? How can we enter the world of the directors of the Whitby and Pickering Railway Company, the Stephensons, Henry Belcher and his friends in the Whitby Literary and Philosophical Society, "The Townsman", and the writers of Pigot's Directory?

The years between c.1780 and 1865 have been termed "The Age of Improvement". Key improvements took place in agriculture through new farming and land management methods. Trades and crafts were transformed by mechanization and steam power, the expanding canal system, regular post and coach services, the development of roads and the introduction of public railways.

In social affairs, a concern for moral and material improvement brought about a ferment of reform and conflict. Wars with France, America, China and Russia, an Act of Union of the Irish and British Parliaments, the extension of Catholic civil rights, the abolition of slavery, first steps towards a fully representative democracy, universal schooling, and the founding of civic universities are but a few of the momentous events at this time.

Proposals for a Whitby to Pickering railway emerged when the effects of improvements and reforms were creating dramatic changes in power and influence. The years following the French Revolution and Napoleonic Wars were a time of working class unrest. They have been described as a 'challenge to order' and summarised as a preoccupation with 'Cash, Corn and Catholics'. Several of the newly industrialised northern cities, especially Manchester, were in a turbulent and unstable condition witnessing riots, strikes and the savage suppression of protest. Whilst economic concerns amongst all classes can be identified as the main cause of conflict, an underlying loathing of corruption was finding increasingly overt means of expression amongst workers in the towns and cities. It was not until 1825 that an upturn in trade and industry restored relative stability. It proved to be a temporary lull. Agitation for reform continued. The Catholic Emancipation Act was carried in 1829 making changes to the electorate in Irish counties possible and enabling Catholics to sit as MP's and hold most public offices.

The significance of corn as an issue was that a law had been passed in 1815 that was designed to protect and regulate its price in the interests of landowners. The 'price of bread' both literally and metaphorically went to the heart of the rural and increasingly urban communities' existence. Rumbling disquiet persisted until 1846 when the Corn Laws were repealed.

This victory for free trade captured the spirit of the times, a mood mirrored in free enterprise for railway development. Ironically, one of the most prominent supporters of railways and free trade, William Huskisson (1770-1830) was fated to be among the first passengers to be killed in a railway accident. The circumstances of his death at the opening of the Liverpool and Manchester Railway in 1830 has tended to obscure his achievements as a leading statesman when President of the Board of Trade, Secretary of State, and Leader of the House of Commons. As an economic expert, he made a major contribution to creating a climate in which railways and free enterprise might flourish.

Freedom of Ideas

A further form of freedom was also being progressively championed; the freedom of ideas. Increasingly vocal demands from reformers to expand educational opportunities came to the forefront of debate. The ensuing struggle was prolonged and bitter as it went to the core of class attitudes to authority, hierarchy, and territory. The interests of competing religions made this potent mix yet more volatile. The formation of the Whitby Literary and Philosophical Society is a key example of a practical response to these issues demonstrating the commitments and liberal values of its members.

Another way of considering background influences on the townsfolk of Whitby and Pickering during the debate about a railway is to recall some key terms in use at the time. A significant discussion focused around the idea of "estates". War with France was about the proper place of the three "Estates of the Realm"- the first estate (in France) being the clergy, the second comprising the nobility, and the third encompassing "commoners". In England, these terms were adapted to define "Lords Temporal, Lords Spiritual, and Commons".

Thomas Carlyle (1795-1881) reflects in his highly influential *On Heroes and Hero Worship* (1841) on Edmund Burke's (1729-97) views on limiting the authority of the King, the idea of a representative democracy, and the role of political parties. He comments that, "Edmund Burke said....there were three Estates in Parliament, but in the Reporters' Gallery yonder, there sat a fourth Estate more important than they all" – a telling prediction of our world today. Edmund Burke, radical philosopher and leading politician was MP for the neighbouring town of Malton near Pickering from 1780 to 1794.

Talk of 'estates' (from Old French meaning 'status'), was particularly apt in another sense for by the latter half of the 19th century it was estimated that in England, 363 individuals each owned 10,000 acres of land. Taking England and Wales together, approximately 4,000 persons owned half the land. The situation in previous decades would have been little different. Landed property owners held most offices in government, obtained commissions in the army and navy, determined the appointment of lesser clergy, and not infrequently ensured preferment for members of their family and friends. Most public offices, titles, and honours were available for purchase and many became virtually hereditary.

All of these factors would undoubtedly have shaped the interests and decisions of those most closely involved in proposing a railway from Whitby to Pickering.

Towards a Modern Democracy

Although business entrepreneurs in the newly developing industries were making fortunes, they could not rival the influence of landowners in wealth, power, or prestige. As Members of Parliament were unpaid apart from receiving "expenses", they had of necessity to be wealthy. Nevertheless, in the 1820's, as two thirds of the constituencies were under the direct influence of a landowner - usually a peer, wealth alone was not sufficient. For example, seven peers influenced the election of fifty-one MP's and a quarter of the House of Commons came under the control of peers or sons of peers. Violence and corruption regularly accompanied elections when contested and a goodly proportion went uncontested. Between 1832 and 1850, sixty-nine results of elections were set aside because of corruption.

Whilst the dominance of the landowners was not complete, the parliamentary agenda reflected their interests. The intense attention paid to the Game Laws is a telling example. Armed poaching attracted seven years transportation and between 1827 and 1830, one in seven of all criminal convictions were made under the Game Laws.

Aristocratic families were not the only landowners. The established church (by 1801, the "United Church of England and Ireland") was a major landed property owner also. Before the later reforms, some Bishops had incomes greater than government ministers. The Bishop of Durham for example had a living worth £19,000 per year when ministers received £5,000. However, both figures are generous when compared with three hundred parish clergy each receiving £50 per annum.

The continuing influence of the Church of England on government is shown by grants for church building. In 1818, these amounted to £1m followed by a further £0.5m six years later. Between 1800 and 1850, in excess of 2,500 churches were built. Meanwhile, without such support, over 16,000 Methodist chapels were constructed over the same period.

The restrictions on opportunity extended most severely to Roman Catholics and Protestant Non Conformists – the "Dissenters" as they were called. Until 1829, Roman Catholics could not become a Member of Parliament or Justice of the Peace, vote in British elections, or take a seat in the House of Lords. Dissenters were also nominally barred from holding public if not parish office. Unmarried women could own property but not sit as an MP or vote or go to university.

Education and the Economy

The influence of the established church on government most notably affected education. Until c.1828, there were but two English universities, Oxford and Cambridge. Church of England clergymen staffed them almost entirely and to take a degree would mean subscribing to the Thirty Nine Articles of Religion. During the 1820's a substantial proportion of around 3,000 undergraduates were destined to teach in parish and village schools, "public" or private academies, or grammar schools.

Such influence was considerably strengthened through the *The National Society for Promoting Religious Education.* Founded in 1811, it was the mainspring for providing Church of England schooling. Its mission was to found a church school in every parish in England and Wales. Its objects were;

> "that the National Religion should be made the foundation of National Education, and should be the first and chief thing taught to the poor, according to the excellent Liturgy and Catechism provided by our Church".

By 1831, there were approximately half a million children in Sunday Schools and twice that number in National Society schools. The movement towards state schooling did not take root until forty years later. Marriage registers yield a clue to prevailing levels of literacy where a third of all males and half of females used a mark in 1839.

However, the privileges of the established church were soon to be curtailed. By 1836, when the railway was fully opened, the reform of the church had begun in earnest. This was inescapable through the success of non-conformist religions. By 1850, when Bishops' incomes had been equalized, state grants modified, parish boundaries rationalised, residency requirements imposed, and restrictions introduced on clergy engaging in trades, it was estimated that half of all churchgoers were in fact dissenters.

J S Fletcher in his "Making of Modern Yorkshire" reminds us of the cultural climate around this time. He quotes from a debate in Parliament in 1847 when the prime minister proposed making a government grant of £100,000 to promote education - a miserly sum compared with the national income of around four hundred and fifty million pounds. The proposal met with customary hostility. It was countered by an impassioned address from Thomas Babington Macaulay (1800-1859), progressive politician, lawyer, and reformist writer;

"You tell us that schools will multiply and flourish exceedingly, if the government will only abstain from interfering with them. Has not the government long abstained from interfering with them? If it were true that education, like trade, thrives most where the magistrate meddles least, the common people of England would now be the best educated in the world. Our schoolmasters would be eminently expert in all that relates to teaching as our

15

cutlers, our cotton spinners, our engineers.....Is this the case?....Nearly one third of the men, and nearly one-half of the women, who are in the prime of life, who are to be the parents of the Englishmen of the next generation.......cannot write their own names.....Tens of thousands who are able to write their names have in all probability received only the wretched education of a common day-school. We know what such a school too often is; a room crusted with filth, without light, without air with a heap of fuel in one corner and a brood of chickens in the other; the only machinery of instruction a dog-eared spelling book and a broken slate; the masters, the refuse of all other callings; discarded footmen, ruined pedlars, men who cannot write a common letter without blunders, men who do not know whether the earth is a sphere or a cube, men who do not know if Jerusalem is in Asia or America. And to such men, men to whom none of us would entrust the key of his cellar, we have entrusted the mind of a rising generation and, with the mind of the rising generation the freedom, the happiness, the glory of our country"

Meanwhile, the country's economic fortunes fluctuated year-by-year. Some idea of the prevailing pattern can be gathered from the growth of three main commodities; coal, pig iron, and cotton. Between 1780 and 1830, coal production quadrupled, pig iron increased by eleven-fold and cotton by a remarkable forty-four times. Over the same period, the population grew from around ten million to sixteen million. Life expectancy appeared to vary by class and by urban or rural location. The variation ranged from thirty-five to fifty-five years for "gentlefolk" and fifteen to thirty eight years for "labourers"

Economic growth was not smooth. After the defeat of Napoleon in 1815, government expenditure halved and several hundred thousand men were demobilised. In 1825, a catastrophic recession saw the failure of approximately ninety private country banks. Poor relief tripled to six million pounds annually. However, alongside far-reaching changes brought about by the new factories and mills that spread across towns and cities, there was the remarkable rise of railways and an extraordinary movement towards reforming the conditions of everyday life.

For the inhabitants of Whitby, creeping industrialisation and the decline of traditional handcrafts created a need to look outward. New ways of using the available resources had to be found. Exploiting alum, jet, stone, and whale oil for street lighting were just some of the starting points. In Pickering, largely dominated by agricultural affairs, greater accessibility and exposure to new ideas would quicken the pace of development. In both cases, education and re-education were the keys to progress. At Whitby, a group of enlightened thinkers and planners formed themselves in a voluntary partnership to engage in both tasks. This effort was matched by capital seeking a home for investment.

A Timeline of National Events

c.1750	Beginning of the "Industrial Revolution"
1756-63	Seven-Year War with France
1760	George III becomes King
1771	Opening of first cotton mill
1775	First British Building Society
1775-1783	American War of Independence
1788	First edition of "The Times"
1792-1815	Napoleonic Wars
1797	Introduction of Income Tax
1801	Creation of the "United Kingdom"
1806	Bank of England founded
1807	First gas street lights in the world, Pall Mall, London
1811	The "Luddites" organise widespread sabotage of steam powered looms; 12,000 troops sent to Yorkshire
1812-1814	War with America
1815	Corn Laws introduced to protect British farmers
1820	George IV ascends throne
1825	Opening of Stockton and Darlington Railway
1829	Roman Catholic emancipation
1828	Duke of Wellington, Prime Minister
1830	William IV crowned King
	Liverpool to Manchester Railway opened.
1832	Parliamentary Reform
1833	Factory Act regulates working hours for women and children
1835	First elected town councils
1836	Whitby to Pickering Railway opened. (At this time there were around 400 miles of track laid; by 1871, c. 13,000 miles had been opened.)
1837	Registration of births, marriages, and deaths
1838	London to Birmingham Railway
1843-47	The years of "Railway Mania"- over 200 Acts for new railways passed.
1844	Gladstone's Railway Act defines minimum national standards
1854	Crimean War

Early Victorian Voices

To imagine what everyday life was like for a passenger on the Whitby and Pickering railway, we need to hear the voices of those who were living at the time. One such voice is Dr Augustus Bozzi Granville (1783-1872) who provides us with two commentaries. The first (below) tells us about his journey from Scarborough to Pickering in 1836 and the usefulness of the newly opened "rail-road" to which "Pickering owes its present prosperity". In chapter nine, Dr Granville outlines his views on the medical benefits of railway travelling.

17

Three years after Augustus Granville made his journey from Scarborough to Pickering, Henry Belcher recorded his experiences of the journey taking us onwards to Whitby on the railway itself. His account appears in chapter seven.

Neither writer could have envisaged how radically altered this journey would be in the space of a few more years. Yet in all likelihood, Henry Belcher would have been party to the ambitions of Stephenson and Hudson when they outlined their plans for a steam railway from York to Scarborough in the summer of 1839. He would certainly have had the vision to see the opportunities this project would bring for the directors of the Company. Moreover, given Henry Belcher's widespread influence, it seems inevitable that he would have shared confidences with George Hudson about developing Whitby as a spa and bathing place in the wake of Scarborough's example. Nevertheless, the scale and rapidity of change could scarcely have been imagined. It took seven years or more to get the Whitby and Pickering railway up and running. The York to Scarborough line, including its new branch line to Whitby via Pickering and the conversion of the original horse-drawn section to steam working, took less than half that time.

Dr Granville's Journey from Scarborough to Pickering in 1840

Dr Augustus Granville travelled through Pickering on his grand tour of *Spas of England and Principal Bathing Places*. He had practised medicine in London for twenty-three years when he embarked on his travels in the summer of 1839. The accounts of his journeys are full of personal observations and anecdotes, as these notes about his visit to Pickering and its new railway reveal;

> "*After an excellent breakfast at a neat inn at Snainton, I changed my vehicle and driver, and set off for Pickering, along an enchanting by-road; though the road itself is neither smooth nor in good condition, from the friable materials, the calcareous grit of the county, employed in making it, as well as keeping it in repair.*
>
> *The smart lad who sat by my side first pointed out to me Mr Osbaldeston's villa on our right, passing which and before reaching Allerston, I beheld on my left, from the crest of a hill, the rich champaign country, still called the Marshes, with New Malton in the distance, and Castle Howard at the foot of the Howardian hills; the whole bounded by the Wolds, south of the York road.*
>
> *Next he introduced to my notice Thornton Dale, placed in a hollow, with a trout stream crossing the road and Mr Hill's park, in the vicinity of which we chanced to meet a fair country lass travelling unattended, on horseback, in the fashion of the county. One cannot speak satisfactorily of the appearance of the several villages through which we passed. The houses of the yeomanry, built of yellow coloured stone so general throughout this oolitic district, did not give one the idea of comforts within. My quick-tongued companion alleged as a reason for it that the inmates were not in easy circumstances, owing to low wages and hard work. Being himself the son of poor farming people at Brompton in the*

The Gothic Saloon, Scarborough-replacing the Old Spa washed away in a violent storm in February 1837.

neighbourhood, he admitted that he had been kept at the school in that village, at Sir George Cayley's expense, for nearly six years, where he learned but little reading and writing, and was just able at the end of that time to manage his bible and no more. I inquired if people drank much in these parts, "Yes, a goodish little," was the answer, "And what is it they do drink?" – "Why all sort, ale and rum, and brandy, and gin, and sometimes three or four young farmers, who can afford it, will club together for a bottle of wine, and drink that instead, to be thought gentlemen like."

To the north of the market place at Pickering, an ancient broad carriage-way with the remains of a line of lofty elms, which once formed part of a great avenue, leads to one of those undulations or swells in the limestone formation, which like so many ribs, descend from north to south, down the lofty moorland into the vale of Pickering. On the summit, of one of these, the remains of Pickering Castle are still visible, though in a very dilapidated state; the walls of circumvallation, in some places lofty, and in others depressed, following the undulation of the ground, mark still the extent of the castellated territory. The view from the hill into the vale of Pickering would be exceedingly beautiful were it not for the unsightly stone fences and boundaries, which, with straight and right angular deformity, offend the eye, and have considerably spoiled in this, as in most parts of Yorkshire, the picturesque appearance of the country.

Pickering owes its present prosperity to the rail-road which placed it in immediate communication with Whitby. Its inexhaustible quarries of limestone

The Old Road and the New

would have been useless but for the new facility thus acquired of disposing of that produce, By bringing York, too, in nearer communication than before with the Port of Whitby, there being but twenty five miles of coach-road between the terminus at Pickering and the metropolitan city of the county, the German Ocean has been, as it were, approximated to the Irish sea.

Of the reality of this fact, I met with an illustration in the person of an American skipper who having put into the Port of Whitby from the Baltic, had found letters summoning him instantly to return to his native land, with or without his vessel. He had consequently left the latter in charge of his mate, and mounting one of the carriages on the single line of horse-trail to Pickering at five o'clock in the morning, reached that place in time for the coach to York, where I saw him get out and immediately enter the carriage train on the rail-road to Leeds, on which I was myself preparing to travel at the time. It was then about noon. Leeds we reached in a little more than an hour, and my hurried skipper, who had allowed himself scarcely a moment's breathing-time, took coach again as far as Littleborough, where he would arrive at four o'clock, quite in time for one of the afternoon trains on the new rail-road, which from that place conveys the traveller in three quarters of an hour to Manchester. Thence, I need not say that our transatlantic traveller intended to proceed by one of the numerous trains which leave for Liverpool, so as to reach that seaport at the expiration of an hour and a half, quite soon enough to enjoy a hearty repast, the first refreshment on that day, and ship himself off in one of the steamers, which, at the close of a long day in July, drop down the Mersey with the evening tide, ready to take advantage of the land-breeze that is to waft them into the Atlantic.

Thus a man who rose in the morning, on the eastern coast of England, his face turned towards Russia, would, ere the sun of the same day had set, be seen quitting the western coast of England, his face turned towards America. Such is one of the miracles of rail-road travelling!"

Dr A B Granville *Spas of England and Principal Bathing Places: 1: The North* - 1841

CHAPTER 2

THOUGHTS ON A RAILWAY FROM WHITBY INTO THE INTERIOR.

This publication appeared in 1831, two years before Royal Assent was given for a railway from Whitby to Pickering

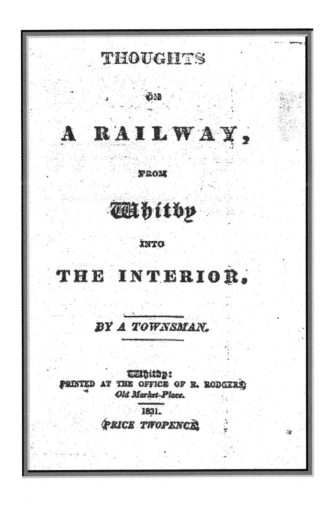

THOUGHTS

ON

A RAILWAY,

FROM

Whitby

INTO

THE INTERIOR.

BY A TOWNSMAN.

Whitby:
PRINTED AT THE OFFICE OF R. RODGERS,
Old Market-Place.
1831.
(PRICE TWOPENCE.

My Fellow Townsmen,

I believe there will need but little apology from me, for introducing to your notice any suggestion on a subject in which you are all deeply, interested— the Revival of the Trade of our Town.

Among the different plans which the pressure of our situation has elicited, that of a Railway into the interior, has held, and still continues to hold, the most prominent place.

But respecting the direction which that Railway should be carried, to secure the greatest and most durable benefit to our trade; I have reason to think considerable difference of opinion exists, even among those who have been most active in forwarding the project in general.

Having considered the subject for some time back, and, having the advantage of a good local knowledge of the district, I have not the least hesitation in expressing my decided opinion, that a Railway from here to Pickering, or the neighbourhood, with a branch on the line already surveyed, as far as Lealholm-bridge, would be both a great and immediate benefit to our town; and tend, not only to the increase of our present branches of trade, but open new channels for the employment of the dormant capital and industry of Whitby.

And first, by running into the vale of Pickering, it would secure the supply of that fertile and populous country, as far as Malton, with Timber, and other Baltic and American goods, as well as Groceries, Spirits, Wine, &c. Sea Coals, likewise, for the use of Farmers along the line, would be required to a considerable extent. The return Trade in Agricultural produce, for shipment, might also be expected to be very large.

The Trade in Lime, from Newton-Dale would alone form an important item of Revenue. By forming a Depot for that article at Lealholm Bridge, the supply, not only of the Dales, but of Scaling, Wapley, Lofthouse, and parts adjacent, would be secured; and a great quantity of Moor Coals, for burning the Lime-stone, would be carried back from the Moor Pits to Newton-Dale and Pickering.

Whinstone, from Goathland Head, would be another considerable article of traffic in both directions; upwards, from Silhoe, for the repair of the Highways at and near Pickering; and downwards, from the Quarry below Beck Hole, for shipment at Whitby, as it is clearly ascertained that large contracts for this article might be, at any time, obtained.

Freestone of different qualities, and to almost any extent, might be thus brought, at a cheap rate, for shipment, and for home use.

By the adoption of this line, Timber, from Lord Feversham's estates, in the neighbourhood of Helmsley, which now costs £2 2: a Ton, carriage, would be brought for about £1 2s making a reduction in the price of that article, of £1 a Ton. Supposing the ships built here to require, on an average, 200 tons of Timber, including waste, this would be a saving of £200 in each vessel. Besides, as the Raff Merchants would be obliged to keep much larger stocks of foreign timber than at present, the builder would have an opportunity of purchasing, at a low rate, such wood as suited his immediate purpose, without the necessity of keeping a large dead stock on hand. These advantages, in addition to the low rate of wages here, would enable us to build ships at as cheap a rate, as any other port on the coast.

Timber would likewise be brought here to be shipped for other places. It is well known that a great deal of Ash Timber, and sometimes oak, is carried from about Pickering to Scarborough, to be sent from thence, by sea, to Sunderland, Newcastle, &c., the whole of which would, undoubtedly, come down to Whitby.

The branch to Lealholm-bridge, would secure the entire trade of all the Dales in the vale of Esk, together with Rosedale, Farndale, &c., the supply of every description of goods, and the return of agricultural produce; and, as there is abundance of water power at Lealholm, the erection of extensive flour mills, or other manufactories, would be almost certain to follow, and increase the amount of traffic on the road.

There is every reason to believe, that this Road might be made, at a light expense, by way of Goathland and Newton Dale; and there is little doubt, upon a fair calculation of the expense, and probable trade, that it would yield an annual return, after deducting expenses, of 6 or 7 per cent.

Upon comparison of this with the Stockton line, there can scarcely be a question as to which would be most advantageous to Whitby at the present time. If, indeed, there was a CERTAINTY that Coals could be brought down to Whitby at as low a rate as to rival Stockton as a Shipping Port, then, it might perhaps be advisable to proceed with that line; but, as this, to say the least of it, is a very disputable point, and one in which we should, at all times, lay at the mercy both of the proprietors of the Pits and the Stockton & Darlington Railway Company, the question is, Which of the lines would afford the larger amount of general trade? And, therefore, be more beneficial to those engaged in business at Whitby. By forming the Stockton line, we should have to compete with the extensive Commercial Establishments of that place; with men already well versed in wholesale business, and, from the extent of their trade, able to furnish Goods at the lowest possible rate; while, on the other hand, our Merchants and Tradesmen, owing to their very limited sales, would be quite unable to meet their rivals on equal terms. Even at the best, the trade would always be a divided one.

No such disadvantage, however, presents itself on the Pickering line: we should then have an extensive opening for business, without any competitor; besides which, it is reasonable to suppose that this line, running so directly into the heart of the country, would, at no distant period, be carried further—to Malton, and perhaps to York, or Leeds.

Should it be thought proper, at a future time, to proceed with the Stockton line, part of it would be already formed, and the experience gained in making this line, would greatly assist in calculating both the expense and probable return of the other.

To shew the importance of forming Rail-road communications in a district so hilly and difficult of access as that in our neighbourhood, I may, although it is not directly connected with my subject, mention a singular fact – In Farndale, an extensive dale about 20 miles form Whitby, most of which is the property of Lord Feversham, there is a considerable number of very good Oak Trees, suitable for Ship-building, which have been stript of their bark, and left standing; the expense of carriage, owing to the badness of the roads, being more than the value of the Timber.

These remarks might have been extended to greater length, but enough has, I trust, been said to excite your attention to the subject; and feeling confident that the more strictly a comparison between the two lines is instituted, in the same degree will the superior advantages of the line I have pointed out appear.

I REMAIN
YOURS, &c.,
A TOWNSMAN.

Whitby, December 9th, 1831

From the Office of R. Rodgers, Old Market Place, Whitby.

CHAPTER 3

PERSONALITIES AND POLITICS

Webs of Influence

F IT HAD NOT BEEN FOR THE collieries and the development of their wagon-ways in the north east and the web of connections between families in Darlington, Whitby, and London, building a railway from Whitby to Pickering might never have happened.

As early as 1797, iron rails mounted on stone blocks had replaced wooden rails in at least one colliery in the north east of England. This made the transport of coal from the pithead to the River Tyne much easier by reducing the rolling resistance of the wagons. Thus, one horse could now haul four coal wagons by eliminating rough road surfaces. Using one narrow trackway rather than a whole road width meant that further economies could be made. The additional attraction of "travelling engines" was that they were capable of hauling a load four or five times that of a horse, at four times the speed.

Adopting these advances at Stockton and Darlington, promised significant advantages in hauling coal from collieries in the west close by Darlington to the docks at Stockton some 31 miles to the east. Initial thoughts were to use a rope and horse-drawn system. Edward Pease, from a wealthy Quaker family and the driving force behind proposals for this alternative method, visited nearby Killingworth colliery at George Stephenson's invitation. Stephenson, aged thirty two, had persuaded the co-owner, Sir Thomas Liddell, to allow him to experiment with a self-propelled steam engine. The idea was to eliminate fixed engines used in rope hauling and reduce the expense of using horses. Pease was impressed by what he saw.

The No 1 engine at Darlington

So, at the point at which the Stockton and Darlington Railway was formed in 1818 (Motto: "At Private Risk for Public Service"), influential local businessmen, professionals and landowners were beginning to appreciate the promise of investing in rail-roads. As a result, nineteen men from Whitby bought shares in the railway to the present day values of approximately four hundred thousand pounds out of an estimated total cost of around five million pounds.

Henry Belcher (1785-1854), a Whitby solicitor who later became the main champion and promoter of the Whitby-Pickering line, invested today's equivalent of around £5,000. His counterpart at Darlington acting for the Stockton and Darlington railway was Francis Mewburn (1785-1867), "the first railway solicitor". Mewburn steered proposals for a public railway through Parliament between 1819 and 1821. He then served as solicitor for the Stockton and Darlington Railway Company until his retirement in 1860

Mewburn's brother, John Mewburn, became a curator of the Whitby Literary and Philosophical Society in 1829, four years before Royal Assent for the Whitby and Pickering Railway Company was granted. In this way, the legal brains behind each of these pioneer railways had close associations with promoters and shareholders living in both towns.

It was very probably one or more of these people who invited George Stephenson to become personally involved in the design and construction of the Whitby to Pickering line. Soon afterwards, he became a founder member of the Whitby Stone Company that was to become a significant user of the new railway. The Company subsequently supplied limestone blocks to his son Robert, then engineering the London to Birmingham Railway; permission for both railways having been granted in May 1833. We shall follow the fortunes of the Stephensons at Whitby and Pickering in the next chapter.

For the moment, we may note that this network of connections did not end there. The years 1832 and 1833 proved to be a watershed for the promoters of the line for it not only witnessed the final stages of planning a railway to Whitby and Pickering but also ushered in a new system of voting. The numerous anomalies in the national system of government were finally tackled by reform, although several more decades were to pass before the stains of corruption and patronage were brought under a greater degree of control.

Democracy comes to Whitby

Whitby benefited through the allocation of one representative member in the new Parliament that would shortly be deliberating on the proposal to form a railway. The qualification for a vote was a male householder with a £10 rent or more. In Whitby, this gave voting rights to 425 electors out of a town population of around ten thousand. Henry Belcher was the returning officer for the election that took place on 6th December 1832.

This eagerly awaited date involved much jockeying for position. In anticipation, a public invitation called for a candidate to stand for election. One hundred and twenty two notables, supported by nine Whitby ministers nominated Richard Moorsom Jr. His manifesto read,

"Retrenchment and Economy, every possible reduction of Taxation, the Abolition of Slavery, Free Trade to India and China, and assistance and support to the Extension of the Railways"

Moorsom was the son of a Justice of the Peace and Deputy Lieutenant for the North Riding. At that time, a JP wielded considerable power and influence, effectively acting as a local lawmaker. The Lord Lieutenant of the district (The Earl of Zetland, Lord Mayor of York) normally recommended the appointment of JPs who were typically drawn from prominent landowners. A minimum qualification to become a JP was landed property of £100 a year (based on average earnings, approx £70,000 today). Nationally, around two thousand JPs were, in all but name, chief executives of their locality with duties ranging from levying taxes to regulating factories. A substantial proportion consisted of clergymen.

Moorsom's Storehouse, Whitby, constructed with whale jawbones from a sketch by George Weatherill in R. Weatherill, *The Ancient Port of Whitby and its Shipping*, 1908

Moorsom had already shown an interest in politics through his publications on slavery and shipping. His family connections with the Admiralty (his uncle was captain of HMS Revenge that fought at Trafalgar and brought home the news of victory) and Moorsom's nomination in 1823 as the first president of the Whitby Literary and Philosophical Society, would suggest that he was well favoured. He was not, however, to have it all his own way. Another candidate emerged – Aaron Chapman (1771-1850) - a London merchant and son and grandson of the leading partners of the Simpson Chapman banking house (later to become a branch of Barclays Bank).

Today we may think of banks as remote corporate bodies with an international management. In Moorsom's day, banks in Whitby and Pickering sprang up from successful shopkeepers, factory owners, and traders. Simpson Chapman & Co were Whitby drapers and grocers, Robert and John Campion of Campion's Bank were manufacturers of sailcloth, wine merchants, and ship owners. Such merchants gained a reputation for steady and attested local service. Gradually, their transactions took on an aspect of borrowing and lending by making advances to known individuals and offering safekeeping for cash. Whitby in particular had several banks. At least one had lavish premises that cost the equivalent of £700,000 today. At Pickering, soon after the railway arrived, the original shambles in the marketplace where the town's butchers were originally located, included a bank

So, in the background to decisions about the launch of a railway, a contest of influence developed involving a variety of commercial interests, a network of traders, some Quaker families, and the landed gentry. These intricate relations stretched across the region to London and beyond. Most notably, Joseph Pease one of the sons of Edward Pease and manager of the Stockton and Darlington line, was elected under the reformed voting system as Member of Parliament for South Durham to become the first Quaker MP. By this time, he owned many Durham collieries and was the buyer and planner of the new town of Middlesbrough with partners including Thomas Richardson, a relative of the Whitby banking business. In these ways, the interests of Whitby had strengthened immeasurably in the space of a few years.

The Railway and the New Parliament

The electoral battle that ensued at Whitby in 1832 spotlights some of the opinion-leaders of the day. Moorsom represented the "Whigs" variously billed at the time as the "Blues". Chapman championed the "Tories" under their colours, the "Pinks". These colours may be a little confusing to the modern reader. However, at this time political parties were not managed as they are today and had barely emerged as distinctive organisations. The use of colours as symbols offered a means of marking differences and sharpening distinctions in the minds of the new voters.

The "Whigs" became known as the "Liberals" later in the nineteenth century. Indeed the eldest son of the founding Liberal Prime Minister, W E Gladstone, was Whitby's MP for twelve years (1868-1880). The label "Whigs" derived from the name given to Scottish cattle rustlers and horse thieves and was originally coined as a term of abuse by the Tories. Whig sympathies lay towards developing industry and commerce, holding the monarchy accountable to the people, and supporting religious tolerance. They might conveniently be described as a "country party" as opposed to a Tory "court party". Their grip on government during the formative years of the Whitby and Pickering railway was one factor in its successful completion.

The "Tories" became the modern day "Conservatives" mainly through the use of the term by Sir Robert Peel (1780-1850), best known for his contribution to founding a national police force (the "Bobbies" or "Peelers") starting with London in 1829. Tory leanings were towards the King, the House of Lords, and the established church – in short the "establishment".

Whilst the main springs of efforts to develop the Whitby and Pickering railway were located in Whitby, events in the neighbouring town of Scarborough should not be overlooked, especially the influence and activities of Sir George Cayley (1773-1857). Whilst he is best known for his pioneering experiments in

30

aeronautics, his philanthropic spirit also encouraged a deep involvement in educational affairs and the practical uses of scientific discoveries. Between 1832 and 1834, at a critical time for the fortunes of the Whitby and Pickering railway, he served as Member of Parliament for Scarborough. At that time, Cayley's intensely inventive mind turned to railways. The directors of the railway at Whitby could hardly have had a better advocate. In 1830, he attended the opening of the Liverpool and Manchester Railway and a year later published an article on "Practical Hints on Railway Travelling". His contribution, no doubt prompted by the death of William Huskisson, aimed to improve railway safety

After the passage of the Whitby and Pickering Railway Act in May 1833, Cayley wrote a letter to the *York Herald* proposing a railway to link Scarborough with York. The route he suggested broadly follows that of the present day line. Six years after Cayley's letter, the two George's - Stephenson and Hudson - outlined their plans for a railway at a meeting held in Scarborough Town Hall in 1839.

By this time, another farsighted contender, Sir Frederick William Trench (1775-1859) took a seat as an MP for Scarborough. Connected by marriage to the Duke of Rutland, he was closely involved in the reconstruction of the Scarborough Spa – a chief attraction of the town at the time. He was also a motivating force for the construction of the Thames Embankment built some forty years after he first proposed it. There is some evidence to point to a connection between this grand design and the bijou project built to replace the Old Spa at Scarborough (see page 19).

At Pickering, located in the neighbouring north riding constituency, two MP's were elected to the new Parliament; Hon William Duncombe (1798-1867) later 2nd Baron Feversham of Duncombe Park, Helmsley and Edward Stillingfleet Cayley (1802-1862) of Wydale House, Brompton by Sawdon. The town of Pickering is approximately half-way between these two villages. Both of these MP's were actively engaged in politics at the time. Duncombe championed the reform of factory working conditions and in 1830 declared that it a duty to "mitigate the sufferings" of the "industrious and working classes". Some years later, he presented the Ten Hour Act in the House of Lords limiting the daily working hours of women and children in textile mills.

In the same year, Edward Cayley, son-in-law of Sir George, published a wide-ranging treatise "On Commercial Economy". He traces in detail and at length the effects of industrial development, advocates a "variety of employment", and urges action to counteract the excesses of "machinery....providing an endless supply to a glutted market.....with less human labour...(as) . an evil of growing magnitude". He concludes his analysis of the economic situation of his day with a number of proposals for parliamentary reforms.

With associates such as these, it is hardly surprising that the passage of the Whitby and Pickering Railway Company Bill met with little opposition and that

31

subsequent developments proceeded according to plan. Elsewhere, vigorous and sometimes violent opposition accompanied proposals to build a railway.

Electors and Speculators

The junketing of the Blues and Pinks in Whitby was heralded by a flood of publications. Over 180 pamphlets and leaflets emerged during the year from 1831 to 1832 providing a lively backdrop to the detailed business of planning a railway to Pickering.

The rival parties organised three public feasts. Two days after the Reform Bill received Royal Assent in June 1832, one thousand five hundred tickets were distributed to celebrate Chapman's visit to the Angel Inn Yard in the town. The "Blues" responded in the following month with a beef, plum pudding, and ale public feast attended by two thousand people.

The Chapman "Pinks" replied with redoubled vigour. A grand procession to the rousing refrains of three bands marched from the town. They gathered in a well chosen field to ensure an uninterrupted view from the rival candidate's house. In the harbour, two fully rigged ships decorated in pink matched the sashes, rosettes, banners and ribbons of Chapman's supporters. By a quarter to three in the afternoon of July 12th 1832, some 176 plum puddings, 40 gallons of sauce, 5 gallons of French brandy, 2773 lbs of beef, 995lbs of ham, 773 lbs of veal, and 299lbs of mutton were consumed. Over one thousand gallons of ale provided "unalloyed felicity" for up to six thousand guests, with the exception of the ladies. For them, tea and cake prevailed to ensure that "females ..... partake of a beverage that cheers but not inebriates".

Toasts to King William IV and Queen Adelaide and to the town were accompanied by renditions of the national anthem and "Rule Britannia." Speeches included optimistic estimates of the future success of a railway based upon a recent report from George Stephenson. Dancing and foot races followed with the most determined revellers repairing to the Angel Inn after fireworks at 9.30pm.

The Angel Inn (by 1851 known as the Angel Hotel), is situated on New Quay Road in the centre of the town, adjacent to the harbour. The Angel Yard was a starting point for stage-coaches and Royal Mail posting chaises and was a hub of activity. The Angel was the focal point for social gatherings of all kinds. It offered an Assembly Room for prosperous patrons to arrange social functions, dinners, balls and soirées and featured a "Rose Room". On the ceiling around a painting of a rose ran the legend "Be it spoken under the rose" reminding those present that anything discussed in that room should not be repeated and should be treated as strictly confidential. No doubt many discreet conversations took place at this spot about the prospect of a railway to Pickering.

A plaque on the east wall of the Angel confirms that it was here on Wednesday 12th September 1832 that decisions were taken to build a railway to

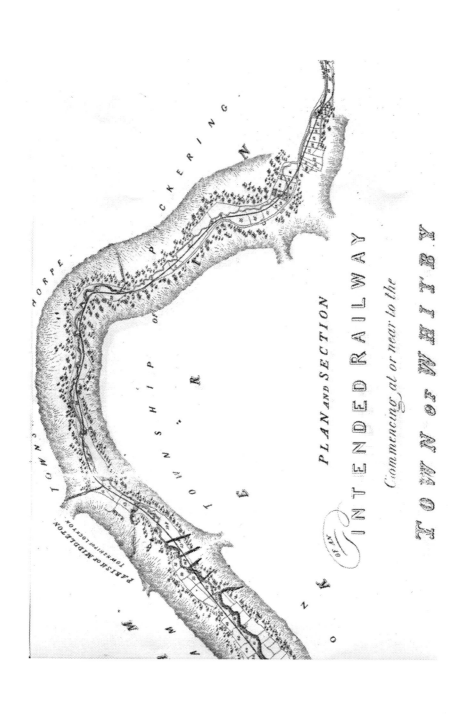

PLAN and SECTION

of an

INTENDED RAILWAY

Commencing at or near to the

TOWN of WHITBY

Pickering. A share list for the Whitby and Pickering Railway Company opened with prospective investors speculating on a 10% return. Thirty thousand pounds was subscribed immediately. The election verdict came exactly three months later, on the 12th December; Chapman for the "Pinks" – two hundred and seventeen votes, Moorsom for the "Blues"- one hundred and thirty nine. Aaron Chapman served for fifteen years as Whitby's MP and was returned three times unopposed. He also became one of the first directors of the Whitby and Pickering Railway along with four of his relatives.

Fourteen of the twenty-five directors listed in the Act granting permission for the railway were also members of the Whitby Literary and Philosophical Society including its chairman and deputy. Seven of the directors were senior partners in three of the four Whitby bank and represented in London by some of the leading finance houses. There was therefore ready access to investment funds locally and sponsorship in the capital city. In these ways, the politics of the Society, the nation, and the railway became powerfully intertwined. George and later, Robert Stephenson, took a leading role in its development with Aaron Chapman in support. The redoubtable Henry Belcher who promoted the entire enterprise, ably advised them.

Whitby and 'The Genius of Stephenson'

George Stephenson (1781-1848)

34

Horse-drawn coal wagon, on a wooden rail, 1765

The Stockton and Darlington railway, launched in September 1825 and extended to Middlesbrough in 1828, offered a model for tackling Whitby's declining fortunes. As nineteen Whitby men had invested in this first public railway from its beginnings in 1818, it is not surprising that they soon considered a possible line connecting Whitby with Stockton and Darlington. However, earlier investigations into the possibility of a canal linking Whitby with Pickering offered an alternative solution to the problem of improving inland communications.

It was not until 1831 that a survey was commissioned from Thomas Storey, engineer and general traffic manager for the Stockton and Darlington railway. Storey's report was debated and considered inconclusive and so the promoters of the line sought a second report from George Stephenson. Formerly chief engineer of the Stockton line and fresh from his triumphant completion of the celebrated Liverpool and Manchester Railway, he presented his findings in the early summer of 1832.

George Stephenson's general achievements will be familiar and need little introduction. However, the details of his career offer a reminder of the skills and vision that he brought to Whitby and Pickering. His son, Robert, also made a significant contribution to both Whitby and its railway.

Stephenson was the second of six children (two girls and four boys) living in one room, "an ordinary labourer's dwelling-its walls … unplastered, its floor…of clay, and…bare rafters…exposed overhead" His childhood was spent with his parents as none of the Stephenson children went to school. A wooden tracked wagon-way on which horses hauled coal passed right outside his front door. It inspired a growing interest in engineering, and as a pastime he made mechanical models from clay, cork, and string.

After a brief spell as a herdsman and farm worker, he gained employment with his father at Wylam Colliery near Newcastle Upon Tyne picking stones out of the freshly mined coal. Later, aged fourteen, he worked as an assistant engineman stoking the fire that fuelled the pit pump. At the age of eighteen, he had still not learned to read or write. At three pence a week, he went to a night school for three nights for lessons in spelling and reading. For four pence a week, he was able to learn arithmetic.

By the age of twenty-one, he had acquired sufficient means to marry and take a quayside cottage in Newcastle, close by the fixed engine that he operated to move ballast from the collier brigs lying alongside. A year later, his only son Robert was born on 16th October 1803. Three years later, after a move to the nearby Killingworth Colliery, tragedy overcame his family. His wife died shortly after giving birth to a daughter who had survived for only a few months.

George Stephenson's blotched signature from the marriage register 1802

Leaving his son Robert for a time in the care of a neighbour, he travelled on foot to Scotland after receiving an invitation from a spinning works owner to improve the large mill engine installed there. He walked back to Killingworth, this time with £28 in savings (approximately £1,500 today) in recognition of his invaluable services. His savings did not last long as nearly half went on paying off his father's debts. These had built up from an engine house accident that left his father with serious burns and the loss of his sight. The remaining savings went towards moving his parents to a cottage at Killingworth.

At this time, the Napoleonic wars made life most unpredictable. The possibility of being drafted to the militia or navy loomed and Stephenson seriously considered emigrating to the United States along with his sister and her husband. However, his skills with engines were attracting attention and having solved a notoriously difficult problem pumping out a nearby mine, his reputation as an "engine doctor" and "pump doctor" began to grow. As a result, in 1812 he became engine-wright at Killingworth High Pit at a salary of £100 a year, the use of a horse and the right to act as a consultant for other clients.

Years of experimentation followed on ways of improving existing "loco-motives" in several northern collieries. At Lord Ravensworth's expense, Stephenson designed and supervised the construction of his first "Travelling

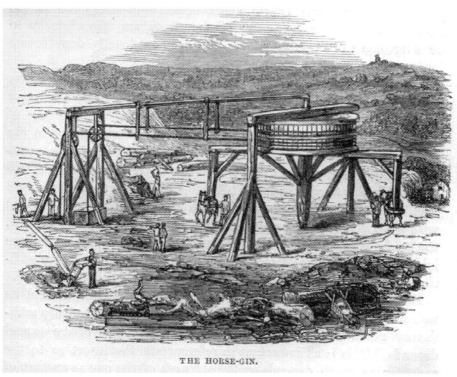

THE HORSE-GIN.

Two views of colliery horse-drawn 'gins' or engines used for winding men, coal and other materials up and down shafts.

37

Engine" in the colliery workshop. By adopting new methods and materials, he completed his new engine in July 1814. In the following year, he patented an improved version that proved to be a turning point in the history of transport.

The Rise of the Iron Horse

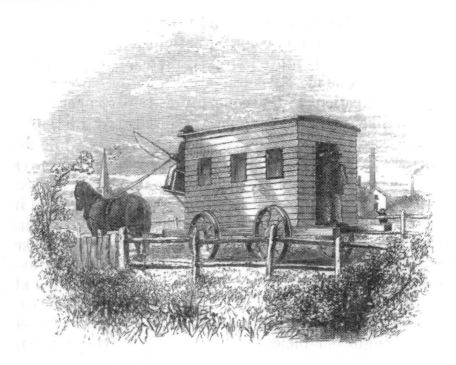

George Stephenson's 'Experiment' Railway Coach 1825

Stephenson produced several of these travelling engines and modified a wagon-way using horses to one using "iron horses" at Hetton Colliery near Durham. Opened under the supervision of his son Robert in 1822, it became, at eight miles in length, one of the longest rail-roads to connect a coal mine with a port. The experience gained, especially with the design of the rails and their supports, made further advances in performance possible.

Incorporating such features into the Stockton and Darlington line meant that by the time of the opening ceremony in September 1825, George Stephenson had spent over ten years developing railways principally for hauling coal. Passenger traffic received little attention until the obvious success of the line prompted experiments in this new direction. Appropriately enough, Stephenson named his first passenger coach "The Experiment". Seating up to 18 passengers on two wooden benches, its double-ended design avoided the need for turning at either end of the line. Travelling in this fashion, the directors made

**An advertisement for the horse-drawn coach
on the Stockton and Darlington Railway**

their journey on the opening day and one month later in October 1825, a revolutionary public passenger service began to operate to a published timetable.

Earlier in the same year, Stephenson gave expert witness to a parliamentary committee assessing a Bill for the construction of a double line railway from Manchester to Liverpool. By this stage, Stephenson had supervised or improved nine railways and with his son had constructed over fifty steam engines including around sixteen locomotives. Two major points were vigorously contested by the committee; the idea that a travelling engine could achieve twice the speed of a stage-coach and the possibility of a rail-road crossing a twelve mile area of bog known as "Chat Moss". The Bill failed at its first presentation but passed on a second occasion. After further controversy, Stephenson became engineer-in-chief with a salary of £1.000 per year and went to live in Liverpool.

Stephenson's in-depth knowledge of designing passenger coaches, overcoming challenging gradients, making good and economical speed with steam powered engines, and tackling boggy ground, were all areas of special relevance to the Whitby and Pickering railway project. His three-day interrogation by the committee for the passage of the Bill for the Liverpool to Manchester line was also to stand him in good stead for his many future projects including his report to the Whitby shareholders six years later.

In the interim, he became incredibly busy. For several years between 1825 and 1830, he was not only designing every detail and managing the Liverpool-Manchester project, but also training pupils in the absence of experienced staff.

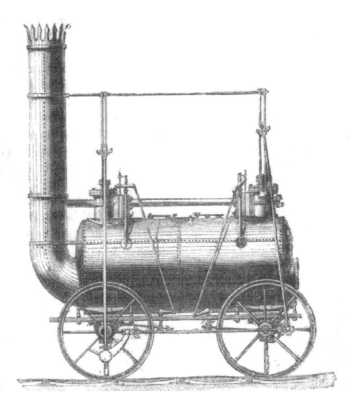

A travelling engine used on the Killingworth Railway c.1825

One of his closest associates, Fred Swanwick, (1810-1885) was the son of a boyhood friend. Swanwick drove one of the engines at the Grand Opening of the Liverpool and Manchester Railway and at the age of twenty-four, took over from Stephenson at Whitby in July 1834. One year later, he presented a bust of his mentor to the Museum and remained a member of the Whitby Literary and Philosophical Society until 1853.

Remarkably, it was to be as late as 1828 for a decision to be made about the means of transporting passengers and goods on the Liverpool to Manchester line. At the launch of the Stockton and Darlington line, horse-drawn coaches carried passengers whilst wagons hauled coal by steam power. The question arose as to whether to adopt this pattern for the Liverpool and Manchester line. Twenty yeas later, a similar dilemma presented itself at Whitby.

Horses or Steam? The Rainhill Trials

The directors of the Liverpool and Manchester inclined towards an all-steam option and they commissioned Stephenson to build a locomotive on a trial basis. They nevertheless remained to be convinced that travelling engines could

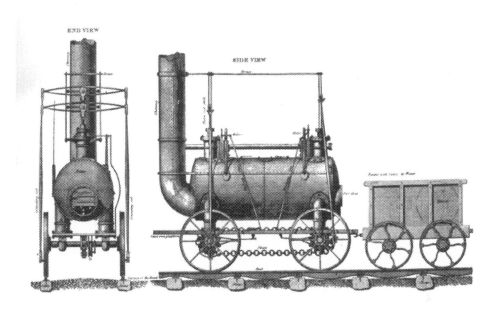

George Stephenson's 'Patent Locomotive Engine' 1826

be the mainstay of the system as opposed to a fixed engine arrangement. The directors therefore decided to offer a £500 prize to identify the most suitable locomotive. A number of rigorous conditions were specified;

"to draw....day by day, twenty four tons weight....at ten miles per hour.... Effectually consume its own smoke,....be supported on springs....ready for trial at the Liverpool end....not later than 1ˢᵗ October 1829....price ....must not exceed £550"

The famous "Rainhill Trials" were duly run over several days commencing on Tuesday 6ᵗʰ October 1829. Five competitors entered including one "locomotive" powered by a pair of horses on a treadmill – quite possibly a tongue in cheek entry contrived by Thomas Brandreth (1788-1873). He was one of Stephenson's friends and business associates from their Stockton and Darlington Railway days together. Bearing in mind the commentary of Stephenson's biographer, Samuel Smiles (1812-1904) on George's "fondness for frolic", there may well have been an element of teasing wit in this entry.

Brandreth, an Etonian and barrister, had sought special permission to enter his invention in the Trials. His "Cycloped" was invited to make an additional run to provide amusement during a lull in the proceedings. Brandreth and Stephenson had previously collaborated on the design of a "Dandy Cart". This contrivance was essentially a wagon on which a horse could jump aboard whilst the remaining wagons freewheeled on down-hill stretches of a line. The cart served the serious purpose of allowing horses to rest and regain strength.

Stephenson's 'Rocket' 1829

"Cycloped", whilst perhaps being a fanciful entry, may nevertheless have provided a useful object lesson to demonstrate the limitations of horsepower in favour of steam power. Its appearance was certainly timed for a critical moment when vision, commercial risk and Stephenson's vested interests were in conflict.

Each competitor made a number of return trips over a measured distance to represent the expected working route between Liverpool and Manchester. Various events overtook the entrants who were presented to meet this "ordeal" in the style of a horse race – in this case an "iron horse" race. Broken pumps, burst cylinders and one of the horses falling through the floor of its "engine" left George and Robert Stephenson's "Rocket" declared the winner. Their iron horse had reached an unprecedented average speed of 15mph with reliability and economy. The decision was confirmed to adopt steam engines.

The first steam trip taking Board members from Manchester to Liverpool took place on 14th June 1830. The return journey took an hour and a half. The comparable journey by stage-coach took more than three hours and proved to be twice as expensive. On this momentous occasion, the Whitby connection was prominently represented in the person of Captain William Scoresby Jr. (1789-1857), son of the renowned whaling Captain William Scoresby Sr (1760-1820). Both father and son were born in Cropton, a small village between Whitby and Pickering. William Scoresby Jr (later the Reverend Scoresby) had forged a glittering career as an arctic mariner-scientist. Now, at the age of forty-one, he was invited to minute the speed of the "Arrow", one of a new generation of improved locomotives, riding on the footplate alongside its driver, George Stephenson.

Both men were ideal representatives of the spirit of Victorian enterprise. Stephenson by exploring the limits of mobile steam powered engineering, Scoresby by publishing pioneering studies of the Polar seas – *"An Account of the Arctic Regions and the Northern Whale Fishery" (1820)* and *"Journal of a Voyage to the Northern Whale Fishery (1823)* that earned him a coveted Fellowship of The Royal Society in 1824. Several of the geographical features Scoresby discovered in his exploration of four hundred miles of the east Greenland coastline were named after his Whitby friends and notables including Mewburn, Moorsom, and Simpson.

Whitby Whalers among the Icebergs in the Davis Straits
(From: R. Weatherill. The Ancient Port of Whitby and its Shipping, 1908)

Reports on a Proposed Rail-Road to Pickering

These elaborate associations between Whitby worthies and George Stephenson may help us to understand why an engineer of his standing should have troubled with a rail-road that was hardly cutting-edge, particularly at a time when his fame was approaching its height. This railway, designed to be horse-drawn on a single track, was not at the outset intended for steam traction. It would not therefore offer any immediate opportunities to deploy his latest technology.

One answer, apart from the pressures doubtless brought to bear by Whitby subscribers in return for their early support of the Stockton and Darlington line, might have been Stephenson's innate relish for a challenge. This proposed railway was undoubtedly going to provide plenty of this, as Whitby is crowned by hills comprising steep and sudden gradients. The surrounding contours rise from around 10 feet above sea level at Whitby to over 900 feet at the summit with intervening dips of approximately 669 and 560 feet, finally descending to 100 feet at Pickering. The area also contained considerable expanses of uncharted bogs.

Another clue to George's interest in the line may lie in his entrepreneurial instincts. His report to a committee of subscribers and prospective shareholders completed in July 1832 was discussed at Whitby two months later. In it, Stephenson refers to the "agricultural and mineral riches" along the proposed route from Whitby to Pickering and notes the availability of various stones e.g. whinstone, freestone, and limestone used in agriculture, repairing roads, and building. Somewhat more cryptically, he alluded to other hidden riches;

"As soon as the main line is completed, there is no doubt that the Company will find it their interest to lay down several short branches into the rich mineral districts adjoining the line, and that these branches will prove valuable feeders....... I have thought it better, however, for the present, to abstain from adverting to them more particularly"

Stephenson may well have been taken by the lure of ironstone in an age increasingly dependant on its use. Deposits were known to exist at Grosmont village some six miles along the intended route from Whitby. Iron had long ago been smelted at monastic sites in the area and other workings indicated ironworking as early as the first century AD. He was also very familiar with one of the main blast furnaces at Bedlington Ironworks near Killingworth colliery and Birtley Iron Company's premises not far from Hetton Colliery. He could well envisage opportunities arising from by-products of the railway. Within a year, he had capitalised on this possibility by becoming one of the founder members of the Whitby Stone Company when the Railway Company was formed in 1833. Soon afterwards, a trial load of ironstone was sent to Birtley and limestone was supplied to his son, Robert.

George Stephenson's Final Years

George Stephenson's involvement in the Whitby Stone Company was an example of his widening interests in industries allied to railways, most notably at

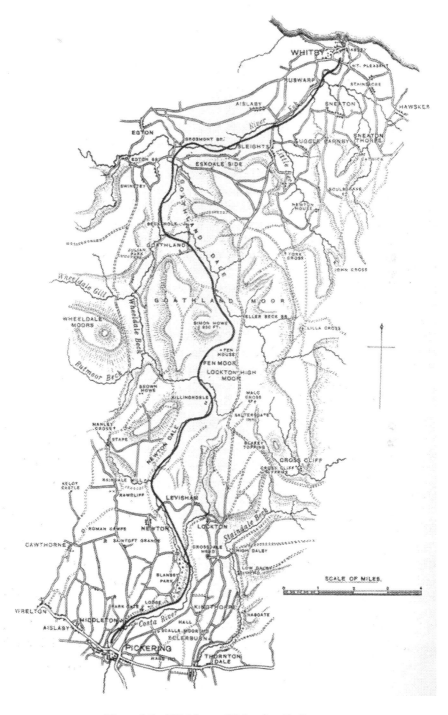

Plan of the Whitby to Pickering Railway

45

Clay Cross near Chesterfield. Here in the year following the opening of the line between Whitby and Pickering, he formed a Company to exploit coal deposits found in excavating a tunnel for a railway linking Leeds and Derby. It was to be his retirement project.

Aged fifty-seven, he bought a substantial mansion a few miles away. With four partners, he opened a coalmine, ironworks, lime quarry, and lime works. One of his business associates was George "The Railway King" Hudson, of which more later. Unlike Hudson who was not devoid of charity but rather more occupied by lavish hospitality and publicity stunts, Stephenson retained an active social conscience.

George Stephenson's last ten years at Clay Cross are a testimony to a life in which railway engineering merged with a wider social vision. Four hundred houses were built there and from being a small hamlet, Clay Cross grew within a few years to employ around one thousand people. With a population exceeding 1,500, George Stephenson created a system for the welfare and education of his workers. His private secretary and assistant, none other than Fred Swanwick, came to live at nearby Chesterfield and supervised the project.

In return for a modest contribution, free education, including access to lectures, reading rooms, newspapers and a library at his newly established Workmen's Institute was provided together with free medical aid and sick and disablement pay for workers and their families. Stephenson introduced such innovations many years before the founding of national welfare institutions. The arts were not forgotten either; two bands, a choral society, and a cricket club were maintained with prizes awarded for those with horticultural interests.

George Stephenson's funeral of took place in August 1848, some three years after Hudson had purchased the Whitby to Pickering Railway. His burial took place in The Holy Trinity Church, Chesterfield where his grave is marked by a simple stone inscribed with the initials, 'GS'. In sharp contrast, eleven years later, his son Robert found his final resting place amongst national heroes in the sumptuous surroundings of Westminster Abbey.

Robert Stephenson

Without his son, many of George Stephenson's early achievements would not have been possible. Deeply influenced by his father's struggle to gain an adequate education, Robert Stephenson was groomed to become both a future partner and adviser.

After early years at the local village school, Robert went at the age of eleven to a select private academy in Newcastle five miles away, making the daily journey on the back of a donkey. His father scraped together the considerable cost – almost half of his wage at Killingworth Colliery – by working in his spare time cleaning clocks and watches, mending shoes and cutting out cloth.

Robert Stephenson (1803-59),
Railway Engineer and Member of Parliament for Whitby from 1852 to 1859

When Robert was fifteen, he began an apprenticeship at Killingworth. Between 1821 and 1823, he assisted his father to survey the Stockton and Darlington and Liverpool to Manchester lines and spent six months at Edinburgh University "for purposes of scientific culture", rewarding his father's investment with a prize for mathematics. Robert had also taught himself shorthand so that he could take down the lectures he attended verbatim. Neatly transcribing his notes into notebooks, he was then able to share the latest thinking of eminent scientists of the day with his father as a means of securing George's own continuing education.

The crowning achievement of all this experience was the founding of a factory to make steam engines. Although other sites produced locomotives, this was the first purpose built locomotive factory in the world.

Robert Stephenson at the age of twenty became the managing partner of Robert Stephenson & Co at Forth Street, Newcastle. This venture jointly funded by himself, his father, Edward Pease and Michael Longridge of the Bedlington Ironworks, began supplying locomotives in 1824, initially to the Stockton and Darlington Railway. Robert, at a salary of £200 a year took full charge of production, with his father advising on design from a house in nearby Eldon Street.

Forth Street Works, Newcastle c.1824

This arrangement did not last long. Robert decided to risk all and go off to South America. Various interpretations have been put forward to explain this sudden break with his father. His situation as an only child in thrall to his father's preoccupations from an early age contrasted sharply with the lure of a distant land with uncharted and fabled opportunities. This tempting prospect may well have been the spur to test his mettle on his own terms. Another factor may have been the economic circumstances emerging at the time. Whilst share prices were soaring in Mexico and South America, England experienced a financial crisis soon after his departure with around fifteen per cent of the country banks becoming bankrupt.

Robert had been head-hunted by a wealthy Quaker city financier and cousin of Edward Pease. The assignment was to lead an expedition to set up mines on the Magdalena River in Columbia – not for lowly coal but mines for gold, silver, copper and tin. What young man of talent and vision could have passed over such an undertaking?

Against his father's and factory business partners' wishes, he sailed from Liverpool to Columbia in June 1824 returning three years later to once again run the locomotive works in Newcastle. He supervised the construction of eight locomotives for the Liverpool and Manchester line and drove one of them at the opening ceremony on 15th September 1830.

Three years later, Robert Stephenson became chief engineer for the construction of the London to Birmingham Railway at a salary of £2000 per year and moved to London. It was to be the first main railway line out of the capital. A triumphal arch at Euston of solid granite over 21 metres high marked the gateway only to be demolished amid much controversy in 1962. The line linked at Birmingham with the Grand Junction Railway being built under the supervision of his father and so provided a through route to Manchester and Liverpool.

Engineering the Early Railways

From 1830 until the opening ceremony eight years later, Robert Stephenson was the main champion and driving force for the London to Birmingham Railway. It was a monumental undertaking. Six times more costly than the Liverpool to Manchester line and 112 miles in length, it commanded much public fascination and opposition in equal measure. The engineering necessary was new and untried. More than half of the contractors became bankrupt in the process. Their experiences however proved invaluable for the railways that followed including the Whitby and Pickering railway.

Some idea of the challenge of engineering these early railways can be gathered from Samuel Smiles account of the construction of the Blisworth Cutting and Kilsby Tunnel;

Blisworth Cutting

"The Blisworth Cutting is one of the most formidable grooves ever cut in the solid earth. It is a mile and a half long, in some places sixty-five feet deep, and it passes through earth, stiff clay and hard rock....One third of the cutting was stone, and beneath the stone lay a thick bed of clay, under which were found beds of loose shale so full of water that almost constant pumping was necessary at many points to enable the works to proceed.....Steam engines were set to pump out the water; two locomotives were put on, one at either end of the cutting, to drag away the excavated rock and clay; and eight hundred men and boys were employed along the work, in digging, wheeling, and blasting, besides a large number of horses.......twenty five barrels of gunpowder were exploded weekly (amounting to) three thousand barrels"

MAKING THE RUNNING.

Kilsby Tunnel

"The chief difficulty of the undertaking was the execution of the tunnel under Kilsby Ridge.....two thousand four hundred yards long passing one hundred and sixty feet below the surface (the length of the 1836 tunnel on the Whitby and Pickering railway is approximately 130 yds) But the works had scarcely been commenced when it was discovered that.......there existed an extensive quicksand under a bed of clay forty feet thick...there was nothing for it but (to place) numerous additional shafts and pumping engines over the line of the tunnel where it crossed the quicksand.....As for the contractor, he abandoned the work in despair, and died shortly after; it was said the anxiety killed him.....A line of pumping engines having an aggregate power of 160 horses was erected at short intervals over the quicksand in the direction of the tunnel......the pumping went on for eight continuous months, in the midst, as it were, of two almost perpendicular walls of water and sand on either side (the workmen) proceeded with the building of the tunnel....the excavators and bricklayers working night and day until the work was finished....The water pumped out of the tunnel....would nearly be equivalent to the contents of the Thames at high water, between London and Woolwich"

SHAFT OF KILSBY TUNNEL.

The Railway Builders

"The labourers who executed these formidable works were in many respects a remarkable class..." the railway navvies as they were called... (shortened from 'navigator' derived from the construction of canals, referred to as 'navigations')......Their experience in all sorts of earthwork, in embanking, boring, and well sinking-their practical knowledge of the nature of soils and rocks, the tenacity of clays, and the porosity of certain stratifications- were very great; and, rough-looking as they were, many of them were as important in their own department as the contractor or engineer...Joining together in a 'butty gang', some ten or twelve of these men would take a contract to cut out and remove so much 'dirt'...fixing their price according to the character of the 'stuff' and the distance to which it had to be wheeled and tipped....In times of emergency they would work twelve and even sixteen hours....and the quantity of flesh meat which they consumed was sometimes enormous; but it was to their bones and muscle what coke is to the locomotive-the means of keeping up steam."

51

"Such has been the improvement in these mechanical giants, that as much power is now obtained from one bushel of coal, as in earliest periods was to be had from seventeen bushels"

THE "TIP."

Rail-roads in the Countryside

Other contemporary writers including George Eliot and Charles Dickens colourfully capture the mood of the times. George Eliot's (1819-1880) setting of "Middlemarch" in the 1830's gives a flavour of the impact of the railways on everyday life in rural areas;

"As he said, 'Business breeds'. And one form of business which was beginning to breed just then was the construction of railways. A projected line was to run....... Where the cattle had hitherto grazed in a peace unbroken by astonishment;.......... The submarine railway may have its difficulties; but the bed of the sea is not divided among various landed proprietors with claims for damages not only measurable but sentimental. In the hundred to which Middlemarch belonged, railways were as exciting a topic as the Reform Bill or the imminent horrors of Cholera, and those who held the most decided views on the subject were women and landholders. Women both old and young regarded travelling by steam as presumptuous and dangerous, and argued against it by saying that nothing should induce them to get into a railway carriage; while proprietors, differing from each other in their arguments......... were yet unanimous in the opinion that in selling land, whether to the Enemy of mankind or to a Company obliged to purchase, these pernicious agencies must be made to pay a very high price to landowners for permission to injure mankind. But the slower wits............. took a long time to arrive at this conclusion, their minds halting at the vivid conception of what it would be to cut the Big Pasture in two, and turn it into three-cornered bits, which would be "nohow".......'The cows will all cast their calves ....if the railway comes across the Near Close; and I shouldn't wonder at the mare too, if she was in foal. It's a poor tale if a widow's property is to be spaded away, and the law say nothing to it. What's to hinder 'em from cutting right and left if they begin? It's well known, I can't fight.' ....The best way would be to say nothing, and set somebody on to send 'em away with a flea in their ear, when they came spying and measuring.......... Let 'em go cutting in another parish. And I don't believe in any pay to make amends for bringing a lot of ruffians to trample your crops.........the more spokes we put in their wheel, the more they'll pay us to let 'em go on'. ......This reasoning was perhaps less thorough than he imagined, his cunning bearing about the same relation to the course of railways as the cunning of a diplomatist bears to the general chill or catarrh of the solar system. But he set about acting on his views in a thoroughly diplomatic manner, by stimulating suspicion........In the absence of any precise idea as to what railways were, public opinion..... was against them; for the human mind in that grassy corner had not the proverbial tendency to admire the unknown, holding rather that it was likely to be against the poor man, and that suspicion was the only wise attitude."

"Middlemarch" Ch.56 (1871)

MAKING AN EMBANKMENT.

Rail-roads in the Towns and Cities

Charles Dickens's account of building Robert Stephenson's London to Birmingham railway is memorably described in *Dombey & Son;*

"The first shock of a great earthquake had, just at that period, rent the whole neighbourhood to its centre. Traces of its course were visible on every side. Houses were knocked down; streets broken through and stopped; deep pits and trenches dug in the ground; enormous heaps of earth and clay thrown up; buildings that were undermined and shaking, propped by great beams of wood. Here, a chaos of carts, overthrown and jumbled together, lay topsy-turvy at the bottom of a steep unnatural hill; there, confused treasures of iron soaked and rusted in something that had accidentally become a pond. Everywhere were bridges that led nowhere; thoroughfares that were wholly impassable; Babel towers of chimneys, wanting half their height; temporary wooden houses and enclosures, in the most unlikely situations; carcases of ragged tenements, and fragments of unfinished walls and arches, and piles of scaffolding, and wildernesses of bricks, and giant forms of cranes, and tripods straddling above nothing. There were a hundred thousand shapes and substances of incompleteness, wildly mingled out of their places, upside down, burrowing in the earth, aspiring in the air, mouldering in the water, and unintelligible as any dream. Hot springs and fiery eruptions, the usual attendants upon earthquakes, lent their contributions of confusion to the scene. Boiling water hissed and heaved within dilapidated walls; whence, also, the glare and roar of flames came issuing forth; and mounds of ashes blocked up rights of way, and wholly changed the law and custom of the neighbourhood. In short, the yet unfinished and unopened rail-road was in progress; and, from the very core of all this dire disorder, trailed smoothly away, upon its mighty course of civilisation and improvement"

Dombey & Son (1849) Ch. 6

MAKING A CUTTING.

Closer to hand is Dickens' personal opinion of the Whitby and Pickering Railway. In a letter to his close friend, the novelist and writer Wilkie Collins (1824-1889), Dickens recalls his early experiences on the railway prompted by Collins' more recent (1861) visit to the town;

"In my time that curious railroad by the Whitby Moor was so much the more curious, that you were balanced against a counter-weight of water, and that you did it like Blondin. But in these remote days the one inn of Whitby was up a back-yard, and oyster-shell grottoes were the only view from the best private room. Likewise, sir, I have posted to Whitby. "Pity the sorrows of a poor old man."

Letters of Charles Dickens, 2nd ed. 1880

Dickens wittily likens his journey on the rope drawn incline from Beck Hole to the Vale of Goathland to the first crossing of the Niagara Falls by tightrope. "The Great Blondin" had accomplished this feat shortly before the date of the letter sent to Collins. (Dickens had visited "the vast immensity" of the Niagara Falls in April 1842 commenting that "It would be hard for a man to stand nearer God than he does there")

It is also possible that Dickens was recalling his visit to Mulgrave Castle near Whitby, seat of the Marquis of Normanby in April 1844. He dedicated *Dombey & Son* to the Marchioness of Normanby (1798-1882) having met the family on several occasions on visits to Canada, London and Paris. Another possibility relates to the time Dickens spent accompanied by his wife on their visits to the Smithson family in Malton, seven miles away from Pickering. Charles Smithson (1804-1844) was a close friend who he visited for three weeks in July 1843. Charles Dickens' younger brother was also in the town about that time whilst working as a civil engineer on the York-Malton-Pickering-Scarborough railway from offices Hudson established in Malton to construct the line.

Robert Stephenson and Whitby

Robert Stephenson's completion of the London to Birmingham railway at the age of thirty-five confirmed his reputation as a leading engineer of his day. Many more commissions followed in Britain and abroad. His skills broadened to include the construction of numerous bridges including the Britannia Tubular Bridge (1845-50), the Conway Tubular Bridge (1848), the Newcastle High Level Bridge (1844-1849), and the Royal Border Bridge over the Tweed at Berwick (1850) All of these bridges were supreme examples of high quality design and innovative technology.

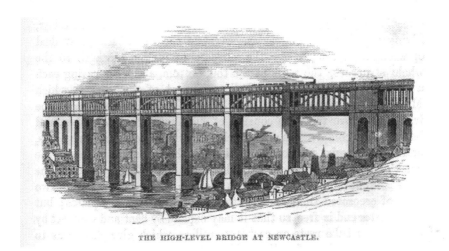

THE HIGH-LEVEL BRIDGE AT NEWCASTLE.

At the height of his powers, his personal life unravelled through a disastrous business transaction and the death of his wife. He had married Fanny Sanderson from a London middle class family on his return from South America in 1829. She died from cancer after a two-year illness in 1842. Despite her last request, Robert Stephenson never re-married.

In 1847, he became MP for Whitby and on the death of Henry Belcher in 1854 became the first non-resident president of the Whitby Literary and Philosophical Society. Three years later, amongst many other honours, he received an honorary degree at Oxford University with his close friend, Isambard Kingdom Brunel (1806-1859). Two years later, both of these great railway engineers died within a few days of each other, Brunel in September and Robert Stephenson on the 12th of October 1859.

CHAPTER 4

BUILDING THE LINE

Surveying and Levelling

 EMOTE AND SMALL THOUGH THE TOWN OF WHITBY was, it had managed to orchestrate support from some of the greatest railway engineers of the 19th century. The chief conductor was Henry Belcher whose account of the line follows in chapters five and seven. He was the legal brains behind the project and solicitor for the Company from its formation until its takeover by Hudson's York and North Midland Railway Company in 1845. Belcher's chance encounter with George Dodgson, an assistant surveyor laying out the line, led to the unique account of the *"Scenery of the Whitby and Pickering Railway"* and its ceremonial opening on Thursday 26th May 1836, (see chapter five).

Three years previously, the first general meeting of the Whitby and Pickering Railway Company took place at the Angel Inn Whitby on 1st October 1833. A successful application in May of that year, had secured an Act of Parliament granting permission to construct the railway, By August, preliminary contracts were agreed. Additional survey work could then begin in earnest.

Powers granted to the Company to proceed were considerable;

Of all the tyrannical powers in the country, a railway Company is the most formidable. It applies to Parliament to be endowed with powers which the common law denies to the Sovereign herself; it seeks for authority by which, without leave, and in defiance of it, it may invade property, having purchased it at a price which, from local associations or circumstances, may be far below its value to the possessor; it levels grounds and houses without remorse, be they grange or cottage; or, what is worse, it cuts close by and utterly mars the estate without actually touching it; and fells down oaks which ancestors may have planted, and destroys for ever that which may be most dear to its proprietor. And all this must be submitted to, because the public weal is paramount to private considerations.

F S Williams *Our Iron Roads* 1852

The preceding era of canal building had encouraged the widespread use of the skills and techniques involved in land surveying. Passing on these skills was accelerated by the growth of collieries and their wagon-ways. Detailed land surveying was often arduous and had to take place at times when there would be the least disruption to crops. Proposals for a railway had to meet a November 30th deadline for parliamentary scrutiny to take place in the following session. Plans and sections to a scale of three inches to the mile also needed depositing with specified institutions and individuals. This meant working through the autumn months whilst also allowing sufficient time for the drawings to be engraved, printed, and distributed. Draughtsmen and lithographers frequently worked day and night to meet deadlines (see chapter six).

Surveyors were in short supply. To meet frantic demand, advertisements appeared for complete training in fourteen days for sums ranging from three to five guineas a head. Opportunities for 'quackery' and unscrupulous operators were extensive. The tasks involved in surveying could be, and in several instances proved to be, hazardous especially in places where opposition to a railway was strong. At least one surveyor was jailed for drawing a gun in self-defence whilst another committed suicide apparently after incurring the wrath of George Stephenson. Blockades, posses of armed gamekeepers, varying degrees of violence, and court cases were commonplace events. On the Liverpool and Manchester survey, hiring a prize-fighter to guard the theodolite ensured a certain measure of security!

Subterfuge was frequently called for to enter land at nightfall or on occasions when owners were absent or otherwise engaged. The Sabbath was a good time to avoid the wrath of churchmen. Dissuading irate landowners from taking extreme measures led to the practice of hiring protection from hand picked "navvies" who had a stake in the line progressing smoothly. Decoy parties frustrated the most determined opposition. Even poets were moved to pen verses. Wordsworth enclosed one in a letter to Gladstone objecting to a proposed railway to the head of Windermere. It began with the words; "Is there no nook of English ground secure from rash assault?"

The main task for land surveyors after the granting of Royal Assent was to interpret the plans for the selected route, peg out the line, and provide further records for construction work at key places. Both Thomas Storey and George Stephenson would have identified a route that made best use of the natural features, crossing rivers and streams at a point closest to their source, aiming for as straight a line as possible. Hard won experience had proved the wisdom of avoiding "gentlemen's seats and pleasure grounds" wherever practicable.

Before the advent of Ordnance Survey Maps of Yorkshire c.1850, surveyors and engineers would have doubtless drawn upon the work of Christopher Greenwood who produced a fine 1 inch to 1.37 miles map of the 'County of York' from his surveys between 1815 and 1817. Greenwood and his son then went on to publish their "Atlas of Counties of England" between 1829

A LEVELLING PARTY.

and 1834 which greatly aided the work of the early railway builders. Undoubtedly, Storey and Stephenson would have consulted the map prepared for a proposed Whitby-Pickering canal in 1793. The maps and plans of the Whitby Harbour engineer, Frederick Pickernell (1796-1871), may also have proved invaluable.

It was however Fred Swanwick, Stephenson's young apprentice engineer who was delegated to carry out detailed work on the proposed line. He was accompanied by several assistants including the twenty-two year old, George Dodgson, of whom more later. Dodgson had been sent from Liverpool to assist in making detailed plans, maps, and elevations that had to be produced to the statutory deadlines. His pay would be around one guinea a day at a time when an agricultural labourer would receive a daily wage of around thirty-two old pence. Given the challenge of the North Yorkshire moors and surrounding terrain, undertaking this work was not straightforward; Charlotte Brontë's letters refer to a hurricane in Yorkshire and adjacent areas in December 1833!

Dodgson's tasks involved identifying the form and features of tracts of land, making accurate plan-view drawings, determining a baseline level, and using this baseline to plot the surrounding features. The aim would then be to achieve the nearest approximation to level running combined with the least demanding gradients. Engineers expected surveyors to cover around three miles a day. Some flexibility in this regime shortly disappeared with the increasing rigour demanded by the introduction of national standards.

The investors in the Whitby and Pickering Railway had been shrewd in engaging Stephenson to direct developments and to seek a follow-up to Storey's initial report. Thomas Storey, formerly a colliery 'viewer' or engineer had limited experience of developing railways. Indeed everyone involved, surveyors, engineers, directors, contractors, and solicitors were, in varying degrees, all intrepid pioneers.

It was also sound judgement on the part of the promoters that oversight of all contracts would be carried out by the Company secretary and by the directors under advice from the Stephensons (father and son) and from Fred Swanwick, the latter's most experienced and trusted colleague. All the documentation for a successful application had to satisfy a myriad of legal detail both locally, to make sure every aspect of the plans and sections were accurate, and nationally to navigate the complexities of parliamentary procedures.

Surveyors and solicitors needed to achieve the closest co-operation to ensure success. Serving statutory notices on everyone affected by the plans was a complex matter. The notices needed returning in every case in order for the resulting lists of assents to proposals to be both trustworthy and complete. One inaccuracy or one objection would be enough to create expensive and intractable delays. Signatures obtained from interested parties, letters of support from prominent individuals, and the preparation of impressive petitions, all played their part in achieving a smooth and uncontested passage through the committee stages in Parliament.

Although less stringent requirements applied to the earliest applications for railways, the professional standards that Henry Belcher brought to this work proved to be of the highest order as there was no opposition to the Bill.

His enduring legacy is the book he wrote to launch the line illustrated by Dodgson (see below). It is not only a unique document in the history of Victorian railways, but is a testimony to Belcher's outstanding qualities of leadership and vision.

The Company directors met fortnightly. Their first task was to divert the River Esk at Larpool in order to reduce the number of bridges needed. The necessary engineering work took a creditable four months.

Nevertheless, nine wooden bridges required building over the river, eight of them sited within three and a half miles of each other. The largest was over 95 metres long (George Stephenson had recently engineered sixty-three for the Liverpool to Manchester route!).

Another early decision was to purchase land for a double line where possible as an investment for possible future expansion beyond the approved single line. Deciding upon the type of rail and fixings to adopt was also a tricky business at a time when these details were still under development. This issue was settled in favour of a design "newly invented by Mr Robert Stephenson".

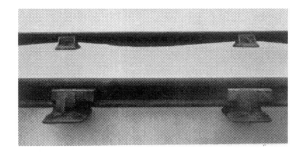

Malleable iron rail of 1825 and steel rail of the present day

Despite calls for the suspension of work at Pickering during the winter months, construction continued with arrangements made for offloading rails arriving at Malton by boat and by sea at Whitby. Progress for the first six and a half miles at both ends of the line moved on apace. By New Year's Day 1834, the directors of the Whitby and Pickering Railway Company ceremoniously opened the new River Esk cut.

The Grosmont Tunnel

The Tunnel at Grosmont constructed c.1835.

By March 1834, two thirds of the contracts were agreed including the completion of a tunnel, 130 yds long, 10 feet wide, and 14 feet high. Constructed of brick and locally quarried stone it provided an entry into the Vale of Goathland. Only a few farms and buildings marked the locality and for a time, it was simply dubbed "Tunnel.".

The discovery of ironstone and the coming of the railway created a mini – boom. The resulting settlement was then called 'Grosmont' after 'Growmond' the nearby 13th century priory and the related Grandimont Abbey in Normandy, France. It is possible that the site of the present Co-op and Post Office played some part in serving the needs of the earliest constructors of the line and for stabling the horses that worked the line. The present "Station Tavern" (formerly the Station Hotel) provided much grander premises. The original building was completed in 1836 in time for the opening of the line and named the "Tunnel Inn"

In the previous summer, the first horse-drawn railway coach, "The Premier" (see page 72) began a service to the Tunnel. It ran from the Company offices situated on part of the shipyard of Fishburn and Brodrick located about half a mile down stream from the present Whitby railway station.

Francis Whishaw's account of *The Railways of Great Britain and Ireland* (1842), dedicated to "the Railway Capitalists of the United Kingdom," provides us with a detailed account of the first coaches to use the line;

"The carriages are of two kinds, open and closed. The open carriages cost £100 each, and the closed £280, the latter weighing about 2.75 tons. The wheels are 3 feet diameter. Each carriage is drawn by one horse, as on the Edinburgh and Dalkeith Railway, the driver sitting in front, and having power to stop the carriage by a lever attached to the brake, conveniently fixed at the side of the carriage." (The Edinburgh to Dalkeith railway was the first railway to serve the capital city of Scotland. Opened originally as a horse-drawn coal carrying tramway to the Firth of Forth, it carried passengers from June 1832.)

Some idea of the scene surrounding the inaugural passenger rail-road service from Whitby to Pickering may be gathered from the following description written by Richard Weatherill (1844-1923), son of the book-keeper for the Whitby and Pickering railway, George Weatherill;

"Great numbers of the smaller craft owned at Whitby were employed in the coasting and coal trades, which found occupation for immense fleets from other ports as well as from Whitby.....Six hundred vessels have been seen to pass Whitby on one day. I myself have counted 400 in sight at one time from our cliffs.... In these (1908) days of steamers a 5.000 ton vessel will have perhaps 25 men for a crew, but 5,000 tons carried by the old sailing vessels required some 30 vessels and about 200 men. The larger vessels traded to the Baltic, Mediterranean, and America, the largest of all going to India, China, and Australia. Several of these latter were licensed India-men, carrying passengers as well as cargo......and guns......the graving (dry) docks on both sides of the river were seldom unoccupied, whilst there were usually several vessels in the harbour waiting "turns" for dry dock repairs. Before the ships went to the docks, the ballast........was discharged into lighters (*flat bottomed barges*) till they came out, when it was re-shipped. At the Church Street docks (*on the East i.e. Abbey bank*) the vessels' massive bows and figure heads standing out over the palings with the bowsprits and jib booms stretching across the street were always an interesting sight, and the sound of the carpenter's calking hammers (*making a boat watertight*) was a local characteristic. The ship carpenters and others worked from 6 a.m. to 6 p.m., the Town Hall bell ringing at those times for them to finish the working day. When leaving work they took home as much firewood as they could carry under an arm."

R. Weatherill The Ancient Port of Whitby (1908)

Part of the original rail used on the Pickering to Whitby line-note the absence of cross sleepers to allow easy movement for horses.

By the summer of 1835, a second-class coach was brought into service for Saturday 'market people' for journeys to and from Grosmont at a fare of 6d. The experience of the first month suggested that another first class coach should be built, much lighter than "The Premier" and be ready for the finished route to Pickering.

Arrangements were made for charging tolls to people walking along the line. Rails, mostly laid on stone blocks, were brought in from various suppliers from as far afield as Worcestershire, South Wales and Northumberland. A section of the original rail used is on display at Pickering Station (see above).

With the pace of construction quickening, the directors busied themselves with purchases of more wagons, a weight house, and a coach shed. There were difficulties in purchasing sufficient horses and the directors themselves were urged to buy any suitable they might find.

Apart from the diversion of the Esk, the necessary cuttings, embankments and bridges, and the tunnel at Grosmont, two other major obstacles remained; the steep hill from Beck Hole to Goathland and the crossing of Fen Bog.

Stephenson's Inclined Plane

To ascend the steep hill from Beck Hole to Goathland, machinery to form a self-acting inclined plane was purchased from Robert Stephenson in the sum of one hundred and forty six pounds, four shillings, and six pence on 5th February 1836. The ascent from Beck Hole cut a curve through woodland for nearly a mile, opening out onto the village green near the village school at Goathland. The average gradient was 1 in 15 but the steepest section, requiring mechanical assistance for over 1,500 yards, was approx. 1 in 11.

George Stephenson designed a self-acting system that counterbalanced three coaches coupled together with a water tank on wheels that ascended or descended by means of a rope. By 1841, seventeen self-acting inclines were in service in the northeast. Later modifications to the counterbalanced incline at Goathland incorporated a stationary steam powered winding engine.

Describing the inaugural journey, the treasurer of the railway, Thomas Clark, provides this account of the Beck Hole incline that Dickens had likened to doing it "like Blondin";

"On the signal being given to "go on", at a merry speed, the train proceeded, and soon arrived at the inclined plane-the horses were detached and some delay necessarily took place, which afforded to the passengers an excellent opportunity for inspecting that which had been decried by those not very favourable to the undertaking, as an insurmountable obstacle to the operations of the Company, no pains having been spared to invest the "inclined plane" with a most formidable and terrific character. The ladies and gentlemen, however, who had never seen the place before were surprised and agreeably deceived in their expectations, for on the signal being given three carriages loaded with passengers glided up the steep ascent with a pleasing, rapid, and easy pace; and both on going and returning many were heard to declare that the ascending and descending of the incline so far from being in any way disagreeable, was certainly as pleasant as any other part of the day's journey. The other carriages followed in succession, and the band during the time played enlivening airs to the manifest delight of a large assemblage of people collected about the top of the inclined plane and who with colours flying and firing guns welcomed the visitors, whilst the most sincere wishes for the prosperity of the undertaking were elicited from all present"

H. Belcher *Scenery of the Whitby and Pickering Railway* (1836)

A more technical description is supplied by the noted railway historian, G W J Potter;

"The rope wheel which was fixed in a horizontal position at the top of the incline was of 10 feet diameter and 5 inches in depth; and was made with a rim of hollow section to receive the 4.5 inch rope, The latter ran on sheaves, 10m inches in diameter, set in iron frames which were let into stone blocks; there being 174 of these sheaves placed at intervals of 8 yards all along the incline......In 1836 the time taken to haul a coach up the incline by this method was usually 4.5 minutes. (around 11 mph) A few years later this plan was abandoned, and a steam engine was placed at the Goathland end of the bank."

G W J Potter *A History of the Whitby and Pickering Railway* (1906)

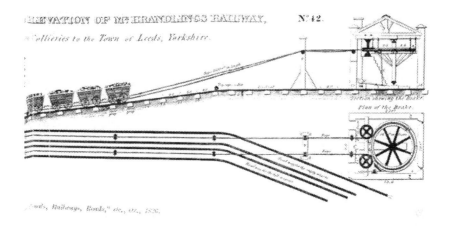

Typical layout of an Inclined Plane

The frontispiece of the first edition of Potter's excellent history of the line is entitled, "Far from the Madding Crowd"- a reference to the title of Thomas Hardy's fourth novel. It features a watercolour of a moorland scene by Gordon Home, artist and author of several books on Yorkshire published in the opening decades of the 20th century. Home's history of Pickering provides a first hand account of one of the workers on the railway from the Pickering end;

"Will Wardell....as a boy of twelve acted as a postillion to the horse railway. Postillions (a means of driving and controlling the coach by riding one of the horses) were only employed for a short time, the horse or horses being soon afterwards driven from the coach. As a rule they employed one horse from Pickering to Raindale, where there was a public-house; then two to Fenbogs, and one to Bank Top above Goathland. If the wind were fair the coach would run to Grosmont by itself, after that one horse took the coach to Whitby. If more than one horse were used they were yoked in tandem; five were kept at Raindale, where Wardell lived.....two coaches "The Lady Hilda" and "Premier"...were painted yellow and carried outside, four in front, four behind, and several others on the top, while inside there was room for six. Wardell helped to make the present railway, and has worked for fifty-five years as a platelayer on the line. He remembers Will Turnbull of Whitby who used to act as guard on the railway coach, and in the same capacity on the stage-coach from Pickering to York. He made the journey from Whitby to York and back daily, the coach running in conjunction with the railway coach".

G Home The Evolution of an English Town (1905)

William Wardell at his home in Pickering in June 1905, aged 78yrs.

Fen Bog and Chat Moss

After ascending from Beck Hole onto the village green at Goathland, the line crossed over the moor and approached the summit. Here, the Stephensons and Fred Swanwick encountered the fourth major obstacle. They had already diverted a river, built a tunnel and constructed a mile-long inclined plane. Now they had to build across a morass of marshland and mire known as "Fen Bog";

"Fen bog....over which the railway is carried for about a mile (is) the site of the summit level. The spring which feeds this bog is one of the sources of Pickering Beck, which uniting with the Derwent, pours its waters into the estuary of the Humber, and joins the

66

sea, after a course of nearly a hundred miles, though rising out of the side of a hill which commands a view of the German Ocean, only a few miles distant."

H. Belcher *The Scenery of the Whitby and Pickering Railway* Ch. IV

**Work in progress constructing the Chat Moss crossing
– a system similar to that used to cross Fen Bog.**
–

Fen Bog is situated in Newtondale and has peat deposits up to eighteen metres deep. It presented the surveyors and engineers with a considerable challenge. However, Messrs Stephenson and associates brought with them invaluable experience of the crossing of Chat Moss when they were building the Liverpool and Manchester line a few years earlier.

Chat Moss was considered an impossible barrier to cross. Critics and engineers at the time spoke plainly;

"perfect madness…this man (George Stephenson) has applied himself to a subject of which he has no knowledge and to which he has no science to apply…..a railroad certainly cannot be safely made over Chat Moss without going to the bottom of the Moss…..everyone knows that iron sinks immediately on its being put upon the surface…culverts which have….the next morning disappeared….There is nothing, it appears, except long sedgy grass, and a little soil to prevent (the rail road) sinking into the shades of eternal night…..etc….etc…etc."

Undeterred, Stephenson approached this formidable task by constructing a floating road. In essence, this was an elongated raft of cross sleepers on a matting of heath and branches of trees covered with a few inches of gravel. A parallel footpath formed in a similar fashion made a trackway to bring materials for the permanent line. Samuel Smiles comments that;

"The wagons carried about a ton each, and they were propelled by boys running behind them along the narrow iron rails. The boys became so expert that they would run the four miles across at the rate of seven or eight miles an hour without missing a step; if they had done so, they would have sunk in many places up to their middle."

The softest parts of the bog were made sufficiently firm to bear the weight of the construction by a combination of drains and double depth hurdles interwoven with heather. The drains were constructed by laying empty tar barrels nailed together and covered over with clay to form an underground sewer.

The greatest difficulty arose at the Manchester end. Here it was necessary to form an embankment, but as fast as it was built up it sank into the bog. The weekly chart of excavation and embankment set against expenditure and displayed in the directors' room began to show no progress. Alarmingly, on some occasions, the fortnightly audit showed less progress than had appeared a fortnight or month before. Alternative methods of piling and building a viaduct of timber proved so costly as to raise the possibility of having to abandon the project.

Stephenson persevered against every dire prediction including the notion that railways themselves were at an end. The organisation of his efforts was itself an innovation. Finding labour, training assistants, building wagons and managing the supply lines all had to be accomplished in the absence of experienced contractors with readily available plant. Tipping hundreds of thousands of cubic metres of material into the bog was required until an embankment formed. This prodigious effort successfully allowed the first experimental train of passengers to cross over Chat Moss on 1st January 1830, drawn by none other than the "Rocket" of Rainhill fame.

By the Side of Stephenson: Steaming over Chat Moss in August 1830

From the pages of a diary kept by an attractive young actress performing at Liverpool at the time, we can form a vivid picture of what it was like to be travelling on a trial run of the first intercity steam passenger service.

"While we were acting at Liverpool an experimental trip was proposed upon the line of railway which was being constructed between Liverpool and Manchester,…. The Liverpool merchants,…. had accepted the risk of George Stephenson's magnificent experiment, (and)….. had the adventurous imagination proper to great speculators, which is the poetry of the counting-house and wharf…..They were exultant and triumphant at the near completion of the work, though, of course, not without some misgivings as to the eventual success of the stupendous enterprise.

My father knew several of the gentlemen most deeply interested in the undertaking, and Stephenson having proposed a trial trip as far as the fifteen-mile viaduct, they, with infinite kindness, invited him and permitted me to accompany them; allowing me, moreover, the place which I felt to be one of supreme honor, by the side of Stephenson.

He was a rather stern-featured man, with a dark and deeply marked countenance; his speech was strongly inflected with his native Northumbrian accent, but the fascination of that story told by himself, while his tame dragon flew panting along his iron pathway with us, passed the first reading of the "Arabian Nights," the incidents of which it almost seemed to recall……I listened to him with eyes brimful of warm tears of sympathy and enthusiasm, as he told me of all his alternations of hope and fear, of his many trials and disappointments, related with fine scorn how the "Parliament men" had badgered and baffled him with their book-knowledge, and how, when at last they thought they had smothered the irrepressible prophecy of his genius in the quaking depths of Chatmoss, he had exclaimed, "Did ye ever see a boat float on water? I will make my road float upon Chatmoss!" ….. and so the railroad was made, and I took this memorable ride by the side of its maker, and would not have exchanged the honor and pleasure of it for one of the shares in the speculators………

And now I will give you an account of my yesterday's excursion. A party of sixteen persons was ushered, into a large court-yard, where, under cover, stood several carriages of a peculiar construction, one of which was prepared for our reception. It was a long-bodied vehicle with seats placed across it, back to back; the one we were in had six of these benches, and was a sort of uncovered charabanc. The wheels were placed upon two iron bands, which formed the road, and to which they are fitted, being so constructed as to slide along without any danger of hitching or becoming displaced, on the same principle as a thing sliding on a concave groove. The carriage was set in motion by a mere push, and, having received, this impetus, rolled with us down an inclined plane into a tunnel, which forms the entrance to the railroad.

This tunnel is four hundred yards long (I believe), and will be lighted by gas. At the end of it we emerged from darkness, and, the ground becoming level, we stopped. There is another tunnel parallel with this, only much wider and longer, for it extends from the place which we had now reached, and where the steam-carriages start, and which is quite out of Liverpool, the whole way under the town, to the docks. This tunnel is for wagons and other heavy carriages; and as the engines which are to draw the trains along the railroad do not enter these tunnels, there is a large building at this entrance which is to be inhabited by steam-engines of a stationary turn of mind, and different constitution from the unfavourable ones, which are to propel the trains through the tunnels to the terminus in the town.

…. We were introduced to the little engine which was to drag us along the rails. She (for they make these curious little fire-horses all mares) consisted of a boiler, a stove, a small platform, a bench and behind the bench a barrel containing enough water to prevent her being thirsty for fifteen miles,--the whole machine not bigger than a common fire-engine. She goes upon two wheels, which are her feet, and are moved by bright steel legs called pistons; these are propelled by steam, and in proportion as more steam is applied to   the upper extremities (the hip-joints, I suppose) of these piston the faster they move the wheels; and when it is desirable to diminish the speed, the steam, which unless suffered to escape would burst the boiler, evaporates through a safety-valve into the air. The reins, bit, and bridle of this wonderful beast is a small steel handle, which applies or withdraws the steam from its legs or pistons, so that a child might manage it. The coals, which are its oats, were under the bench, and there was a small glass tube affixed to the boiler, with water in it, which indicates by its fullness or emptiness when the creature wants water, which is immediately conveyed to it from its reservoirs. There is a chimney to the stove, but as they burn coke there is none of the dreadful black smoke which accompanies the progress of a steam vessel.

This snorting little animal, which I felt rather inclined to pat, was then harnessed to our carriage, and, Mr. Stephenson having taken me on the bench of the engine with him, we started at about ten mile an hour. The steam-horse being ill adapted for going up and down hill, the road was kept at a certain level, and appeared sometimes to sink below the surface of the earth, and sometimes to rise above it. Almost at starting it was cut through the solid rock, which formed a wall on either side of it, about sixty feet high. You can't imagine how strange it seemed to be journeying on thus, without any visible cause of progress other than the magical machine, with its flying white breath and rhythmical, unvarying pace, between these rocky walls, which are already clothed with moss and ferns and grasses; and when I reflected that these great masses of stone had been cut asunder to allow our passage thus far below the surface of the earth, I felt as if no fairy tale was ever half so wonderful as what I saw. Bridges were thrown from side to side across the top of these cliffs, and the people looking down upon us from them seemed like pigmies standing in the sky.

…..We were to go only fifteen miles, that distance being sufficient to show the speed of the engine, and to take us on to the most beautiful and wonderful object on the road. After proceeding through this rocky defile, we presently found ourselves raised upon embankments ten or twelve feet high; we then came to a moss, or swamp, of considerable extent, on which no human foot could tread without sinking, and yet it bore the road which bore us….. but Mr. Stephenson has succeeded in overcoming it.

A foundation of hurdles, or, as he called it, basket-work, was thrown over the morass…… Upon this the clay and soil were laid down and the road does float, for we passed over it at the rate of five and twenty miles an hour, and saw the stagnant swamp water trembling on the surface of the soil on either side of us. ......He explained to me the whole construction of the steam-engine, and said he could soon make a famous engineer of me, which, considering the wonderful things he has achieved, I dare not say is impossible. His way of explaining himself is peculiar, but very striking, and I understood, without difficulty, all that he said to me. We then rejoined the rest of the party, and the engine having received its supply of water, the carriage was placed behind it, for it cannot turn, and was set off at its utmost speed, thirty-five miles an hour, swifter than a bird flies (for they tried the experiment with a snipe). You cannot conceive what that sensation of cutting the air was; the motion is as smooth as possible, too. I could either have read or written; and as it was, I stood up, and with my bonnet off "drank the air before me." The wind, which was strong, or perhaps the force of our own thrusting against it, absolutely weighed my eyelids down. When I closed my eyes this sensation of flying was quite delightful, and strange beyond description; yet, strange as it was, I had a perfect sense of security, and not the slightest fear.

At one time, to exhibit the power of the engine, having met another steam-carriage which was unsupplied with water, Mr. Stephenson caused it to be fastened in front of ours; moreover, a wagon laden with timber was also chained to us, and thus propelling the idle steam-engine, and dragging the loaded wagon which was beside it, and our own carriage full of people behind, this brave little she-dragon of ours flew on. Farther on she met three carts, which, being fastened in front of her, she pushed on before her without the slightest delay or difficulty; when I add that this pretty little creature can run with equal facility either backward or forward, I believe I have given you an account of all her capacities.

Now for a word or two about the master of all these marvels, with whom I am most horribly in love. He is a man of from fifty to fifty-five years of age; his face is fine, though careworn, and bears an expression of deep thoughtfulness; his mode of explaining his ideas is peculiar and very original, striking, and forcible; and although his accent indicates strongly his north-country birth, his language has not the slightest touch of vulgarity or coarseness. He has certainly turned my head."

Fanny Kemble Records of a Girlhood 2nd ed. 1880

So, when George Stephenson presented his report to prospective investors in the Whitby to Pickering line two years later, he was very confident that Fen Bog would not present much of a problem. By a combination of sheaves of heather wrapped in sheep fleeces, hurdles interlaced with heather, and drains and pilings of Baltic fir, the crossing of Fen Bog was successfully achieved.

Equally remarkable is the survival of the original survey drawings by Swanwick and Dodgson. They were discovered in a folio edition of the *"Scenery of the Whitby and Pickering Railway"* donated to that gem of a library which today, along with its Museum, comprises the Whitby Literary and Philosophical Society. Originating from the widow of Fred Swanwick after his death in 1885, the *"Drawings of the Fen Bog"* depict in pencil and watercolour the necessary arrangements for the drainage of the bog and construction of the line over it. In meticulous detail, the structure of the hurdles necessary to provide a base, appear as fresh as the day they were drawn.

The engineering of the sections following Fen Bog were no less difficult. According to Henry Belcher, the next five miles through Newton Dale presented;

"for the whole way a succession of the most difficult ground over which a railway has ever been attempted to be made. In fact the whole of this length had to be formed over broken or boggy ground – in the course of moorland streams – through heaps of stones and earth, that had subsided from the neighbouring cliffs and hills – and in addition to all this, with so considerable an inclination, that many persons thought it would present a complete interruption to the rate of travelling which was to be expected;"

71

From the summit to Pickering, is a descent of over 430 feet. On arrival at the steepest part, the horses were removed. The carriages were coupled and then ran at speeds approaching 30 mph to the level ground some three and a half miles from Pickering. Travelling at this speed would have been a most memorable and unprecedented experience, as Fanny Kemble's diary (above) testifies. For Queen Victoria, travelling on her first journey by rail from London to Windsor, it was "half an hour free from dust and crowd and heat and I am quite charmed by it". Speed and convenience were shortly to become the watchwords too for the local wonder of the passengers of the Whitby and Pickering Railway Company.

The First Ten Years: 1836-1846

Henry Belcher reported in 1836 that the railway had cost £80,000 to build but ultimately the cost was considerably more. At over £4,400 per mile (sufficient for each built mile to employ two labourers for a lifetime), it was completed for over twice George Stephenson's original estimate. By comparison with the major lines of the day e.g. the Grand Junction Railway linking Liverpool and Manchester with Birmingham costing c. £20,000 per mile and the London to Birmingham line at c.£46,000 per mile, this was a modest sum. The

The 'Premier' horse-drawn coach after an original sketch by George Weatherill.

total cost of the line was however considerable in relation to the local economy; in present day terms in excess of sixty million pounds based on average earnings.

Accounts of passenger fares for the whole journey varied over time. For the inaugural journey, the first class "Premier" coach cost five shillings whether inside or outside. For subsequent travel, the fare was four shillings inside and three shillings outside. The first class fares for the twice-daily shorter journey from Whitby to the Tunnel Inn, were one shilling and three pence inside and one shilling outside and the second class fare for "the market people" was set at six pence.

The single journey time by regular coach took approximately two hours at an average speed of ten miles an hour. Even when the surrounding roads became snowbound and impassable, the line remained open with minimal delays of up to an extra hour.

Between June 1835 and March 1836, 12,000 passengers had travelled from Whitby to the Tunnel Inn and 10,000 tons of stone sent via Whitby to London to be used in building works including the new London Bridge. In the two months after the whole route was opened, over 8,000 passengers were carried including the "first gentleman's carriage.....on a truck". It belonged to the 86yr old uncle of Whitby's MP, Aaron Chapman.

The design of the passenger carriages, trucks and wagons used on the line were only a short step away from existing stage-coaches and coal wagons. Each carriage was drawn by one horse (except for some short sections where two were required) with six passengers inside and as many as could squeeze on top. The sketch (above) of "The Premier" by George Weatherill, the railway booking clerk who allocated numbered tickets and seats, shows space for a further four passengers in front and four behind. The driver can be seen perched on a seat with a footplate and lever to brake the carriage as described by Whishaw. The four, three-foot diameter cast iron wheels had their outer surfaces hardened to improve wear. Essentially, this arrangement was a modified stage-coach placed on a superior type of truck. Open carriages were also employed together with wagons with sheet iron bottoms and trucks on which private carriages and other goods could be carried.

One suitably grand private carriage would doubtless have been that of the Duke of Sussex. His journey on the line is captured in a "Loyal Address", delivered on behalf of the directors of the Whitby and Pickering Railway Company, quite possibly by Henry Belcher;

May it Please Your Royal Highness...The Managing Directors of the Whitby and Pickering Railway Company gladly avail themselves of the opportunity presented by the arrival of your Royal Highness at Whitby to express their sense of the gratification which they derive from the circumstance of your Royal Highness visiting this part of the County of York and travelling upon the Whitby and Pickering Railway.

Original manuscript document in the library of the Whitby and Pickering Literary and Philosophical Society. n.d.

It is intriguingly unclear whether the "circumstance" was general or specific, private or public, especially as this popular member of the royal household brought a colourful history to the town.

Prince Augustus Frederick of Hanover, Duke of Sussex (1773-1843), was the sixth son of George III and Queen Charlotte. He spent most of his time as a young man on the continent at a time when "The Grand Tour " of mainland Europe was a fashionable 'finishing school' for the families of the privileged and wealthy. At the age of thirteen, he entered the University of Göttingen and remained there until 1804. Whilst living in Rome in 1792, he met the second daughter of the fourth Earl of Dunmore. A year later, they married illegally. The young prince had not sought the permission of his father, George III, and as the marriage contravened the Royal Marriages Act of 1772, the king declared it void in 1794.

His continental education had encouraged enlightened and liberal attitudes that found little favour in court circles until the accession of his brother William 1V in 1830. A year later, the duke again married illegally. He strongly supported the reform agendas of the day including the abolition of slavery and Catholic emancipation and became an ardent advocate of the arts and sciences. He amassed a huge library filling ten rooms at Kensington Palace with over 50,000 volumes and was actively engaged in his presidencies of the Society of Arts and the Royal Society. He was a favourite uncle of Queen Victoria and gave her hand in marriage to Prince Albert in 1840. The duke died three years later, requesting in his will that he be buried in a public cemetery.

It remains to be unravelled as to why Whitby should have received this royal visitor. The original document of the loyal address bears no date but must lie within the range 1836-1843. It is possible that as the first grand master of the United Grand Lodge of England, he may have had some contact with one of the oldest lodges of freemasons in the country; Lion Lodge No. 312 at Whitby. One of his predecessors as president of the Royal Society was Sir Joseph Banks (1743-1820) who had strong connections with William Scoresby Jr. The reputation of the Stephensons, the scenic beauties of the line, or the social diaries of the Normanby's or Cholmeley's, may all have played their part.

Despite royal visitors and the sum total of their efforts, the directors could not make ends meet. From its beginning, the line was in debt, initially £13,000, requiring a further loan of £30,000 to clear. It became increasingly obvious that a merger was its only hope of financial success. It was a rude awakening for the original subscribers who had anticipated a seven and half per cent dividend on their investment.

Enter The Lord Mayor of York

George Hudson (1800-1871)

By 1844, the "Great Railway Mania" had begun in earnest with eight hundred new miles of railway approved by Parliament. When the time came to submit plans for new railways, riots, disorder and subterfuge were widespread. On the deadline day of the 30th November 1845, roads and railways to London became impassable with upwards of 800 rival groups racing to Whitehall. In one case, a competitor's plans found refuge inside a coffin in order for them to be safely conveyed by the very railway Company that was hostile to the bid! The

75

supremely successful railway speculator, George Hudson dominated this feverish climate.

Hudson was born on a farm at Howsham on the River Derwent about twelve miles from Pickering. There were strong connections with Whitby as the principal seat of the Chomley family was situated in Howsham. As lords of the manor of Whitby, the family owned Whitby Abbey together with its lands and significant parts of the town including Abbey House built on the proceeds of the alum industry. Colonel George Chomley was a member of the Whitby Literary and Philosophical Society and a director of the railway.

Hudson's first employment was as a stable lad and later as a draper's assistant in a shop in York. However, at the age of twenty-seven, his life dramatically changed direction by inheriting a sizeable fortune in cash, land, and property after the death of his great uncle. The legacy is very difficult to calculate at present day values but may be conservatively put in the region of two million pounds.

As one of the wealthiest residents in York, 'George Hudson Esq' soon acquired influence. He immersed himself in politics when the Reform Act of 1832 brought democratic parliamentary elections to York and became the local Tory party's treasurer. A year later, he was a founding director of the York Union Bank and treasurer of a committee formed to bring a railway to the city.

In 1835, a plan to form a "York and North Midland Railway" was proposed. George Stephenson was engaged by Hudson as its supervising engineer after, it is said, the pair had met at Whitby. Fred Swanwick, latterly of the Whitby and Pickering railway, surveyed the line. By the end of the same year, local democracy came to York and Hudson was elected one of the aldermen of the city. Two years later, he became the first Tory Lord Mayor of York.

By the time of the official opening of the York and North Midland line in 1839, York became linked to London via Rugby and Derby with an extension to Leeds. A train left York at 7.30 a.m. and arrived in London at 9.30. p.m., almost halving the time it took for the fastest mail coach and horses to make the same journey. Hudson was by this time chair of the Company with George Stephenson as a shareholder and member of its Board. In July of that year, Hudson and Stephenson announced to shareholders that they were exploring the possibility of a new railway from York to Scarborough with a connection to Pickering and Whitby.

On October 19th, they announced their plans to a public meeting in Scarborough. The unrivalled talents of a hugely successful businessman and the most celebrated railway engineer of his day were now firmly linked in the new enterprise of developing the fledgling seaside tourist industry. Meanwhile, the directors of the Whitby and Pickering railway had always envisaged the development of their line. One of the reasons for the overshoot from the original estimates had been the purchase of land for double line working. With two such powerful advocates, their immediate strategy was a foregone conclusion.

The "Railway King" in Whitby and Scarborough

George Hudson turned his attention to Whitby in earnest by forming the Whitby Building Company in 1843. He unveiled ambitious plans to develop the land overlooking the sea on a cliffside site opposite the Abbey. An improved railway plus newly built accommodation and services might prove to be a winning combination.

Typically, he also had grand plans for entering Parliament. Aaron Chapman, the sitting MP for Whitby was in his early seventies and heading towards retirement. Rumours circulated that Hudson had already made a deal with the local Tories to become their candidate at the next election. However, the Tories of Sunderland spotted their own opportunity. After an election, won by Hudson largely on his promise of a new dock and providing a railway to match, he became the town's MP in 1845. His purchase of the Whitby and Pickering Railway took place in the same year.

The original idea of developing the West Cliff fields at Whitby, today resplendent with handsome buildings of stone and crescents in the style of Georgian spas looking seaward along the cliffs, are a striking reminder of Hudson's visionary zeal. He had formed the Whitby Building Company with several of his friends as shareholders including the York-based architect George Townsend Andrews (1804-1855). Soon afterwards, in 1845, Henry Belcher published an influential pamphlet on the "Advantages of the West Cliff at Whitby for Building Purposes". There is some evidence to suggest that Belcher had a stake in the hotel planned for this location, quite possibly the present day Royal Hotel. Planning for this prestigious development went on apace under Hudson's direction in tandem with the purchase of the Whitby and Pickering railway for £80,000 –much less than it cost to build.

The splendid buildings that today appear with their multi-storied terraces of brick including "Hudson Street" are served by the "Khyber Pass", a dramatic access road, built c. 1850 to provide a convenient way of reaching the beach and harbour below. It came to be named after the bloody history of the British invasions and retreats from Afghanistan (1838-42 and 1878-80) along the thirty-three mile mountain passage through the Hindu Kush Mountains from the borders of modern day Pakistan.

Hudson's plans for the construction of a railway from York to Scarborough progressed in parallel with the West Cliff developments at an equally rapid pace. The proposed new line included a branch to connect with the Whitby and Pickering railway at Rillington, just outside Malton. Hudson engaged Robert Stephenson as its engineer and aimed to open the new route in time for the thirtieth anniversary of Waterloo.

Work commenced in July 1844 even before the granting of Royal Assent. The main base was at Malton and despite design changes and difficulties with peat bogs at the Scarborough end, progress was fast by any standards. Some idea of just how fast can be gathered from the fact that the foundation stone for Stephenson's Ouse Bridge was not laid until March 1845 and the single-track line was opened to Scarborough and Pickering on 7th July only four months later.

Ancillary works on stations and widening for a double track continued for some time afterwards. George Andrews was the architect initially responsible for the notable station buildings at Malton, Pickering and Whitby and the especially fine examples at York and Scarborough, although what we see today includes subsequent alterations and extensions.

A steam passenger service operated to Pickering from October 1845. Its fine Andrews designed station complete with its white and purple glass-covered roof was lit by gas from its own gas works nearby. (Part of the original still survives serving now as a hairdressing salon). Horse-drawn working continued from Pickering to Whitby for a short time until the line's conversion to a double track for locomotives. The effects of this change are evident in the fact that it took twenty horses and ten men to shift 120-ton loads of ironstone from Grosmont to Whitby. The return journey took four hours. The introduction of steam working greatly reduced the cost and the return journey was accomplished in one hour.

The existing horse tunnel at Grosmont had a second tunnel for steam trains built alongside. Cast iron replaced timber bridges, modifications were made to curves, and the rope incline was replaced by wire enabling the first steam locomotive to enter Whitby on 1st July 1847. A further eighteen years were to pass before removing the rope incline in 1865 and building a four and a half mile deviation line.

It is interesting to note the contrasting styles of these two tunnels (above) built alongside each other but separated in time by just over a decade. The first has a grace and charm that is wholly absent in the functional form of the second. They illuminate the underlying attitudes of the early and mid-Victorians to the impact of structures on the environment and the decisions made by individual owners and their architects and engineers. Frederick Williams who wrote *Our Iron Roads* in 1852 uses the example of a tunnel, built in the same year as the second Grosmont tunnel, under the parkland of Shugborough Hall, Shropshire in 1847;

The entrances to tunnels should be various in style, yet consistent with the style of work. They should be massive, to be suitable as approaches to works presenting the appearance of gloom, solidity, and strength.......a light and highly decorated structure, however elegant and well adapted for other purposes, would be unsuitable in such situations; it is plainness combined with boldness, and massiveness without heaviness, that in a tunnel entrance constitutes elegance; and at the same time it is economical.....The appearance of the mouths of some tunnels, especially when thrown out into prominent relief by a pleasant and well wooded landscape stretching around and behind them, is by no means unattractive. As a proof of this statement, a better illustration could scarcely be furnished than of the Shugborough Park tunnel, on the Trent Valley Railway. The north face of this structure forms a noble archway, deeply moulded, flanked by two square towers, the whole being surmounted by a battlemented parapet. The lofty trees, covered with the richest foliage, rising from the elevated ground through which the tunnel is pierced, give a depth of tone and artistic effect to the whole scene at once imposing and beautiful, and form a remarkably fine feature in the scenery of the railway.

Shugborough Tunnel

In addition to the various modifications to the line to accommodate double tracked steam working, the railway station at Whitby was re-located closer to the town centre on the site of another former shipyard. Robert Stephenson opened the new station in July 1847 and shortly afterwards became the town's MP.

A year later, Hudson completed the purchase of the West Cliff fields. By this time, he had been elected Lord Mayor of York for the third time. Amongst his other public offices, he was MP for Sunderland, Lord-Lieutenant of Durham, Magistrate for the North Riding of Yorkshire and Freeman of the Merchants' Company of York.

His house at No. 1, Albert Gate, Knightsbridge, London was one of the largest and most lavish in the city. So large indeed that the satirical magazine *Punch* suggested a railway system would be needed to service the warren of rooms, cellars, and storeys! His London residence was grandly complemented by one of England's earliest Palladian villas at Newby Park adjacent to his Baldersby estate in Yorkshire between Thirsk and Ripon. These estates were but two of several he purchased amounting to around 15,000 acres.

By this stage in his astonishing career, George Hudson controlled almost a third of all the railway lines then built and it seemed there was little left beyond his influence although not everyone was convinced. Thomas Carlyle's highly influential publications as historian, biographer, and essayist were highly critical. He wrote a vitriolic attack on "King Hudson", whose "Rayless Majesty" had been elevated through "balderdash and beer". When at the height of the "Railway Mania" proposals were mooted for a statue in Hudson's honour, Carlyle condemned the idea as a " Brazen Image", that should be thrown "down a coal shaft"!

A Fading Vision.

Two years after steam locomotives entered Whitby, Pickering, and Scarborough, Hudson's enterprises did indeed hit the buffers. The "Giant Humbug" as Dickens had referred to him, met a stream of allegations about the financial affairs of the companies he presided over. Investigating committees were formed and a parliamentary enquiry launched in response to claims that he had bribed Members of the House.

It was 1849 and Hudson's 'annus horribilis'. As the reports of investigations circulated to the directors of his companies, he tendered his resignation, one after another, and sought refuge in Newby Park. In York, Hudson Street was to be re-named Railway Street.

A decade of litigation, claims and counter claims of breaches of contract, failing health, and disposals of assets followed. These events were leavened only by the opening of the new dock at Sunderland and his re-election there as an MP in 1857. He had escaped possible imprisonment by a combination of self-imposed exile in France and Spain, parliamentary privilege, and successful court settlements.

Opinions at the time were divided about his culpability. His contemporaries commented; "a large part of the invective poured out upon him came from quarters, of the purity of which there was little to boast. The fox that loses his tail is persecuted by all the foxes; the rook that is maimed is cawed out of the rookery". A writer in the *Illustrated London News* remarked that "Mr Hudson is neither better nor worse than the morality of 1845. He rose to wealth and importance at an immoral period…whatever may be the hue of the error he committed, it is rather too much to expect of him that he should be purer than his time or his associates. The commercial code of 1845 was, as far as railways were concerned, framed upon anything but moral principles."

By end of the 1850's, in the decade before Hudson's death in 1871, the West Cliff developments at Whitby were well advanced and this, together with the steam railway, led to him being credited as a major benefactor to the town. His several invitations to public functions there included a dinner in his honour. He responded by saying that he believed that, "the day is not far distant when I shall be able to carry out and accomplish all that I proposed for the benefit of your place". At the annual dinner of the Whitby Agricultural Society in 1858, he was regaled with the view that he was; "the mainspring – the moving power- of everything to make Whitby what it is". A year later, the tumbrels were set to roll.

The End of an Era

The chief protagonist at this time was H.S. Thompson, who headed the North Eastern Railway Company. Formed from Hudson's York and North Midland, the new Company was subsequently responsible for operating the steam railway service to Whitby and Pickering.

Thompson, as chairman of the York and North Midland following Hudson's resignation, pursued him through the courts. The death of Robert Stephenson in October 1859 offered an opportunity for Thompson to stand as Liberal parliamentary candidate for Whitby. Hudson was now in Paris after his shock defeat in Sunderland a few months earlier. Bereft of parliamentary privilege, he declined to stand on this occasion but signalled his intention to offer his candidacy at the next general election. It was a standoff that was to last but a few years.

Whitby returned Thompson as its first Liberal MP by the narrow margin of 39 votes. The next general election arose six years later and coincided with the opening of the new Whitby to Pickering deviation line in 1865. The same year also marked the death of Charles Hudson, George Hudson's brother. He had campaigned vigorously on George's behalf since moving to Whitby to live on the West Cliff development and manage the newly built Royal Hotel.

George Hudson was persuaded to stand as Tory candidate against Thompson. He arrived in Whitby to be greeted at 'his' railway station by enthusiastic supporters, addressing them later from an upstairs window at the Angel Inn and again at St Hilda's hall. The North Eastern Railway was not popular in the town and the deviation line was yet to deliver its promised improvements. It looked likely that Hudson would triumph.

On the day before the poll, a ruse was re-enacted that had misfired at Sunderland some years before. On the grounds of failing to meet an alleged debt associated with North Eastern Railway's interests, Hudson was arrested on Monday 10th July, taken to York Castle, and imprisoned there for three months. Thompson lost the election by an even narrower margin of 23 votes to a last minute replacement candidate - Charles Bagnall (1827-1884), Ironmaster at the flourishing Grosmont Ironworks. Hudson was destined to fight for his reputation to the last. The final twist of this tale of misfortune for Hudson was that Thompson had been born at Newby Park.

Whatever the rights and wrongs of his dealings in his public and private life, George Hudson was both a visionary Victorian and in the case of Whitby, a luminary influence. When he died in December 1871, *The Times* editorial commented;

"he was a man who united largeness of view with wonderful speculative courage, …This is the kind of man who leads the world…..The world will court rich men, but there is one whom it will court still more and that is he who is supposed to be able to make all men rich. This was Mr Hudson's position"

On the day of his funeral, shops in Whitby closed as they were also along the route of the cortège in York. The opening of the deviation line in 1865 might well serve as his memorial signifying both enterprise and risk. A more poignant and enduring symbol of Hudson's daring may however be the unfinished arc of the superb Royal Crescent on the West Cliff which looks out over Whitby as if with one eye closed.

Henry Belcher: The Forgotten Diplomat

If "diplomacy is to do and say the nastiest thing in the nicest way", this might well stand as the family motto of civilised solicitors everywhere. Henry Belcher was certainly one of the best. His command of the founding, development, formation, and championing of the Whitby and Pickering Railway has, through the intervening years been largely forgotten, overshadowed by the glamour of railway technology and the romance of the landscape and places which he – if not alone – united.

Given that the Whitby and Pickering railway was one of the earliest scheduled passenger railway services in England, Henry Belcher might more reasonably be remembered as the second railway solicitor after Francis Mewburn of Stockton and Darlington fame. At the first Annual General Meeting

Henry Belcher (1785-1854) Solicitor of the Whitby and Pickering Railway and author of *"Scenery of the Whitby and Pickering Railway" (1836)* and *The Stranger's Guide for a Summer's Day Excursion from Scarborough to Pickering and thence by the Railway to Whitby (1843).*

of the railway Company on Thursday 17th October 1833 it was resolved that;

"Mr James Walker and Mr Henry Belcher be the Clerks to the Company, but without salary beyond the fees incidental to the office and that they also be the Solicitors to the Company".

Some idea of Belcher's grasp of detail and the precautionary zeal of a lawyer is enshrined in thirty-three legally binding penalties drafted into the Company's Regulations. Their sweep and scope can be judged from the following; *Number 26. No driver shall stop his wagons that he may feed his horse, or eat his dinner, or do anything else.*(!)

Belcher was born near Manchester, coming to Whitby about 1820 to form a partnership of "Clarke and Belcher" and later of "Belcher and Walker" solicitors. At this time, he had premises in Sandgate and acted as Whitby's coroner and steward to the lord of the manor. At the passage of the Reform Act in 1832, Henry Belcher became the Borough's Returning Officer. Together with his brother Charles, whose name appears as one of the directors of the railway in the Act laid before Parliament, they are both listed as founder subscribers of the newly formed Whitby Literary and Philosophical Society. In January 1823, Henry became a vice-president of its Council and its second president fifteen years later, in 1838.

Five years later in 1842, he published a pamphlet on the inefficient state of "schools for the poor" in the neighbourhood. This was written at a time when schooling was not compulsory, when schools were largely denominational and thinly spread, and when pupils had to pay for their own education. Typically, Henry Belcher made a spirited and practical response to his own convictions by founding the "Whitby Institute of Popular Arts, Science and Literature" and becoming its first president in 1845. The Institute aimed to "place its advantages within reach of all classes" by providing a reading room and library specialising in "Art, Science and General Literature". It held weekly meetings "for mutual improvement", occasional meetings for "musical and other rational entertainment", classes for instruction, and lectures on "all subjects of popular interest". At the core of its formal constitution was the rule that "Neither Politics or Controversial Theology be entertained".

Its first premises in Whitby were in Flowergate with accommodation provided for a housekeeper. Henry Belcher donated one hundred and fifty volumes to its library together with other donors including Robert Stephenson who specified certain titles for purchase on his behalf including two volumes on molluscs and four volumes on architecture. In the year following Henry Belcher's death, it was resolved that the Institute and the Whitby Literary and Philosophical Society take steps to build joint premises in his honour.

Belcher's public works demonstrate that he was a man of wide interests and a notable patron of the arts. Perhaps his most accessible achievements for us today are the books he wrote and published to promote the Whitby and Pickering railway. His first publication, reproduced in the following chapter, ranks as a significant contribution to our historical understanding of the natural history, topography, culture and economy of the locality. His account of a journey from Whitby to Pickering on the newly formed railway in the early nineteenth century has immortalised his voice and enabled us to share in the outlook of his class of fellow Victorians.

A related, and much less well-known publication reproduced in chapter seven, chronicles a journey in the opposite direction travelling from Scarborough to Whitby. It was written in 1843, just before Hudson and Stephenson's steam railway opened. George Haydock Dodgson, one of Stephenson's assistant surveyors, illustrated both publications. Belcher had spotted him sketching in Whitby and the story of this encounter and its aftermath is told in chapter five by a direct descendant of the Dodgson family.

Henry Belcher also encouraged and was closely associated with another widely celebrated Whitby watercolourist. George Weatherill (1810-1890) was employed in Belcher's practice as a clerk and a book-keeper for the railway. It is typical of his visionary influence that Henry Belcher commissioned Weatherill, well before his rise to fame as an artist, to provide four lithographed "views" for a booklet written in 1839 to raise funds for a church at Grosmont. Belcher writes; "there is only one drawback to prevent this interesting neighbourhood becoming a desirable place of residence, now that the Whitby and Pickering railway has made it so easy to access, and that is the circumstances of there not being any church within several miles"

H Belcher *Some Account of the Ancient Priory of Grosmont, in the Vale of Esk, near Whitby, with two views of the ruins as they appeared before being removed.* 1839

Belcher's efforts bore fruit and in September 1841, he wrote verses for the laying of the foundation stone. The church, dedicated to St Matthew, opened in June 1842 and silver Communion Service was given by Belcher to mark the occasion. (The present church was erected some thirty years later to accommodate the greatly expanding population from the growth of the local ironstone industries. The stained glass east window from the original church recorded the contribution of Henry Belcher.)

Henry lived to complete the purchase of the Whitby and Pickering railway by Hudson and to witness the tribulations that later befell the Railway King. He died in the year that Britain opened hostilities against Russia and embarked upon the Crimean War, the year that London experienced a cholera epidemic with the loss of 10,000 lives, and the year that saw the opening of the Canada Great Western Railway.

Henry Belcher served as the second President of the Whitby Literary and Philosophical Society from 1838, soon after the railway opened, to his death in 1854 at the age of sixty-nine. His remains were interred in St Mary's Churchyard, Warwick. A memorial address given at the Whitby Literary and Philosophical Society in April 1854 recorded;

"its sense of the courtesy, impartiality, and ability invariably manifested by him in the discharge of his duties, as well as of the important services rendered by him in the furtherance of the objects of the society.........

Henry Belcher was no ordinary man. Indeed Whitby will not soon see his like again. His urbanity and courteous manners rendered his society agreeable and welcome to every grade of society. He was in fact, the genuine type of the true English gentleman"

CHAPTER 5

ILLUSTRATIONS OF THE SCENERY ON THE LINE OF THE WHITBY AND PICKERING RAILWAY IN THE NORTH EASTERN PART OF YORKSHIRE FROM DRAWINGS BY G. DODGSON (1836).

This book launched the artistic career of George Dodgson. As a young man, he was an assistant surveyor employed by George Stephenson to prepare elevations, plans, and maps for the construction of the Whitby and Pickering railway. His drawings of the scenery of the line were sent to London for engravings to be made. The printer then published the text with illustrations from the engraved plates. An account of George Dodgson's life follows in Chapter Six written by his direct descendant, Hugh Dodgson.

Henry Belcher, the solicitor for the railway, wrote and edited this book, commissioned the drawings, and invited contributions from his associates. Many of the early Victorian spellings of place names will be readily recognisable e.g. Glazedale (Glaisdale), Staiths (Staithes). Others such as Goathland Beck (now Eller Beck), North Dale Beck and Newton Dale Beck (now Pickering Beck) may not be so obvious. A limited railway directors' folio edition was also published without text containing all of the main illustrations.

In the year before the full route was completed, a coach ran on the line up to the Tunnel Inn and back with, as Belcher comments, "the exception of Sundays". He continues;

"In the course of the first three months upwards of 6,000 persons travelled to and fro; and so universal and so decided was the admirations expressed at the beauty of the scenery thus thrown open, that the idea of having an illustrated description of the Railway was at once adopted; and the following pages, with the accompanying views, are published, in humble expectation of giving to the Whitby and Pickering Railway an interest in public estimation, on other grounds than those which are usually attached to similar undertakings"

(Ed.)

ILLUSTRATIONS

OF

THE SCENERY ON THE LINE

OF THE

WHITBY AND PICKERING
RAILWAY,

IN THE NORTH EASTERN PART OF

YORKSHIRE.

———◆———

FROM DRAWINGS BY G. DODGSON.

———————

WITH A SHORT

Description of the District and Undertaking,

BY HENRY BELCHER.

" ————— On it runs,
Winning its easy way—
Thro' glens lock'd up before."   Rogers.

LONDON:

PUBLISHED FOR THE PROPRIETORS,

BY LONGMAN, REES, ORME, BROWN, GREEN, AND LONGMAN,
PATERNOSTER ROW.

1836.

INTRODUCTION

THE project of submitting to the public an account of a Railway, in the form proposed in the following pages, may appear somewhat extraordinary and paradoxical, especially as the Railway to be described is of little importance, compared with the numerous undertakings of the same kind in other parts of the kingdom. It is true that the town of Whitby with its venerable Abbey, and the magnificent coast scenery in its neighbourhood are not unknown: and it is equally true, that they are justly admired by all who, not deterred by the difficulty of approach from the hilly and dangerous nature of the roads, have hitherto ventured to visit them. Barren and unpromising, however, as may appear the lofty range of moors which encircle Whitby for so many miles, the numerous vales which intersect this district, (but which from the peculiar formation of the country escape the observation of persons travelling by the usual routes) abound with scenery of a highly romantic and beautiful character. These inland recesses are consequently but little known, and have been seldom visited, except by the few, who having a taste for the wild beauties of nature, have had the inclination also to explore the vales and glens where they are to be so abundantly found.

The inhabitants of Whitby have long felt the want of a better communication with the interior of the county, than is afforded by the present moorland roads; and the circumstance of a succession of vallies branching into one another towards the south, and terminating at Pickering, suggested the possibility of the desired improvement being effected by carrying a Rail-road in that direction. The genius of a STEPHENSON having satisfied the public as to the practicability of the measure, the favourable and good feeling of the inhabitants of Whitby and of Pickering, with the aid of friends in other quarters, soon provided the means of carrying that eminent Engineer's plans into operation, and an Act of Parliament for making a Railway from Whitby to Pickering was accordingly applied for, and in May, 1833, received the Royal Assent.

This Railway, passing in a westerly direction from Whitby up the rich valley of the Esk for about six miles, then turns to the south, entering through a short tunnel into the hitherto secluded Vale of Goathland; leaving which, and attaining the summit level at the distance of about twelve miles from Whitby, it runs into Newton Dale, and, threading the romantic windings of that singularly formed chasm, and the rich wood scenery of Blansby Park, arrives at the town of Pickering; developing throughout its course a series of highly beautiful and romantic views.

Whitby Abbey. North Isle

About six miles of the Whitby end of the Railway having been so far completed by the month of June last, as to admit of carriages passing along to that extent, a coach was put upon the line, and has since then run daily (with the exception of Sundays), to the Tunnel Inn and back. In the course of the first three months upwards of 6,000 persons travelled to and fro; and so universal, and so decided was the admiration expressed at the beauty of the scenery thus thrown open, that the idea of having an illustrated description of the Railway was at once adopted; and the following pages, with the accompanying views, are published, in the humble expectation of giving to the Whitby and Pickering Railway an interest in public estimation, on other grounds than those which are usually attached to similar undertakings.

Such being the express object of this work, it is not to be expected that the descriptions will be otherwise than general, or that they will be extended beyond the present appearance and character of the district, except when any allusion to natural history or antiquities may serve to add a charm to any particular places to which those subjects may incidentally apply. —The able Histories of Whitby by Charlton and Young, of Scarbro' by Hinderwell, and of the neighbourhood of Pickering by Marshall and Eastmead, in addition to the recent geological accounts of the Yorkshire Coast by Messrs. Young and Bird, and Mr. Philips, contain so much valuable information as to the antiquities, natural history, geology, and statistics of the neighbourhood, that it would be presumptuous in the Editor of the following pages to attempt adding to the stores of knowledge which these well known works afford. *

The country through which the Whitby and Pickering Railway passes being in itself somewhat singular, there is a consequent peculiarity in the construction of the works of the Railway, which may render some account of it as a matter of scientific contrivance, an interesting addition to that general description of the district, which is more especially the design of the following pages. A Supplemental Chapter on this subject, with some observations as to the prospects of the Railway will therefore be given.

WHITBY,

March, 1836.

* The "PICTURE OF WHITBY," by the Reverend G. Young, of which a new edition is shortly expected to appear, and the "ICHNOGRAPHY OF WHITBY ABBEY," with some account of that interesting edifice, by H. W. Benson, may also be consulted with advantage.

Whitby From the West Pier

CHAPTER I.

WHITBY.

Yon towering cliff, where proudly stand
A ruin'd Abbey's sculptur'd walls,
Points Out to view, from sea or land,
The site of Streonshalh's ancient halls

The scenes where sainted Hilda prayed,
Where Cædmon penn'd his heav'nly lays;
Where holy men their zeal display'd,
And sang their choral hymns of praise.

AT the north-east angle of the county of York, where the small but romantic river Esk pours its tributary stream into the German Ocean, stands the town of Whitby.

Enclosed between precipitous cliffs, and creeping up their sides as they recede along each shore of the river from the sea, the town itself is scarcely to be seen until very nearly approached, though the situation is well pointed out by the ruins of its once stately abbey, which, unlike most other monastic institutions as to site, occupies the highest land in the immediate vicinity, and is visible for many miles in every direction.

The antiquity and importance of that once noble edifice and its attendant establishments, have tended much to confer on the neighbourhood a degree of consequence and interest, that it might not otherwise have acquired; although its claim to historical record rests not on this ground alone.

That the Romans were acquainted with this part, is evident from the traces of their works still visible in the vicinity, and to which some allusion will be made in the course of the following pages. The Saxons and Danes also were alternately in possession of the district; and, amongst the numerous descents upon the eastern coast made by the latter, two places at no great distance from Whitby, each of which to this day bears the identifying appellative of Raven Hill, are noticed in the annals of local history, as situations where they landed their pagan and desolating hordes.

Of the early history of the abbey but little is known, except that it was founded in the year 658, by the celebrated Hilda, and destroyed by the Danes about 200 years afterwards.

Soon after the conquest the Abbey was rebuilt, and, being endowed with extensive estates by the noble families of Percy and De Bruce, and by other distinguished individuals, flourished in splendour and magnificence until the reign of Henry the Eighth, when it shared the common fate of all similar institutions.

At this time the town of Whitby was of inconsiderable extent, consisting only of a few houses scattered along each side of the river; but the sequestered estates of the Abbey having been granted by the crown to Sir Richard Chomley, the spirited exertions of several members of that distinguished family, and especially of Sir Hugh Cholmley, contributed much to the rapid increase of the place; and laid the foundation of its subsequent wealth and importance.

The Abbey, though built at different periods, was when complete in the form of a cross; and consisted of a nave, choir, and side aisles, and a transept with side aisles on the east side only. In the centre was a noble tower 104 feet high, which standing upon an elevation of at least 200 feet above the level of the sea, formed a most conspicuous and highly useful landmark,

> "A beacon o'er the trackless deep."

On the 25th of June, 1830, this stately portion of the Abbey suddenly gave way, after having for many years exhibited symptoms of rapidly increasing decay. Notwithstanding its tottering condition, it withstood year after year the fury of the wintry blast, as if unwilling to be hurried to that destruction which seemed so inevitably to await it; but it was not fated so to meet its doom, for contrary to general expectation, on the calm noontide of a summer's day it fell slowly and majestically, its fragments forming a shapeless heap of ruin, an apt funereal pile, almost on the very spot once sheltered by its hallowed roof.

Notwithstanding the loss of its tower, enough yet remains of Whitby's "cloistered pile" to make it deserving of the attention of the artist, the antiquary, and the man of taste and feeling. The more closely the ruins are examined the more beautiful and curious do they appear; and, varying in general effect with every change of atmosphere, they form a never-failing subject of interest and contemplation. At morn—at noon— at dewy eve, or by "pale moonlight," the spectator finds himself delighted with the scene.— But the evening and moonlight effects are undoubtedly the finest,

> "When the broken arches are black in night,
> And each shafted oriel glimmers white,"

When we may hear the

> "Owlet hoot o'er the dead man's grave,"

and the low murmur of the waves beneath, forming an accompaniment completely in unison with the scene.

The prevailing taste of the present day for geological pursuits has contributed not a little to bringing into notice a neighbourhood that abounds with rare and valuable specimens, and presents, from the peculiar character of its lofty and precipitous cliffs, an unusually fine field for the practical illustration of the science. A Museum established in the town in the year 1823, possesses a most extensive collection of the specimens of the district, and amongst them, a fossil crocodile in a very perfect state, which is considered unique, and has attracted in an extraordinary degree the notice of the curious and scientific.

Independently of its Abbey and its geological treasures, Whitby has long been admired on account of the peculiarity of its situation, and the grandeur of its coast scenery.

To the eastward the cliffs rise abruptly to the height of nearly 200 feet, and trending towards the south, present for several miles a succession of sudden indentations and bold headlands, picturesque in the highest degree both as to form and color, and imposing in point of elevation. Perhaps the general character of this part of the coast is no where displayed to greater advantage, or

---- "the sea girt side,"
"The steepy rock, the frantic tide,"

found in finer combination than at the southern extremity of Robinhood's Bay; where the steep ascent leading direct from the shore along the very verge of the cliff, on which stands the Peak Alum Works, appears backed by several equally precipitous but somewhat loftier cliffs, till the view is closed in by the bold and towering face of the Peak Cliff rising to the height of 700 feet, and forming the abrupt termination of a ridge of land that in former times was the site of Roman and Danish forts, and is to this day distinguished by the name of Raven Hill. Near the summit of this hill stands Raven Hall, the seat of the Reverend Mr. Willis; and from the highest point there is a magnificent and extensive prospect. To the south the ruins of Scarbro' Castle with the far off cliffs of Filey and Flamborough, and a long range of the Yorkshire Wolds are distinctly seen; whilst to the north the expanse of Robinhood's Bay, with the rich amphitheatrical vale of Fyling lies, as it were, at the feet of the spectator, who, raising his eye over the high grounds at the other side of the vale, beholds in the distance the hills bordering on the vale of Cleveland.

To the north of Whitby the views along the coast are not less imposing. The headlands at Sandsend, Kettleness, Staiths, Huntcliffe and Rawcliffe, abrupt in outline, and varying in elevation from two to six hundred feet, present a succession of grand and romantic coast scenery, scarcely to be exceeded in England: whilst the several vallies opening up the country from the sea at Mulgrave, Staiths, Skinningrove and Marske, are replete with picturesque beauties of no ordinary character.

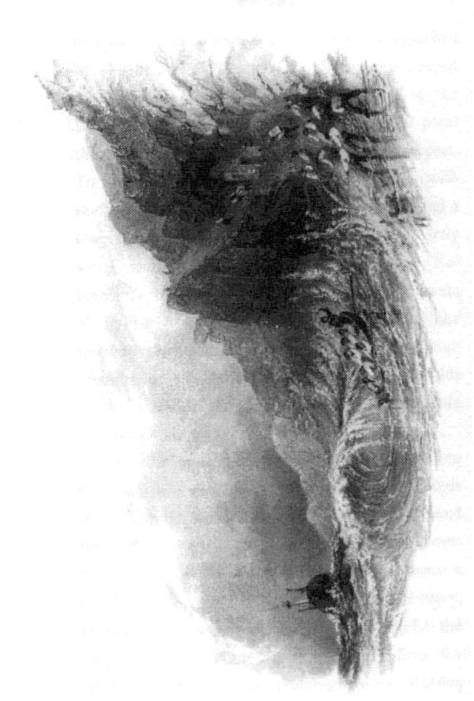

Cliffs at Peak. Robin Hoods Bay.

Mulgrave Castle, distant about four miles from Whitby, is seen embosomed in thriving woods at a considerable elevation above the sea. The grounds, in which are still standing the ruins of the ancient castle, erected according to tradition on the site of a Roman fortress, are justly celebrated for their many natural beauties, as well as for the good taste which has assisted in displaying them to advantage, and making the most romantic situations accessible. Few parks in the kingdom will be found to combine such an extent of fine wood scenery with a near view of the sea, as the one at Mulgrave; and through the courteous liberality of the noble owner there is no difficulty in obtaining permission to explore this part of his domains.

The singularly situated village of Runswick, with its beautiful Bay running deep inland and surrounded by fine cliffs, is highly deserving of a visit; as is also the still more romantic village of Staiths, both of them are within the scope of an easy day's journey from Whitby.

Returning, however, to the more immediate notice of Whitby, it will be found that the scenery along the coast there possesses much that is deserving of admiration. The walk along the scarr under the east cliffs is grand in the extreme: and the small secluded bay of Saltwick, to which it leads, is for its extent the most picturesque of any upon the coast. The frowning lofty cliffs around it are rich in the fossils peculiar, to the upper lias bed; a circumstance that adds much to the interest of a walk along its shores. The field path from Saltwick to Whitby by the top of the cliffs forms a magnificent terrace, commanding a great extent of view both by sea and land.

Turning from the cliff, the ruins of the Abbey strike the enraptured eye, from this point appearing to rise in greater mass than from any other situation, and producing a splendid and overpowering effect. Passing into the high road the spectator, on approaching the church, comes to a turn, whence Sandsend Bay richly burnished by the evening sun, with the lofty and abrupt cliffs of Sandsend and Kettleness, the church crowned hill of Lyth, and in clear weather the distant shore of the county of Durham bursts suddenly on his view, producing an effect indescribable but to those who have experienced it, and to strangers the more surprising from being so unexpected.

Arriving in the churchyard and turning towards the Abbey, a different but not less pleasing effect is produced. That venerable structure now appears lighted up by the beams of the setting sun, whilst the churchyard and intermediate distance are thrown into shade by the buildings that intercept them, thus producing the striking effect so inimitably described in the accompanying view—a view which speaks at once to the feelings, and leads one to exclaim

> How bright and calm above,
> Tho' dark and sad below;
> Like visions of eternal love,
> To solace earthly woe.

Nor is the sentiment weakened by the interesting group introduced into the foreground of the picture, and which tells a more than ordinary tale of sorrow. The sturdy sexton even seems to feel its force and

> _____ pause awhile
> That widow'd love may look once more and weep.

The view from the churchyard is generally admired, and, in a letter under the signature of "Ruswarpius," in the Gentleman's Magazine for July, 1828, is described in so animated and correct a manner, that no apology can be necessary for inserting that description here.—After premising that the ascent from the town to the churchyard is gained by 190 steps, Ruswarpius observes, "From the acclivity extensive prospects present themselves on every side—the tenantless monastic ruins, the wide ocean ever washing the sandy beach, with ships scudding along its bosom in the distance—the woods and castle of Mulgrave— the piers—the concave town, harbour, shipping, and curious draw-bridge" (now removed) "across the river, all immediately beneath the eye—the winding and fertile valley of the Esk, through which rolls in many a serpentine curve the stream of that name, the numerous swelling hills intersecting one another and studded with villas, hamlets, groves, and homesteads, the high and lonely moors beyond covered with dark purple heath, and which seem to frown upon the humble but smiling dales below, the toute ensemble affording panoramic views of mingled beauty and sublimity of which few have hitherto been pictured by the artist, and words must fail to convey an adequate representation."

The town of Whitby itself, though ill built and ill contrived, has much of the picturesque in its appearance, from whatever point of view beheld.—The general effect is not however quite so good since the removal of the curious draw-bridge, which, though injurious to the navigation, and inconvenient and even dangerous to passengers, was nevertheless an object of much interest, as being a good specimen of almost the last bridge of the kind in the kingdom, and an exact model of the structures that had successively been erected in the same situation for several centuries before. A bridge of very different construction, and calculated to afford increased facilities both for the shipping and for travellers, has lately been erected in its place.

The outer piers of Whitby have long been celebrated for the grandeur and insularity of their situation and the excellence of their workmanship. The west pier is particularly admired. Extending a considerable distance into the sea, with an elegant columnar lighthouse at its extremity, this pier forms a favorite promenade with the inhabitants and strangers—and most justly so; for the views along the coast in each direction are from it seen to the greatest advantage, and there is no other point from which the town and harbour display with better effect their peculiar characteristics. Near the battery some steps lead from the pier to the West Cliffs, along which there is a most delightful walk, not so grand

Whitby Abbey from the Church Yard.

as the one on the East Cliffs, but by no means less beautiful, though quite different in character; for the cliffs are little more than half the height, and, excepting at a few points, slope to the beach, which instead of being a floor of rock, as under the East Cliffs, is here a broad extent of sand stretching along the shore for about three miles.— There is a softness and serenity in the view of Sandsend Bay and of the ocean from these cliffs on a calm summer's evening, when the sea appears "as if the sun had melted in its tide," that thrill the mind with rapture, and give rise to the most exquisite feelings of delight. And if, when "the few faint flashes of departing day" gleam along the glassy surface of the deep, and influenced by the sublimity, the repose, the silence of the vast expanse, broken only by the dying murmur of the waves rippling along its shore, these feelings should assume a more serious solemn cast, and there should be a dash of sadness in their tone, yet it must be confessed that it is a sadness by which the heart is made better.

Turning from the coast, the stranger will meet with much to admire amongst the inland scenery within a short distance.

The view of the harbour and town from the road leading to Stainsacre forms, under favourable circumstances of atmosphere, a striking subject for fine effect. And from the upper part of the Larpool Woods also the same objects are seen in different positions, but still in grand and picturesque combination.

Pursuing the road in front of Larpool Hall, the finely situated mansion of Edmund Turton, Esq. a delightful view of the lower part of the vale of Esk, with its winding river, rich fields, and well-wooded declivities, with the high moors in the distance present itself: half a mile further the road descends rapidly into a richly-wooded dingle, which unfolds many picturesque objects; especially a waterfall, which though inconsiderable as to height and body of water, yet possesses so happy an assemblage of all the essentials to a perfect picture, as to be universally admired— and not perhaps the less so, from such a scene being perfectly unsuspected in the near vicinity of a town. A view of this waterfall would have been taken for this work, were it not that there is another in the district of similar character more immediately connected with the object of these pages, and of which an engraving will be given.—The same reason may be assigned for not introducing a print of Falling Foss, a waterfall at Newton House, the sporting seat of John Moss, Esq. of Liverpool—a fall which in point of height is much superior to others, though from the geological structure of the accompaniments not so well adapted for pictorial effect. The extensive plantations at Newton House, with the Hermitage formed out of the living rock, the woodland walks, and the waterfall, form altogether a pleasing object for a day's excursion from Whitby, from whence they are but five miles distant.

Rigg Mill, on the Sneaton Estate, is another romantic specimen of the peculiar glen scenery of the district, and through the contiguous woods and plantations drives have been formed so as to display that scenery to much advantage.

At the north end of the village of Sneaton there are the foundations still visible of the castle, in former times the abode of the Percy's, the princely contributors to the possessions of Whitby Abbey.

The village of Ruswarp, scarcely two miles from Whitby, has ever been the favorite object of a summer's evening walk to those, who prefer an inland stroll to one upon the coast; and there is a degree of rural quiet and seclusion in this little vale, that added to the beauty of the surrounding scenery makes it always pleasing.

" Scenes must be beautiful which, daily seen
Please daily, and whose novelty survives
Long knowledge and the scrutiny of years."

Cowper

West End of Whitby Abbey

CHAPTER II.

ESKDALE.

Along the river's winding shore,
Or o'er its pebbly strand,
A road appears unknown of yore,
By modern science plann'd.

And as up Eskdale's ample range
It skirts each wood and dene,
More grand, more varied is each change,
More lovely grows the scene.

THE previous chapter having been devoted almost exclusively to the scenery of Whitby and the coast, it is now proposed to give some account of the romantic inland vales by which that scenery is backed, and which the formation of the railway has rendered accessible.

Though the valley of the Esk, for the space of three miles from the sea, is known to all persons approaching Whitby by way of Pickering, from the circumstance of the turnpike road to the latter town passing up it to that extent, yet as the course of the railway is by no means the same as that of the turnpike road, the views afforded by the one differ materially from those which may be seen upon the other; and beyond the point, where that road crosses the railway, the latter enters altogether upon scenery that was scarcely known until opened out by that undertaking.

The railway has its commencement on the west side of the harbour of Whitby, at the place once occupied by the extensive ship-building establishment of Messrs. Fishburn and Brodrick; and from whence there is a good view of the east side of the town and harbour, with the venerable Abbey above: but in other respects the line of the railway at its outset presents nothing remarkable, until, passing the quay and warehouse of the Whitby Stone Company on the one hand, and a cluster of cottages on the other, a beautiful and unexpected prospect is displayed. The river suddenly contracted in its extent, winds majestically between steeply rising banks well clothed with wood from the water's edge, except where intercepted on the right by the quay along which the railway is conveyed, forming altogether a singular contrast with the general appearance of the river previously exhibited.

After passing the Weighing Machine House the town and harbour, which, on looking back upon them, from this point appear to much advantage, are altogether lost sight of, and the sylvan vale of Ruswarp begins gradually to come into view.

The railway follows the bold and graceful sweep of the new bed of the river, which when filled by the flowing tide has a noble and picturesque appearance the Larpool woods, and the mansion of Edmund Turton, Esq. proudly rising above them, being on the left, the vale of Ruswarp in front, the plantations and sloping banks of Sneaton with its numerous white cottages and Gothic church, and the more distant village of Ugglebarnby rising gently beyond, on the left; and the extreme distance closed in by the heights of Aislaby Moor on the one side, and the bold eminence of Sleights Moor on the other: nor is the view on looking back less beautiful in its way, though more confined, consisting simply of the sweep of the river, and the rich hanging woods that adorn its banks.
A little further to the left is seen the sequestered dingle of Cock Mill Wood alluded to in the former chapter; with a water mill most picturesquely peeping from amongst "the umbrageous multitude of leaves."
On the space between the railway and the old bed of the river on the right, stands a newly-erected bone crushing and saw mill; the first building emanating from that spirit of speculation which the railway is so well calculated to draw forth and to encourage.
Passing along the flat of Ruswarp Vale, popularly called the Fitz, the village of Ruswarp with its ancient hall, and the pathway through the fields from Whitby are seen on the right.
At the distance of a mile and a half from Whitby the railway crosses, for the first time, the river Esk, by means of a bridge, which forms a conspicuous and ornamental object amidst the surrounding scenery.
From this bridge a general view of the lower part of Eskdale unfolds itself; conveying a pleasing impression of the character of the vale, and giving fair promise of greater beauty as you advance.

A quarter of a mile beyond, the suspension bridge, leading to the Sneaton Estate and erected at the sole cost of the late James Wilson, Esq. M. P., is seen at a point where there is a bold curve of the river, which adds much to its effect.

From hence to Sleights Bridge the railway passes very near the banks of the river, of which several good views are occasionally obtained; and on the opposite hill appear, in succession, the mansions of Joseph Campion, Esq., John Mellar, Esq., and Miss Pennyman, all delightfully situated.

Immediately before approaching the point where the turnpike road to York crosses the railway, the valley of Iburn Dale opens to the left; whilst on the right is a particularly pleasing view, consisting of a bridge of three arches, bestriding "the Esk's fair stream," the luxuriant groups of trees which encircle woodlands, and the well-wooded heights of Aislaby in the back ground.

After crossing the turnpike road, Grove's Hall is to be seen on the right, perched on a steep wooded bank immediately above the river, across which there is a weir with hecks, formerly used for taking the salmon that then abounded in this stream. It is to be hoped that the Esk may again become one of our salmon rivers.

Proceeding a little further, the railway is found to have been taken through an excavation of alum rock; on emerging from which another and a highly beautiful division of the Vale of Esk discovers itself:—

"Wide and wider spreads the vale."

Here, on the left, is the mansion of J. C. Coates, Esq. seated on a gentle elevation of park-like appearance, and surrounded by noble trees:— above stands the village of Sleights.—On the opposite bank, embosomed in plantations, Woodlands, the seat of H. W. Yeoman, Esq. catches the eye,—whilst crowning the well-wooded eminence that rises above, is seen the village of Aislaby, with the mansions of John Benson, Esq. and the late Mark Noble, Esq. looking down on the vale below. The views in this part of the vale are highly pleasing; in front, and on both sides, are extensive woods and plantations, interspersed with richly

Sleights Bridge.

cultivated fields, backed on the north by the heights of Aislaby and Egton north moor, with a long range of stone quarries of cliff-like appearance, and on the south by Sleights Moor,

> "With windy summit wild and high,
> Roughly rushing on the sky."

This high portion of land rising rapidly to an elevation of at least 700 feet above the level of the railway, shews various phases in the course of the next three miles; forming a principal and ever-varying feature in the prospect.
The river Esk is now crossed by a bridge, the second over that stream, and the third in point of number on the railway; and such is the sinuosity of the river's course, that in less than half a mile it is crossed again; and then a little on the left is seen the ruin of Eskdale Chapel.

To those unacquainted with the traditions of the district, and the history of Whitby Abbey, some explanation may appear necessary for introducing the view of a ruin so insignificant in extent, and so wanting in pretensions to the picturesque. The popular legend* connected with this "chapel small, of structure rude," or rather with the hermitage that in days lang syne occupied its site, has been lately made the subject of an elegant and interesting poem by the talented lady of Dr. Merryweather of Whitby. This poem contains several spirited descriptions of the scenery of this part of

> "The lovely vale where Esk meanders down."

"This chapel is of considerable antiquity, being noticed in some of the records of Whitby Abbey as far back as 1224; but nothing is said of the founder. Tradition relates, that the hermitage falling into decay, this chapel was erected;" becoming

*An account of this popular legend is given in the Appendix.

Bridge in Eskdale
No 5

ruinous and too small for the accommodation of the inhabitants, a new and remarkably elegant chapel was erected about seventy years ago, at the neighbouring village of Sleights. The ruin itself has lately become the property of a lady, who seems inclined to protect it from further injury and spoliation.

The approach to the next bridge presents several pleasing views; but the principal attraction is on the left, where a bold sweep of perpendicular rock, the upper parts clothed with fine oak timber, shoots up from the brink of the river to an elevation of nearly two hundred feet,— with Sleights Moor, which here presents a more imposing appearance than from any other point, rising almost immediately and abruptly behind.

Cutting through the Alum Shale.

On the surface of the moor, at some little distance from the excavations that are to be seen near its summit, are some traces of an ancient British encampment.

Till within the last fifteen years an extensive manufacture of alum was carried on in this neighbourhood by the Yeoman family.

A gentle curve of the railway leads to another cutting through the alum shale :— and the scenery at this particular point is well deserving of admiration.

Beyond this excavation the general appearance of the vale becomes more park-like. On a rising ground in front is seen, amongst the trees, the ancient mansion of Newbegin Hall, formerly a seat of the Salvins, but now the property of H. W. Yeoman, Esq. On the left is a foot-bridge over the river, in a most romantic situation, leading by means of a path through the fine hanging woods that climb up the opposite bank to the old alum works.

The river is again crossed by the following bridge,—

In executing the cuttings on this part of the line, both above and below this bridge, as well as in a cutting about a mile farther along, a number of rounded pebbles and masses of whinstone of considerable size were found; strongly indicating that at some remote period this part of the valley has been a lake, whose waters have been gradually displaced by the accumulated deposits of the stream brought down from the hills and dales above. This supposition is further corroborated by the circumstance of the excavated soil, when exposed, immediately producing the indigenous plants of the district.

The Bridge No. 7 now conveys the rail road again over the Esk, into the estates of Mr. Yeoman; and so nearly is the lower portion of the valley here closed in on either side by projecting knolls of rock and woodland, as to be contracted at the bottom to little more than the space required for the passage of the river;* insomuch that the railway has to be supported by a wall along its northern banks. The views on this portion of the line, though confined in extent, are as romantic and singular as at any point in the whole course of the railway through the valley of the Esk.

After leaving the fine sweeping avenue here formed by the removal of trees for the line of railway, and passing over another bridge (the eighth) the valley again expands in full luxuriance. On the right is a fine amphitheatrical range of wood belonging to H. W. Yeoman, Esq., and beyond it lies Cote Bank, a well-wooded estate,

"Whose uplands sloping deck the mountain's side,"

belonging to D'Oyley Saunders, Esq. On the high ground, in the middle distance, stands the ancient village of Egton, a place of importance in former times, and where cattle fairs are still held at regular intervals during the year, and much resorted to. Looking hack from this part of the line the view is very striking, on account of the rich assemblage of wood scenery that presents itself,

"Woods over woods in gay theatric pride."

The river is again crossed by the Bridge here represented; after passing which, and proceeding nearly half a mile, a farm-house and outbuildings are seen on the bank of the river, very near to the railway on the right. This is the site of Growmond, or Grandimont Abbey, "founded," according to Mr. Young, "about the year 1200, by the pious liberality of Johanna, the wife of Robert de Turnham. This lady being heiress to estates in this neighbourhood, granted to the order of Grandimont in France, (a branch of the Benedictines) a mansion in the forest of Egton, to be a cell to their monastery."

The church, of which, according to the same authority, the foundations may yet be traced, has been one hundred feet long, by forty broad. Some of the other buildings extending westward from the church have been converted into the farmhouse and offices above noticed; and in erecting some additional buildings not very long since, the few stones remaining of the Abbey and its appendages were used; so that now no remnants of the ancient buildings are to be seen. The beautiful estate to which these buildings belong, as well as the adjoining one,

*This is the case in several parts of the vale of Esk. One instance has been before noticed, as occurring at the very commencement of the Railway.–Another very beautiful instance will be found at Arncliffe, near Egton Bridge; but the most singular of all, is at a place called Crunkley Gill, near Lealholme Bridge, where the river for nearly a mile runs between two rocky declivities partially covered with wood, and rising very abruptly from the edge of the river to an elevation of at least 150 feet. This place is so difficult of access, as to be little known except to adventurous handlers of the rod and line

have lately become the property of James Wilkinson, Esq.

The situation of this Abbey, like that of Eskdaleside Hermitage, was particularly well adapted for that "love of peace and lonely musing," which characterized the generality of monkish institutions: and as this part of Eskdale is likely to become more populous than hitherto, in consequence of the railway, and the establishment of several works in the immediate neighbourhood, it is to be hoped that another church will, ere long, arise to adorn a situation so eligible for the purpose; and that some well disposed persons, feeling how well

"The calm retreat, the silent shade,
With prayer and praise agree,"

will not permit a neighbourhood, at present far removed from any place of divine worship, to continue so for many years longer.

Near Growmond Abbey farm the railway crosses the river Esk for the last time by a bridge, which in point of romantic character is surpassed by none of the preceding ones, and approaches the Tunnel Inn, which is so situated as to command much beautiful scenery, and to possess numerous advantages in the way of business, arising from its contiguity both to the railway and a public road.—Besides this Inn, several cottages, workshops, and a warehouse have been erected within the last two years, and limekilns are at this time being built at no great distance, the whole bidding fair to form the nucleus of a village, that from the great facilities which the situation affords for speculation in a variety of ways, will most probably spring up in the neighbourhood.

After passing the Tunnel Inn, the railway enters the vale of Goathland; but before proceeding to describe that "happy valley," a few words more must be devoted to the valley of the Esk, of which the traveller on the railway has here to take his leave.

Entrance to the Vale of Goathland

The road that passes in front of the Tunnel Inn leads along the banks of Goathland Beck to Growmond Bridge, a beautiful structure erected over the Esk, immediately below the point where it receives the former stream. After proceeding about two hundred yards beyond the bridge a road turns off to the left, which, following the well-wooded north bank of the river Esk for about a mile and half, terminates upon the Green of Egton, the scenery around which has ever been considered the finest in the whole vale. The richness of the lowlands; — the well-wooded declivities interspersed with green fields;—the cottages and farm-houses peeping from amongst the groups of surrounding trees;—the magnificent wood and rock scenery of Arncliffe and Limberhill, with the river forcing its impetuous course through a channel confined between their precipitous and nearly approaching banks; the splendid prospect from the western ridge of Arncliffe, looking into Glazedale on the one hand, and the east and west divisions of the vale of Esk on the other; with a much loftier range of moorlands than any before alluded to, in the distance ;—all in quick and varying succession attract and delight the eye.

No person who has the opportunity of devoting a day to exploring the varied beauties of this part of Eskdale, should omit to take advantage of it.

On the ridge immediately above Arncliffe Wood are a number of excavations, supposed to be the remains of an ancient British village. Mr. Young, in his history, enters very fully into an account of these and similar appearances in other parts of the district.

At the extremity of Arncliffe Wood is a foot bridge of a single arch of light and elegant form, thrown over the river Esk; and forming a most interesting feature in the lovely scenery around.

The valley of the Esk continues for the remainder of its course towards the high lands, (where its waters take their rise,) beautiful and picturesque; and the several dales of Glazedale, Fryup, Danby,* and Westerdale, that join it on the south, have each their peculiar charms, though all are lovely and romantic in a greater or less degree.

The soil of the lowlands throughout all these values is of a most excellent quality, and very productive; and though apparently shut out from all connexion with the world, these vales possess a numerous, opulent, and respectable population.

*Near the entrance into Danby Dale there are still some remains of a Castle, which owes its origin to the ancient and powerful family of De Bruce.

CHAPTER III.

VALE OF GOATHLAND

The mountain stream impetuous flowing
O'er its wild and rocky bed,
For scenes with richer beauties glowing,
Seems to wish its course were sped.

Thus Youth, with warmth and ardour viewing
Life's delightful fancied way,
Impatient live, for e'er pursuing
Pleasures of a distant day.

THE hills, which inclose this beautiful and secluded vale, so completely overlap each other, as they descend rapidly towards Eskdale, that the communication between the two vallies is altogether concealed. This peculiarity is not confined to the Vale of Goathland, but displays itself in equally as marked a manner at the outlets of the several dales of Glazedale, Fryup, and Danby, insomuch that a person travelling along the central parts of Eskdale is unconscious of there being any vallies, much less vallies of such extent, so immediately branching from it.

The course of Goathland Beck, where it issues from its native valley to join the waters of the Esk near Growmond Bridge, is hemmed in by perpendicular rocks, or steep acclivities; and the only means of entrance into this part of Goathland, before the formation of the railway, was by means of a dangerous and uncertain ford across this rocky channelled stream. Hence Goathland Vale has been hitherto unvisited, and almost unknown, except to the inhabitants of the immediate neighbourhood. This interesting portion of the district is now rendered accessible.

Immediately in front of the Tunnel Inn, but on the opposite side of the river, stands a grove of fine oak trees, occupying the area of a narrow ridge of table land, being the eastern extremity of Lease Rigg, the name given to the hill forming the western side of the lower Vale of Goathland, and which here terminates in a rocky peninsula, nearly surrounded by the doubling of Goathland Beck, above which it is elevated from twenty-five to fifty feet.

This Grove, since the forming of the railway has given the public an opportunity of enjoying its varied beauties, has been most enthusiastically admired; not merely on account of its own peculiar sylvan character and native charms, but because it commands so many and such romantic views of rich hanging woods, with

"Cliffs and craggs,
And bubbling rills, and white cascades between,"

114

on the one hand, and of one of the finest portions of the Vale of Esk, and the lower part of Lease Rigg on the other. There being no underwood, and the trees so happily disposed, as to

"Part admit, and part exclude the day,"

natural vistas appear in every direction, through which the different views are seen with increased effect.

The irregularities in the surface of the ground of this fascinating spot, are occasioned by its having in ages long since been the site of an alum work, of which Mr. Young in his History of Whitby gives a very full account, and contends for its being of a much older date than any of the other alum works in the kingdom.

The interest of this scene is not confined to its picturesque character only. It is rich also in mineral and geological attractions. Placed in the marle stone series immediately above the lower lias bed, the sections of the cliffs on either side of the river exhibit in a very marked manner alternate layers of iron stone, and masses of petrified shells, with the lower has bed beneath. The iron stone is found in three separate beds alternating with the marle stone, and averaging in the aggregate from two and a half to three feet, or more in thickness; and as the ore on trial has been found to be productive, there seems a probability of its becoming a valuable article of traffic, now that by means of the railway it can be readily transported to a place of shipment. The stratum of petrified shells is particularly interesting; and as in one place it forms for a considerable extent the bed of the river, it may be examined with more facility than when in the sectional state. The petrifactions are principally of one kind, the pecten sublævis. The situation of this bed of shells is in itself exceedingly romantic, which, added to its curiosity makes it an object of much interest, and it never fails to call forth the admiration and surprize of those who view it.

A little higher up the bed of the river, and also in the banks on each side, are to be found layers of the stone from which the Roman Cement is made.

Before proceeding to describe the onward course of the railway, a few words must be devoted to noticing the fine views that are to be obtained by ascending the ridge of Lease Rigg, for about half a mile from the grove just described, and through which a road leads up the hill in the direction alluded to. On arriving near the first farm-house in the course of ascent, the spectator on looking around finds himself able to see three beautiful vallies from nearly the same point. Looking towards the west, his eye rests on that fine part of the Vale of Esk, where is situated Egton Bridge and Arncliffe Wood. In the opposite direction the sight ranges over the scenery described in the last chapter, the distant part of the valley being closed by the East Cliff of Whitby, surmounted by the ruins of the Abbey, beyond which extends the dark blue sea. Turning to the south, the lovely secluded Vale of Goathland with its green fields, luxuriant woods, and sinuous stream, lies at his feet.

This ridge of land is also remarkable as being the site of the old Roman road from Dunsley Bay to York; and about a quarter of a mile farther up the hill, are to be traced

115

the remains of a Roman camp through which the road passed, and of which it doubtless was the key. The view from this camp is extensive in every direction, pointing out at once how admirably it was adapted for a military station.

From hence the Roman road took a course nearly south by July Park to Cawthorn Camps, a place of much note, and to which allusion will be made in a subsequent chapter. Some portions of the old road may yet be discovered, and to the curious in such matters, Mr. Young's History of Whitby will be found particularly valuable, as he enters very fully into the history of this road, which seems to have escaped the notice of most of the earlier antiquaries.

Descending again to the north end of the tunnel, and proceeding along the railway, the traveller takes his leave of the Vale of Esk, which in passing through the tunnel, gradually recedes from view with very pleasing effect.

After traversing the tunnel, which is but 120 yards in length, and passing for about the same distance through an excavation at its southern extremity, the lower Vale of Goathland is at once thrown open to the view.

For the space of a mile there is nothing but the generally pleasing character of the vale to notice: and then on the right hand appears an inclined plane, connecting the railway with the quarries of the Whitby Stone Company, situated on the brow of the hill, about a quarter of a mile distant from the railway. These quarries are now wrought to a considerable extent, the stone being of excellent quality, and the railway affording the means of removing it to Whitby, whence it is shipped in great quantities for the London market.

Not many yards beyond the foot of the Stone Company's inclined plane, the railway is carried through the great Whinstone Dyke, by means of a considerable excavation. This Dyke is a most singular feature in the geology of the district. It ranges in nearly a direct line from beyond Cockfield Fell in the county of Durham, to the neighbourhood of Whitby; in many places rising to the surface, but in others concealed by the alluvial formations; and being generally from forty to sixty feet in breadth:—its depth is unexplored. That its origin is to be attributed to the action of fire, and that at some remote period it has been in a state of fusion, seems not to admit of a doubt. The substances in contact with it appear to have undergone a change, occasioned by intense heat; and in the particular instance now under consideration, the alum shale bed on the north side of the Dyke has to a certain extent been changed into a pale yellowish soapy feeling substance, which is supposed to be porcelain earth, and of which the quantity is considerable. The strata through which the whinstone has been upheaved seems to have been completely dislocated by the violence of the eruption.

From hence to Beck Hole (rather more than a mile), the valley increases in picturesque effect, and few as may be, even in this day, the habitations to be seen from the line of railway, there is good reason to suppose that, centuries ago, this valley was not without inhabitants; for in excavating the line of railway at a little distance above the inclined plane, some remains of an urn of baked clay of rude construction, and evidently of very ancient date, were found. This is not the only symptom of former inhabitancy; for on one part of Leaserigg considerable quantities of scoriæ and iron slag are met with, shewing most decidedly that the rich veins of iron ore found in this valley were not

116

only known but also wrought, at a period far beyond the date of any tradition on the subject.

Almost half a mile to the west of the field in which are the remains of iron works, is a pool of water called Randay Mere, formerly of considerable extent, surrounded by barren heath clad acclivities, and presenting a forlorn and solitary, though not uninteresting, scene. The medicinal leech is said to be found here.

The vale now becomes much contracted in extent, and more richly wooded in proportion than before: and a gentle curve of the railway brings into sight the romantic hamlet of Beck Hole, surrounded by an amphitheatre of trees and high ground, that appears to close in the valley.

Beck Hole is situated at the confluence of the two moor land rivulets of Wheeldale and Ellerbeck, whose united waters form the stream that has accompanied the course of the railway from its leaving the Tunnel.

Wheeldale Beck flows from the west through a deep precipitous ravine, whose rocky sides are clothed with pendant woods of wild and luxuriant growth. The winding stream is much interrupted by large masses of rock which form many irregular cascades, and add much to the interest of the scene, though they present formidable obstacles to those who wish to explore it. About half a mile up the valley a small tributary stream is precipitated into it from an elevation of about sixty feet, forming in its descent a singularly beautiful cascade, much broken in its fall by the numerous trees through which it showers down its sparkling and much divided waters—

> "The streams and founts,
> They are flashing down from the mountain brows,
> They are flinging their spray on the forest boughs."

The approach to this singular place is rather difficult, there being no regular road; but probably the pleasure of beholding it is not the less enhanced on this account.

Ellerbeck Glen falls into the main valley from the south-east, and is altogether of a different character from Wheeldale. It is much more confined, and more generally bare of wood; and though the inclosing banks are of less elevation, they are more rocky, and the masses of rock stand more boldly out, and rise more immediately from the water's edge, presenting in some places the appearance of towers, or castle walls. After proceeding nearly half a mile, the features of the glen assume a different character, the banks are higher, and there is more wood: the difficulty of making progress along the deep tangled pathway is increased at every step, and for awhile little is to be seen but a confusion of underwood overhung by large trees, and the stream brawling along beneath them. Half wearied with his scrambles, the adventurous searcher for the picturesque seats himself on some moss-grown stone to rest awhile and contemplate, when

> "the sound
> Of a near fall of water, every sense
> Wakes from the charm of thought."

117

Aroused to further exertion he hastens forward, till

> "shrinking back
> He checks his steps, and views the broken scene:"

Thomason Foss, a water-fall of singularly romantic character presents itself to his view—
This place generally forms the extent of the stranger's scramble, the valley being completely closed in by rocks over which the water falls; but by making a circuit over the rocks to the left, the course of the stream above the fall may be attained; and on pursuing it for a little distance, another cascade scarcely inferior in picturesque attraction to Thomason Foss, will be found.
Near Thomason Foss that truly splendid plant the Osmunda Regalis grows in great perfection. It may be here observed, that all the Vales in the course of the railway are peculiarly interesting to Botanists; many rare plants being found within their range; — of some of which a list will be given in the Appendix.
The enchanting scenery in the neighbourhood of Beck Hole has, for many years past, been a favorite place of resort in the summer season for the young people of Whitby, and their stranger friends, who, in those happy days "when life is in its spring," thought nothing of the difficulty of visiting so romantic a spot, and scrambling amidst its wild recesses; whilst the less adventurous were strolling along the verdant meadows, where

> "The soft ceaseless sound of distant rills,
> Upon the listening ear, came soothingly."

Some too there doubtless are, who, in after life, have recurred to these scenes of early and innocent delight, and felt in all its force that beautiful expression of an anonymous writer, who observes, "I cannot, without a thrill of rapture, recall views that I have seen, never to be forgotten; nor looks, that I have felt in every nerve, that I shall never meet again."
From Beck Hole an inclined plane takes the railway into the upper Vale of Goathland. Having been formed through a wood, the inclined plane presents the appearance of a fine avenue of nearly a mile in length; and the views into the lower Vale of Goathland from several points in the course of the ascent are particularly fine. The inclined plane at the upper end opens upon the Village Green, where on the left hand stands the school; whilst on the right, and at the distance of about half a mile from the railway, is to be seen Goathland Chapel, a plain unpretending modern structure, near the outskirts of the enclosed lands. Not very far from the church to the west, is a place called Killing Pits, supposed by Mr. Young to have been a British village; and to the south-west of this stands Hunt House, a shooting seat belonging to Richard Hill, Esq. of Thornton, the lessee under the Duchy of Lancaster of the manor and extensive moors of Goathland.
A little further than the School House Green the railway crosses a high road which leads to Goathland Mill, very picturesquely situated upon Ellerbeck stream; and

Thomason Foss

where is a waterfall of no mean beauty; and which to those who have not seen Thomason Foss, is worth the trouble of a visit.

The railway is shortly afterwards crossed by another road which leads to a farm-house on the left, known by the name of the Abbot House, which, according to tradition, belonged formerly to the Abbey of Whitby, and was most probably the site of the cell or hermitage which formerly existed in this valley.

Notwithstanding the elevated and exposed part of the country which the railway has now attained, and the near vicinity of the moors, which appear on either hand within a few fields distance, the cultivated land is of good quality, and under excellent management, belonging principally to Mr. Gawan Peirson, an opulent freeholder, whose residence is to be seen amongst some trees on the right, and whose family have long been settled in the vale.

The range of inclosed land in the vicinity of the railway, after lessening field by field, now becomes reduced to a large green field on the left, on which grow a number of detached oak trees, giving it the appearance rather of an outer park, than of the last vestige of cultivated land that is to be seen for several miles afterwards.

The railway proceeds over Goathland Moor, and rapidly approaches the summit level. The rural and luxuriant views of Eskdale and of Goathland—

> "the rivers flow,
> The woody values warm and low,"

are now succeeded by scenes of wildness and desolation. No traces of inhabitancy or of cultivation are to be seen.—A succession of moorland elevations varied only by the channels of the currents formed by the rains or melting snows, is all that meets the eye: yet is the scenery not without interest from the effects of contrast, as well as from its general character; and under some circumstances of light and shade, or the influence of the passing storm, it is even highly picturesque and occasionally sublime—

> The moorland summits wild and bleak,
> Dry rocky channels shew;
> Like furrows on the aged cheek,
> Where tears have ceased to flow.

CHAPTER IV.

NEWTON DALE.

A Dale, which lofty cliffs enclose,
Preserves unseen its winding way,
Till jutting crags high interpose,
As if all onward course to stay:
The weary wanderer starts, to find
His further progress thus confin'd.

Let him pass on—and soon he sees
A sudden turn the way reveal,
Whence brighter vales, hills, fields, and trees,
Will on his wond'ring eyesight steal.—
In life, the distant ills we fear,
Thus nearer seen, oft disappear.

THE elegant author of "Recollections of the East," describes a view of the wilderness in Judea in the following words:—"The eminence that overlooked it was stony and barren, and the scene was sad and silent; in wandering over the valley the stranger often finds himself amidst its jutting rocks and windings, shut out utterly from all human eye and sound. Above him rise the lofty and rocky precipices thinly sprinkled with trees and foliage on one side, while on the other all is barren—the stream dashes along at his feet." Were it allowable to apply this language as the description of the entrance into the upper part of Newton Dale, it would be impossible to find words more appropriate.

The accompanying view shews the entrance into Newton Dale, and it is rather extraordinary that Fen hog, which fills the central part of the view, and over which the railway is carried for about a mile, should be the site of the summit level. The spring which feeds this bog is one of the sources of Pickering Beck, which uniting with the Derwent, pours its waters into the Estuary of the Humber, and joins the sea, after a course of nearly a hundred miles, though rising out of the side of a hill which commands an extensive view of the German Ocean, at only a few miles distance.

After passing over Fen Bog the railway curves round the base of a steep and barren hill, and enters the confines of the higher division of Newton Dale, called North Dale, a place comparatively unknown until the formation of the railway; for it was previously almost inaccessible, and rarely visited except by the hunter or the shepherd: and when approached presented so wild and desolate a scene, as almost to realize what is so feelingly described in the following lines:—

> "All sad—all silent—on the ear
> No sound of pleasing toil is swelling,
> Earth has no quickening spirit here,
> Nature no charm, and man no dwelling."

After passing for upwards of a mile through this solitary glen, all further progress seems arrested by the projecting eminences and cliffs that apparently enclose its southern extremity. This effect occurs in several parts of Newton Dale, both in passing up and down, and adds much to the excitement and interest of the ride along the railway.

On advancing a little farther, the main valley is discovered extending towards the west, and the railway, sweeping rapidly round the foot of a bold and lofty projection on the right, crowned by a large mass of rock, called from a perforation visible near its point, the Needle's Eye, brings the traveller into full view of the middle division of Newton Dale, extending about a mile before him, and of which the general character is peculiar, and singularly picturesque. The only portion of any thing like level ground is that occupied by the railway; and even that has been artificially obtained, whilst on either hand the surface rises more or less abruptly to an elevation of about 500 feet, the upper part of which, from one to two hundred feet in height, consists almost entirely of bold perpendicular ranges of rock, large fragments of which lie scattered about the vale below.

On both sides of this division of the valley, and indeed in the greater part of North Dale also, are alternate projections and recesses, each corresponding to the other in so striking a manner, as to leave no doubt as to their having been in times long past one solid mass, which being riven asunder by some mighty convulsion of Nature, has left the valley as it now appears.

On the north side of this part of the Dale is a fine semicircular range of rock, called Killingnoble Scar,

> "where the hawk
> High in the beetling cliff his eyrie builds."

This Scar has for ages been celebrated for a breed of hawks, which is still to be found there. So far back as the year 1612, on the occasion of a commission from the crown to enquire into and ascertain the privileges and extent of the lordship of Goathland, it appears that evidence was then given, to the effect that "there hath been hawkes bred in Newton Dale, in Killingnoble Scar, which the inhabitants of Goathland were charged to watch for the King's use."

Entrance into Newton Dale

North End

At the foot of this cliff is a small pool of water, generally known by the name of Newton Dale Well; a place which in former times obtained great celebrity, extraordinary virtues being ascribed to its waters; and on Midsummer Sunday a fair was held here, to which the country people from many miles round resorted, performing some superstitious ceremonies to ensure to themselves and families the benefits of this well's salutiferous influence.—Of late years this custom has been given up, and the well has become so much deserted, that its exact site is not readily to be found. From an opening between the contiguous cliffs issues a pellucid stream, possessing strong petrifying qualities, and quickly incrusting every thing within its reach.

The cliffs on the south side of the dale are equally as lofty and precipitous as those on the north; but their bases being well covered with woods, chequered with corn and meadow land, the general effect is different; and thought not so grand, yet, on the whole, it is more pleasing. Indeed it may be remarked as a peculiarity of Newton Dale, that in each of the three divisions, which the sudden turns in its course naturally divide it into, and of each of which, in all other respects the general character is different, where one bank is at all wooded or cultivated, the opposite one is comparatively bare.—Here scarcely a tree or a field is to be seen on the north side of the dale, while the south presents a succession of woods, and a few patches of cultivated land, but not a dwelling is to be seen on either side.*

After passing for about a mile along Middle Dale, and without the appearance of any outlet, the railway takes another sudden turn beneath the projecting point of a bold and extensive range of cliff, and enters into the lower or southern division of the Dale. Here the features of the valley assume a different character. On the right it is inclosed as before by boldly rising hills, with precipitous rocks along the upper parts, but the range of those rocks is comparatively regular and unbroken and thrown further back, and between them and the bottom of the vale lies a considerable extent of undulating land in good cultivation, interspersed with wood and thriving plantations, and sprinkled with farm-houses, that give animation to the scene. On the opposite side the hills rise steeply from the vale, and present, with little exception, a bare and sterile aspect.—The railway passes for about two miles through scenery of this description— until approaching Raindale Mill, where a change takes place in the general character, as well as in the name, of the valley.

From the nature of the soil in the cuttings for the railway, through the several divisions of Newton Dale, it is evident that the present apparent bottom of the valley is not, in several parts, the original one, but that masses of rock and

* It is to be hoped that a situation so singular and picturesque will not long remain without some means of accommodation for the visiters who would soon frequent its lonely haunts, were any place of rest or shelter provided.

Newton Dale Scarrs

earth have time after time fallen from the enclosing cliffs and high grounds, and filled it to the depth of several feet. This has no doubt been the first cause of the formation of Fen Bog, the channel of North Dale Beck having been dammed up, till in the progress of time so raised as again to enable the stream to regain its former course, though upon a higher level.

In Middle Dale there has been at some time an immense mass of cliff and land detached from Killingnoble Scar, and precipitated into the vale below.—The upper part of the rising ground forming the middle distance in the view of this dale, is formed of this *"avalanche."* The rocks, as they were hurled from their native cliff centuries ago, still lie en masse prostrate at its foot, with their stratifications perpendicular to the plane of the horizon, and presenting a singular and interesting spectacle.

In several of the cuttings for the railway in the higher part of the Dale, trees were met with standing in their natural position, and but little altered in substance. In the lower part of the valley several trunks of trees were found that were quite black, apparently from the effects of fire.

Some heaps of scoriæ were also met with in the cuttings in the South Dale—shewing that iron has at some period been smelted here.

On the summit of the hills, forming from the line of railway the apparent southern and easterly boundary of the middle and lower division of North Dale, is an extensive tract of table land, at the easterly extremity of which rises another range of hills, similar in form and general character to those which immediately close in the Dale on the east. Of the upper part of these hills occasional glimpses are caught from several parts of the line.

On arriving at Raindale Mill, a small valley is seen running up to the moors on the right, and about half a mile beyond, there is on the same side a more considerable opening, on the south of which is some elevated ground, where stands the village of Newton. A little to the west upon the brow of the same hill, and in a most commanding situation at about a mile distant from the railway are to be found Cawthorn Camps, the most complete remains of Roman fortifications in the district. The camps are four in number, the largest of them contains an area of 560 feet, by 550. The most westerly camp, though the smallest, is superior to the others in strength and workmanship, and is supposed to have been the latest formed; it is nearly square, and fortified by a double trench. The Roman road noticed in a former chapter passed through the centre of this camp. On the easterly side of this camp, and in fact adjoining to it at its south-east angle, is a camp of singular form, being an irregular oval of 850 feet in length, by 320 in breadth. Mr. Young, in the History of Whitby, gives a very full account of these camps, having evidently bestowed much pains and research in collecting information respecting them.

South Dale
Newton Dale

Raindale Mill

Newton Dale

Soon after leaving Raindale Mill, the railway turns a little to the left, and proceeds for full two miles in a direct line through a cultivated, hut uninhabited valley, called Leavisham Bottoms, and the scenery though richly wooded, being tame in comparison with that of Newton Dale. In one part of this portion of the line is a place called Gale Bog, (from the quantity of sweet Gale that grows upon it,) being a considerable extent of highly decomposed vegetable matter, in a situation hardly to be expected, considering the state of culture of the surrounding land. Doubtless that land presented a very different aspect at the time this bog was formed; for it appears from Leland's account of the district, that though now so profusely wooded, it was in his day bare of that ornament.

Proceeding some little distance beyond the Gale Bog, and crossing a bridge, a small well-wooded valley is seen on the left. This is Leavisham vale, in the upper part of which a church is situated in a very picturesque situation. The small stream that meanders down this rural and secluded dell, here falls into the Newton Dale Beck, and the scenery at this "meeting of the waters," is highly beautiful. Still there are no traces of inhabitants, and from hence to within a mile of Pickering, the railway winds along the bottom of rich hanging woods for four miles successively, one fine sweep following another, relieved occasionally by a solitary green field or a broken line of road, but still not cheered by the sight of a single dwelling. The extensive plantations on the right of the valley belong principally to his Majesty in right of his Duchy of Lancaster; but those on the opposite banks are private property, the most luxuriant of them being part of the Kingthorpe Estate, the property of Captain Fothergill.

So completely is the view on the railway confined to the steep wooded banks on each side, that the traveller is not aware of the great change in the features of the neighbouring district, which occurs at almost every advance, that he is now making through this rich and park like scene.— Leaving the course of the railway, and emerging from the labyrinth of woods through which it winds, he will find on gaining the open ground above, no barren hills or rocky heights beyond, but on either hand rich and well-cultivated fields, gently sloping to the south, and extending into the fertile Vale of Rye,

"luxuriant and unbounded,"

whilst far to the north he sees the dreary heath-clad summits of the moors, that had previously so often bounded his view.

The scenery on the course of the railway within the last two miles of its approach to Pickering, becomes more open and varied; and a farm-house, with some extent of level and cultivated land around it, appearing on the right, shews that a complete change has taken place, even in the natural formation of the valley—and that the traveller is leaving the rocky glen and wooded vale, and fast approaching an open and cultivated country.

CHAPTER V.

PICKERING.

The vale now opens to the sun,
The streams in softer currents run,
The lulls in broader range extend,
And gently to the plains descend;
Whilst in mid view a town is seen,
The swelling trees and fields between—
There too, a castle-crested mound—
Where royalty a prison found,
Where warrior chiefs, in days of yore,
O'er vassal lands stern empire bore,—
Its ruin'd walls, its tottering towers displays,
The wreck of feudal times, the pride of bygone days.

THE last curve of any consequence in the course of the railway, is little more than a mile distant from the town of Pickering, which gradually rises into view; and, as it is approached, a very interesting combination of scenery presents itself. The railway passes near the side of a rivulet, between gently sloping banks covered with well-wooded inclosures and thriving plantations. In the distance on the left are seen the remains of the once powerful castle of Pickering, magnificent and imposing even in decay, standing on a bold eminence of limestone, and commanding an extensive prospect over the surrounding country. A small portion only of the town is to be seen from the railway, the greater part being intercepted by the rising ground on which the castle is situated. On the right a continued profusion of luxuriant hedge row timber confines the view to the immediate vicinity of the town.

Though the early history of Pickering has never been satisfactorily ascertained, yet all the information that has been collected on the subject tends to shew that it is of very great antiquity; and that it was in former ages a place of much consequence.

According to some authorities Pickering was a British town, and founded many years before the Christian æra.—No Roman remains have hitherto been discovered there. The castle presents some proofs of its being of ancient date, and the inner mound is supposed to be of British origin. The castle was probably erected about the middle of the reign of William the Second, whose

Pickering Castle

father retained Pickering in his hands after the conquest. It remained the property of the Crown for many years; and was sometimes the abode, and on one occasion the prison, of royalty— Richard the Second was immured here, before being removed to Pontefract.

After various vicissitudes, during the turbulent times of our Henries and our Edwards, the "Manor, Castle, and Forest of Pickering" became the property of John of Gaunt, in right of his wife, from whom they passed into the hands of Henry the Fourth, and by him are supposed to have been annexed to the possessions of the Duchy of Lancaster.

Leland, in his Itinerary, thus describes the situation and state of this castle— "The toune of Pickering is large, but not well compact togither. The greatest part of it, with the paroch chirch and the castle is on the south-est part of the broke renning thorough the toune, and standith on a great slaty hill. The other part of the toun is not so bigge as this; the brook rennith betwixt them, that sumtyme ragith, but it suagith shorteley agayn; and a mile beneth the toun goith into Costey. In Pickering chiche I saw 2 tumbes of the Bruscs, whereof one with his wife lay yn a chapel, on the south syde of the quier, and had a garland about his helmet. Ther was another of the Bruses biried in a chapel under an arch of the north side of the body of the quier; and there is a cantuarie bearing his name. The Dean of York hath by impropriation, the personage of Pykering, to which diverse chirches of Pykering Lith doith homage. The castelle stondith in an end of the town not far from the paroch chirch, on the brow of the hill, under which the broke rennith. In the first court of it be a 4 toures, of the which one is caullid Rosamonde's toure. In the ynner court be also 4 toures, whereof the kepe is one. The castelle waulles and the toures be meatly welle. The loggings yn the ynner court that be of timbre be in ruine. In this inner court is a chappelle, and a cantuarie prest. The castelle hath, of a good continuance, with the towne and lordship, longgid to the Lancaster bloode, but who made the castelle, or who was owner of it fore the Lancasters, I could not lerne there. The castelle waulles now remaining seme to be of no very old building. As I remember I heard say that Richard III. lay sumtyme at this castelle, and sumtyme at Scardehurgh castelle. "The park by the castelle side is more than 7 miles in cumpace; but it is not well woodid."

The writer of these pages has, however, been favored, through the polite courtesy of the keeper of the Records in the Office of the Duchy of Lancaster, with some extracts from two Surveys of the Honor of Pickering, made at different periods, and which not having been heretofore published, that the Editor is aware of, may prove interesting.

The first survey was in the time of James the First, from which it appears, "That the castle of Pickering being the chief house of the Honor, hath in the outer ward or wall thereof three towers, the one called Rosamund's Tower,*

*Of this Tower a view is given at the end of this Chapter.

Decayed both in lead and timber; the second called Dyet Tower, the timber whereof is reasonably good, but the lead in many places cut and carried away, and the beams and joists thereby wholly uncovered at the end; the third called Milne Tower is in good repair, and the chambers thereof well kept. In the inner wall or Middle Ward, there is one tower called Coleman Tower, with one other room thereunto adjoining, heretofore used to keep the Rolls and Records of the Castle, which are absolutely decayed, both roof and chambers, only some few joists stick still in some parts of the walls, and some of the lead lying thereon, and some of the lead lying on the ground in the bottom of the said tower.

"In the Inner Ward there is an antient house, built upon timber, or posts and pan, (as they call it) now called Motehall, where the courts are usually kept, the upper part of which house above the posts cannot long stand, it is so ruinous, nor can be well repaired, unless that part be wholly taken down, the which part of the said house with the chapple, now used for the juries to be kept in, with the decaies in the outer wall, cannot be amended under one hunder marks at the least in any sort."

The other survey was taken in the time of the Commonwealth, after the castle had been besieged by the parliamentary forces, and when it had suffered much injury, on the western side particularly, from the effect of the cannonade to which it was exposed. As after the castle was taken great quantities of papers and parchments were brought out and scattered about the streets, it is probable that many documents tending to throw light upon the early history of this interesting ruin were then irrecoverably lost.

The second survey alluded to is dated in 1651, and entitled, "A Survey of the Honor of Pickering, with the rights, members, and appurtenances thereunto belonging, situate, lying and being in the county of York, and part of the possessions of Charles Stuart, late King, whereof he was seized in right of the Duchy of Lancaster, and settled upon his Queen as part of her jointure, but now settled on trustees for the use of the Commonwealth of England, and held by them as of the Manor of East Grenwich, in fee and common socage by fealty only."

It then proceeds to state— "The capital messuage is situate on the north side of Pickering town, and known by the name of Pickering Castle; the entrance thereof lyeth on the south, through a Gate House which is somewhat ruined in respect that all the covering is taken away. The outwall only remaineth and in good repair; being passed through the said gate you enter into a spacious court, containing one acre and three roods more or less, in which (on the east side) close adjoining the gate, standeth a ruinous house partly covered with slate, in which were lately three several rooms below stairs, and as many above; but in the time of the late wars all the floors for the chambering have been pulled down by the soldiers, in so much that the whole house is ready to fall, there being hardly any thing left to support the roof. The outwalls being partly built of stone and part of timber, and the spars which are fastened to the main wall of the castle do still remain. Further eastward to the said house along the wall standeth a tower, known by the name of Dyet Tower, in which there hath been three several rooms, with other conveniences thereunto belonging, which with little cost may be made habitable, but the lead, wood, and iron was by Sir Hugh Cholmley (as we are informed) carried to Scarborough Castle. Further along the said wall standeth another tower, north to the aforesaid house, and known by the name of Rosamund's Tower, the walls in good repair, but the wood, lead, and iron taken quite away. On the west side of the aforesaid gate, along the wall, standeth another tower, known by the name of Milne Tower, built within all of hewn stone, with a staircase of the same, containing one room below stairs, heretofore used for a prison, with a room above, lately used for a lodging chamber, but within these six or seven years all the iron, lead, and wood have been taken away, and nothing left besides the outwalls, which are in very good repair, and one rotten beam which lyeth across the top of the tower. On the north side of the said court, opposite to the gate, standeth another gate, which is the entrance over a decayed bridge into the middle castle, and leading into another spacious court, containing two rods more or less. On the north-east of the said gate standeth a fourth tower, known by the name of Colman Tower, containing two rooms, but the floors, covering, and all the wood are taken away. On the west side of the said court standeth a large ruined hall, almost all fallen to the ground, nothing of the timber remaining. At the north end of which hall, eastward, standeth one house covered with slate, and in indifferent good repair, containing one room, and known by the name of the chapple, which is now used for keeping of courts for the honor aforesaid. On the back side of which lyeth a third court, containing two roods more or less, in which hath been diverse buildings, but now ruined and fallen to the ground. In the midst of the whole castle standeth a mount containing, one acre, on which there is a spacious ruined old decayed building, being nothing but ruined walls, which in many places begin to fall down. The said building is commonly known by the name of the Moat. The Moat walls of the said castle (which are there now remaining) as the timber, hewn stone, and slate, we estimate to be worth in ready money (besides the charge of taking them down) £200.

"The ground lying within the walls and ditches of the castle aforesaid, contain in the whole three acres and three roods, which is worth upon improvement per annum £5. Memorandum that all the aforesaid premises are (as we are informed) in the occupation of Sir John Danvers, Knight, but nothing has been shewed unto us to verify the same."

As nearly two hundred years have elapsed since this survey was taken, it may well be supposed that the castle is now in a very ruinous condition. Its grand features, however, may still be traced, and the outer towers are yet in a state to shew in some degree the nature of the domestic accommodations which they afforded when in a less ruinous condition.

"What does not fade? The tower that long hath stood
The crash of thunder, and the warring winds,
Shook by the slow but sure destroyer, Time,
Now hangs in doubtful ruin o'er its base."

The views from the West, or Mill Tower, and from the Keep are exceedingly fine, particularly towards the west, where the eye ranges over a most luxuriant country extending many miles, to the foot of the Howardian Hills on the one hand, and the high grounds about Helmsley, and the moorlands on the other. Towards the north a beautiful view is obtained of the lower part of Blansby Park Valley, with the railway extending up its rich and peaceful bosom.

The Vale of Rye is justly celebrated for its fertility, and along the southern declivity of the hills that bound it on the north there are, besides the market towns of Pickering, Kirby Moorside, and Helmsley, a number of populous villages surrounded by gardens and orchards, that give to the district a character of much importance, both in an agricultural and commercial point of view.

There are several rich and well inhabited vallies also, that communicate with the plain of the Vale of Rye—of these the principal are Rosedale,* Farndale, and Bilsdale, each watered by a considerable stream, and being replete with scenery of a highly picturesque description. In Rosedale are still to be seen the remains of a small Abbey that formerly flourished there, and which add much to the interest of this beautiful valley. Close to the Abbey stands the church, and adjoining to it is the church-yard surrounded by some noble trees, and commanding a fine view of the upper part of the dale. 'Tis a sweet and tranquil spot, favourable to meditation, and the indulgence of those feelings that look beyond the world we live in.

For Peace hath there her spotless throne,
And pleasures to the world unknown;
The murmur of the distant rills,
The sabbath silence of the hills,
And all the quiet God hath given,
Without the golden gates of heaven."
    W.S. Roscoe.

The moors and vallies in this district abound with many beautiful insects. The intelligent son of Mr. Hartas of Rosedale has an extensive collection of specimens of these, and other natural productions of the neighbourhood, and amongst them will be found the following:——The emperor moth–the blue argus–the pearl bordered fritillary–the ghost swift moth–the tortoise shell and

*The Rosedale estate has lately become the property of the Rev. Dr. Penfold, by purchase from the Crown, and is likely, under his hands, to be much improved by the forming of new roads, and the erection of buildings, and especially by the re-building of the church and school-house.

peacock butterflies–and the fox moth.

Old family mansions abound in the Vale of Rye; but in the vicinity of the princely abodes of Castle Howard and Duncombe Park it were in vain to enumerate places that whatever may be their claim to admiration, must sink into comparative insignificance.

The town of Pickering contains a population of nearly 4,000 souls. It is straggling and irregularly built, and does not possess much attraction. The church is ancient and handsome; and, with the ruins of the castle, forms the only object to interest the stranger. A spirit of improvement seems to have sprung up since the commencement of the works of the railway, and as that undertaking has approached the period of its completion, this spirit has displayed itself in a most unequivocal manner, in the enlargement and re-building of several houses and shops, and in the erection of places for the convenience of that trade which the railway is so well calculated to introduce.

CHAPTER VI.

THE RAILWAY.

Hail, Modern Science! Who dares now to scan
The endless powers, that thou canst give to man?
Aided by thee, o'er trackless seas he glides,
Braves adverse winds, and stems opposing tides,
Earth's depths attains, her hidden wealth explores,
Applies to varied use her boundless stores;
On iron roads (o'er levell'd hills convey'd,
Through blasted rocks, or tunnll'd mountains made,)
By steam propell'd, pursues his rapid way,
And ends ere noon, what erst employ'd the day,
Air, water, fire, at STEPHENSON'S command,
Such magic powers unfold, beneath his master hand.

JUSTLY celebrated as is the name of STEPHENSON for the astonishing perfection, to which he has advanced the art of travelling on railways, by means of locomotive engines; yet the peculiar character of the country through which the Whitby and Pickering Railway had to be formed, and the limited means of the Company imposed upon him, and Mr. Swanwick his able assistant, a necessity to forego, in some degree, an adherence to those rules (more particularly as to curves and gradients) which necessarily guide an engineer in the laying out and construction of great public lines of railway.

It should, in justice to all parties, be distinctly borne in mind, not only that there were many formidable natural difficulties in the making a railway from Whitby to Pickering, but, that the district being comparatively unknown to the public, and the prospect of traffic and remuneration being of a nature not likely to be satisfactory except to persons residing in the neighbourhood, and fully aware of its natural and artificial resources, and of the probable effect of calling those resources into action, by means of a railway, the expense of the undertaking had to be borne almost exclusively by the inhabitants of Whitby and Pickering, and their immediate friends; and that therefore, unless a railway could be constructed for an amount, which it was calculated would be the utmost extent, that they could raise; the prospect of procuring one at all must have been abandoned.

Such were, in fact, the instructions given to the engineer, who therefore entered upon his important duties under every circumstance of disadvantage: for instead of having a more than usual supply of means for forming a railway through a district full of natural impediments, and consequently requiring a more than ordinary command of money, he was obliged to contrive such a railway as could, by possibility, be constructed for the given sum to which the promoters of the undertaking confined him to.

Notwithstanding all these difficulties the survey was made, an estimate formed, an act applied for and obtained, the railway commenced, and, in three years from the passing of the act, completed; and all, at an expense that makes the average cost amount to no more than about £4,400 a mile.

The whole length of railway is naturally divided into several portions, each differing materially from the others as to its general characteristics. The first of these may be considered as extending from Whitby to the Tunnel Inn, a distance of six miles and a quarter. This part of the line is carried up the Vale of Esk, down which flows in a very tortuous course a river that is subject to sudden and violent floods, and whose banks are in many parts so steep, and that alternately on one side and the other, as to present the possibility of passing up the valley without a succession of bridges. In one situation the necessity of two bridges within a short distance of each other, has been avoided by diverting the stream of the river, a measure that was the more necessary, as bridges in these situations (for they are both within the range of the tide), would have interfered with the navigation, and must therefore have been contrived with moveable centres, to admit of the passage of vessels.

The railway, at its commencement in the Shipyards at Whitby, is about five feet above the level of high water mark, and is carried for about a mile along the northerly shore of the harbour, where in one part it is supported by a quay wall, and then taken in a direct line across the Vale of Ruswarp to a bridge* which conveys it over the river into the manor of Sneaton. This bridge is altogether formed of Baltic fir; but upon such principles as will give it durability as well as strength, and enable it, for many years to come, to resist the fury of the wintry flood. It is 312 feet in length, being carried across the river in a diagonal direction, and divided into five portions of sixty-two feet span each—the frame work of the whole being supported upon four rows of piles fourteen inches square, (placed obliquely so as to offer the least possible resistance to the natural and tidal currents of the river), and firmly strapped together by iron bands. The expense of this bridge, including the masonry, extras, and cornices, was £1,575.

The execution of the works for the next two miles was attended with much difficulty, owing to the boggy nature of the ground, the prevalence of springs, and the tendency of the banks and cuttings to give way. As this portion of the line has now stood the test of the last winter, and the present spring, without exhibiting any further symptoms of sinking or alteration, it is hoped that all danger is at an end.—About half a mile further is a cutting through the alum rock. The excavation of this was tedious, owing to the hardness of the schistus,

*A representation of this bridge is given in page 33.

but in other respects the substance is favorable for cuttings, as the banks require no support. A considerable embankment succeeds, which, (where not intercepted by the river) runs in nearly a direct line for upwards of a mile, when another cutting through the alum stratum is met with and that to a more considerable extent than the other. This excavation is close to the north bank of the river, which is here inclosed by steep banks on both sides, From hence the railway is conveyed over ground that is nearly level, and twice over the river, until at the distance of about a mile and a half it again approaches its northern bank, which rises so abruptly from the water's edge that it was necessary for the railway to be supported by a high and massive wall of masonry skirting the side of the precipitous bank for a considerable distance. Up to this point the ascent from Whitby is very gradual, not being more than ten feet in a mile; but, from hence to the summit level the gradients increase considerably, and at the Tunnel Inn, six miles and a quarter from Whitby, the elevation of the railway is 120 feet above the level of the sea.

The bridges over the Esk are nine in number, and all formed of Baltic wood. The one at Ruswarp has been already noticed. All the rest, with one exception, are made upon the same principle, and supported by two or three sets of piles, according to the breadth of the stream at the place of crossing; the length of the bearings from one set of piles to another, varying from fifty-five to sixty feet. The vignette in page 27 will convey a good idea of the construction of all the bridges, except the one above referred to, which is carried a distance of eighty feet across the river without any piles at all, and notwithstanding the great length of the main bearers, is found to be full as firm and secure as the others that have the appearance of much greater stability. This bridge cost only £275, exclusive of the stone abutments.

This portion of the railway having been in daily operation for the space of twelve months, and during that time subjected to much heavy traffic, especially in the ponderous article of stone, the bridges have been fairly tried, and it is most satisfactory to find that they have fully answered the expectations of the Engineer, and justified him in adopting a description of bridge that was probably looked upon by many as unequal to the pressure and strain to which it might be exposed.

The natural entrance into the Vale of Goathland consisting merely of the winding course of a rapid stream pent up between precipitous banks, precluded all possibility of carrying the railway into its confines otherwise than by a tunnel. Fortunately the barrier that had to be perforated for the purpose was not of great extent, and the tunnel is consequently but 120 yards in length. It is fourteen feet high, and ten feet wide, and is constructed of the Leaserigg stone. After passing the tunnel, the rise in the line is continued to the foot of the inclined plane, where an elevation of upwards of 200 feet above the level of the sea is attained.

The inclined plane is upon the self-acting principle, and though 1500 yards in length, and the average rate of ascent one in fifteen, it works well, and presents no interruption to the average speed of travelling, but rather the contrary, as the coach is generally run up in four minutes and a half.

From the top of the inclined plane to the summit level, the course of the railway has a very gradual and scarcely perceptible rise. The summit level is attained upon a bog, and, which is rather a singular fact, at a point equidistant from each terminus of the line. Much difficulty has attended the formation of the railway over this treacherous and unstable ground. Judging, however, from the manner in which it has stood the test to which it has been exposed, there is no doubt of its being eventually as firm and durable as any part of the line.

Leaving Fen Bog, the railway enters Newton Dale, which extends in the three divisions of North Dale, Middle Dale, and South Dale, for the distance of five miles, presenting the whole way a succession of the most difficult ground over which a railway has ever yet been attempted to be made. In fact, the whole of this length had to be formed over broken or boggy ground—in the course of moorland streams—through heaps of stones and earth, that had subsided from the neighbouring cliffs and hills—and, in addition to all this, with so considerable an inclination, that many persons thought it would present a complete interruption to the rate of travelling which was to be expected; but happily, upon the railway being brought into operation, such is by no means the case—for with the assistance of extra power in the ascent the average speed may be maintained, even in this most unfavorable part of the line.

After reaching the lower part of Newton Dale, the inclinations in the line from thence to Pickering gradually subside, till at the distance of about three miles and a half from Pickering an almost perfect level is obtained, which continues for the remainder of the way.

The rails used are fish-bellied, fifteen feet in length, and of the weight of forty pounds to the yard. Of some of them the joints are half-lapped, and of others scarfed. The chairs, weighing from fourteen to sixteen pounds each, are fixed to stone blocks of four feet in the cube, and presenting an average surface of four feet square: and it is a strong proof of the soundness of the stone, that in righting the way, from time to time, in that part of the line, that has now been upwards of a year in active operation, scarcely half-a-dozen blocks have been found in an injured state, nor is it found that the stone has been worked away under the seat of the chairs, a defect which exists in many stones, and the absence of which in the Eskdale stone is a satisfactory test of its excellence.

The whole length is twenty-four miles. The regular coach traverses the distance in rather less than two hours and a half, making the average speed nearly ten miles an hour; a rate which may probably be somewhat accelerated, when this novel mode of travelling has been a little longer in practice, and the regulating the speed of carriages is more thoroughly understood by the different persons employed.

The estimated expense of forming this railway was £80,000; but this sum included land for only a single line of railway, and contained no allowance for land and buildings at the termini, or the means of conveying goods and passengers. Iron too, at the time this estimate was made, was but one half the price it has since attained. The final cost was c. £105,000.

The Directors, having every reason to anticipate the necessity of a double line ere many years shall have elapsed, secured the requisite land for the purpose in the first instance, and have also expended several thousand pounds in the purchase of land and buildings at each of the termini, and in providing coaches, waggons, horses, and other conveniences for working the line. Abstracting, therefore, as may very fairly be done, the cost of these several items from the total expenditure, it will be found that the actual cost of the railway, notwithstanding the continued advance in the price of iron, has not much exceeded the original estimate.

As in the cost of this railway public expectation has been so little disappointed, so with respect to the anticipated traffic there is abundant reason to think that a most satisfactory result will be obtained. During the last twelve months the line from Whitby, as far as the Stone quarries above the Tunnel, has been partially open—and in that period, notwithstanding the frequent delays and interruptions consequent upon the completion of that portion of the line, upwards of 10,000 tons of stone alone, have been brought to Whitby for shipment to London; and since the 8th of June, 1835, when a coach began to run daily to and fro between Whitby and the Tunnel Inn, nearly 12,000 passengers have traversed that portion of the line.

Now that the line is completed, the prospect of traffic daily becomes more favourable, and the general feeling in favour of the railway is evidently more sanguine and encouraging. A Company has been formed for conveying lime stone from Pickering to some kilns erected near the Tunnel Inn, and at which considerable trade in that article seems likely to be immediately commenced. Two companies for supplying the town of Pickering and the neighbourhood with sea borne coal imported at Whitby, have been formed, and have already begun their operations, with every probability of transacting business to a great extent.

The shopkeepers at Pickering, and the adjacent towns and villages, are making arrangements for having their supplies of goods by means of the railway, and to facilitate their views a steam packet Company has been formed at Whitby, for the purpose of having goods imported there from Hull and Newcastle with punctuality and dispatch. Indeed, the advantages to be derived from the railway with respect to quickness of communication, and the consequent saving of time to the shopkeepers in the Vale of Rye has already been experienced—cargoes of goods for Pickering, Kirby Moorside, and Helmsley have in two instances arrived at the port of Whitby from London in the course of two days, and by the evening of the third day been ready for delivery from the railway depot at Pickering.

The rich and extensive beds of iron ore that are to be found in the vale of Goathland, promise much advantage to the railway whether from the mere transit and exportation of the ore itself, or from the probable establishment of blast furnaces in a district which possesses so many natural advantages for the purpose.

The whinstone also found upon the line in Goathland is invaluable for the making and repairing of roads, and as it has been tried in the metropolis and much approved, there is a prospect of great quantities being annually sent down the railway for shipment at Whitby; nor is there less reason to look forward to a considerable supply being also required at Pickering where the want of good road material is sensibly felt. In fact some whinstone has already been ordered for the use of the roads in that neighbourhood.

With respect to general merchandize, timber, and agricultural produce, the expectation of a great and increasing traffic, to an extent far beyond what was originally contemplated, is rapidly gaining ground.

The commissioners of the harbour of Whitby are directing their attention to the improvement of that invaluable and favourable adjunct to the efficient working of the railway, whilst on the other hand there is every prospect of the line being extended from Pickering in the direction of Malton and York, so as in the course of a few years to connect the port of Whitby with the central parts of the county, an event which will give to the inhabitants of Whitby, the means of conveying themselves and their merchandize by the various railways now in progress, to all parts of the kingdom, and afford to the country generally, and more especially to the inhabitants of the West Riding, an interesting and ready approach to the most romantic part of the Yorkshire coast, and a fresh outlet for the export of their manufactures to the northern parts of Great Britain as well as to the Continent of Europe.

APPENDIX.

No 1.

ESKDALE.

A TRUE ACCOUNT

OF THE

MURDER OF THE MONK OF WHITBY,

BY

WILLIAM DE BRUCE, LORD OF UGLEBARNBY, RALPH DE PERCY, LORD OF SNEATON, AND ALLATSON, A FREEHOLDER; WITH THE MONK'S PENANCE LAID UPON THEM, TO BE FERFORMED ON ASCENSION EVE, EVERY YEAR, OTHERWISE TO FORFEIT THEIR LANDS TO THE ABBOT OF WHITBY.

In the fifth year of the reign of King Henry the Second, after the conquest of England by William Duke of Normandy, the lord of Uglebarnby, then called William de Bruce, the lord of Sneaton, called Ralph de Percy, with a gentleman and freeholder called Allatson, did, on the 16th day of October, 1159, appoint to meet and hunt the wild boar, in a certain wood or desert place belonging to the Abbot of Whitby; the place's name was Eskdale-side, the abbot's name was Sedman. Then these gentlemen being met, with their hounds and boar staves, in the place before mentioned, and there having found a great wild boar, the hounds ran him well near about the chapel and hermitage of Eskdaleside, where was a monk of Whitby, who was an hermit. The boar being very sorely pursued, and dead run, took in at the chapel door, there laid him down and presently died. The hermit shut the hounds out of the chapel, and kept himself within at his meditations and prayers, the hounds standing at bay without. The gentlemen in the thick of the wood, being put behind their game, followed the cry of their hounds, and so came to the hermitage, calling on the hermit, who opened the door and came forth, and within they found the boar lying dead; for which the gentlemen in great fury, because their hounds where put from their game, did most violently and cruelly run at the hermit with their boar staves, whereby he soon after died. Thereupon the gentlemen perceiving and knowing that they were in peril of death, took sanctuary at Scarborough. But at that time the Abbot being in very great favor with the King, removed them out of the sanctuary, whereby they came in danger of the law, and not to be privileged; but likely to have the severity of the law, which was death for death. But the hermit being a

143

holy and devout man, and at the point of death, sent for the Abbot, and desired him to send for the gentlemen who had wounded him; the Abbot so doing, the gentlemen came, and the hermit being very sick and weak, said unto them, "I am sure to die of those wounds you have given me:" the Abbot answered, "they shall as surely die for the same." But the Hermit answered, "Not so, for I will freely forgive them my death, if they will be content to be enjoined the penance I shall lay on them for the safeguard of their souls." The gentlemen being present, bid him save their lives. Then said the Hermit, "You and yours shall hold your lands of the Abbot of Whitby, and his successors in this manner:—That upon Ascension Day, you or some of you shall come to the wood of the Stray Heads, which is in Eskdale-side, the same day at sun-rising, and there shall the Abbot's officer blow his horn, to the intent that you may know how to find him: and he shall deliver unto you William de Bruce, ten stakes, eleven strout stowers and eleven yethers to be cut by you, or some of you, with a knife of one penny price: and you Ralph de Percy shall take twenty-one of each sort to be cut in the same manner: and you Allatson shall take nine of each sort to be cut as aforesaid, and to be taken on your backs, and carried to the town of Whitby, and to be there before nine of the clock the same day before-mentioned: at the same hour of nine of the clock, if it be full sea, your labour and service shall cease: and, if low water, each of you shall set your stakes to the brim, each stake one yard from the other, and so yether them on each side with your yethers, and so stake on each side with your strout stowers, that they may stand three tides without removing by the force thereof: each of you shall do, make, and execute the said service all that very hour, every year except it be full sea at that hour: but when it shall so fall out, this service shall cease. You shall faithfully do this, in rememberance that you did most cruelly slay me, and that you may the better call to God for mercy, repent unfeignedly of your sins, and do good works. The officer of Eskdale-side shall blow, Out on you, out on you, out on you, for this heinous crime. If you or your successors shall refuse this service, so long as it shall not be full sea at the aforesaid hour, you or yours shall forfeit your lands to the Abbot of Whitby, or his successors. This I intreat, and earnestly beg that you may have your lives and goods preserved for this service: and I request of you to promise by your parts in heaven, that it shall be done by you and your successors as is aforesaid requested; and I will confirm it by the faith of an honest man." Then the Hermit said, "My soul longeth for the Lord: and I do as freely forgive these men my death, as Christ forgave the thieves on the cross." And in the presence of the Abbot and the rest, he said moreover these words, *"Is manus tuas, Domine, commendo spiritum meum, a vinculis, enim mortis redemisti me, Domine veritatis. Amen."* So he yielded up the ghost, the eighth day of December, Anno Domine, 1159, whose soul God have mercy upon. Amen.

*O Lord, into thy hands do, I commit my soul, for from the chains of death hast thou redeemed me, O Lord of truth.

No. II.

Through the kind assistance of W. Campbell, Esq. of Whitby, M.D. the Editor is enabled to supply the following list of some, amongst the numerous plants found in the district of the Railway.

Class.	Order.	Genus. Species.	English Name.	Where found.	Time of Flowering.
I.	1.	Salicornia herbacea.	Jointed glasswort.	On the Esk banks, near the railway Toll-house.	June.
II.	1.	Ligustrum vulgare.	Privet.	Newholm Beck.	July.
		Hippuris vulgaris.	Mare's tail.	Costa, near Pickering.	June and July.
		Circæa Lutetiana.	Enchanter's night shade.	Cockmill Wood.	July.
		Verbena officinalis.	Vervain.	Egton Grange.	May.
		Veronica Montana.	Mountain speedwell.	Near Sleights.	July.
		—— hederifolia.	Ivy leaved, do.	Ruswarp.	May.
		Pinguicula vulgaris.	Common Butterwort.	Newton Dale.	June.
		Salvia verbenaca.	Wild chary.	Newton Dale.	June.
III.	1.	Iris pseudacorus.	Yellow Iris.	Newton Dale.	July.

145

Class. Order. Genus. Species.	English Name.	Where found.	Time of Flowering.
Scirpus pauciflorus	Chocolate-headed club-rush.	Sleights Moor	June.
——— sylvaticus	Wood clubrush	{ Egton Bridge and Rus-warp Mill Dam.	July.
Eriophorum vaginatum	Single-headed cotton grass	Goathland Moors	June.
2. Melica nutans	Mountain melic grass	Common	July.
Poa distans	Reflexed meadow grass	Banks of the Esk	June.
——— maritima	Creeping sea, do.	Runswick Bay	July.
——— procumbens	Procumbent, do.	Runswick Bay	July.
Festuca rubra	Creeping Fescue grass.	Runswick Bay	July.
——— bromoides	Barren, do.	Aislaby Moor	June and July.
——— loliacea	Spiked, do.	Egton Bridge	July.
——— elatior	Tall, do.	Sleights Mill	July.
Bromus scalinus	Smooth rye brome-grass	Iburn Dale	June.
Avena fatua	Wild oat (common)	Corn fields	July.
Lolium arvense	White darnel (not common)	In cultivated fields	July.
Rottbollia incurvata	Sea hard-grass	Boghall	July and August

Class.	Order.	Genus. Species.	English Name.	Where found.	Time of Flowering.
		Sanguisorba officinalis	Burnet	Newton Dale	July.
IV.	1.	Cornus Suecica	Dwarf Cornel	Hole of Horcum	July.
		Scabiosa arvensis	Field Scabious	Newton Dale	July.
V.	1.	Borago officinalis	Common borage (doubtful if wild)	Woodlands	July.
		Convolvolus sepium	Great Bindweed	Eskdale	July.
		——— arvensis	Small Bindweed	Ruswarp	July.
		Primula elatior	Oxlip	Whitby Cliffs, and many other places	May.
		Menyanthes trifoliata	Bog bean	Fenbog and Newton Dale	May and June.
		Campanula latifolia	Giant bell-flower	Esk Banks	July.
		Viola palustris	Marsh violet	Sneaton Low Moor	July.
		Verbascum Thapsus	Great Mullein	Mulgrave Woods	August.
		Euonymus Europaeus	Spindle tree	Newholme Beck	June.
	2.	Scandix Odorata	Great chervil	Esk Banks	April.
	4.	Parnassia palustris	Grass of Parnassus	Newton Dale	August.

Class.	Order.	Genus.	Species.	English Name.	Where found.	Time of Flowering.
		6.	Drosera rotundifolia........	Round-leaved sun-dew......	Randymere, near Beck Hole......	July.
			Glaux maritima	Sea milkwort......	Esk Banks, near the railway Toll House......	June and July.
			Statice armeria......	Thrift......		
			Statice limonium......	Sea lavender......		
VI.	1.		Narcissus, pseudo-narcissus.	Daffodil........	Goathland........	May.
			Narthecium ossifragum ...	Lancashire asphodel......	Aislaby Moor........	June and July.
			Juncus maximus........	Wood rush........	Whitby........	April and May.
			—— liniger........	Flaxen, do........	Whitby........	May.
VII.	1.		Trientalis Europœa	Chickweed winter-green....	Randymere........	June and July.
VIII.	1.		Daphne laureola........	Spurge laurel........	Larpool Wood	April.
	3.		Polygonum bistorta........	Great bistort........	Esk Banks and Iburn Dale	July.
	4.		Paris quadrifolia........	Herb Paris	Larpool Wood	June.
			Adoxa moschatellina........	Tuberous moscatel........	Sleights, &c.	April.
X.	1.		Pyrola media	Intermediate winter-green..	Mulgrave Woods, &c.....	July.
			Lythrum salicaria........	Purple loose strife	Newton Dale........	July.

148

Class.	Order.	Genus. Species.	English Name.	Where found.	Time of Flowering.
	2.	Chrysosplenium alternifolium	Alternate leaved sea green, (not common)	Esk Dale, near Carmount.	April.
		———— oppositifolium	Oppositeleaved, do (common)	Esk Dale, near Carmount.	April.
		Saxifraga granulata	White saxifrage	Cock Mill—Ruswarp	June.
		———— tridactylites	Rue leaved	Cock Mill—Ruswarp	July.
	3.	Arenaria peploides	Sea sandwort	Bog Hall	June and July.
		———— marina	Sea spurry	Bog Hall	July.
	4.	Cerastium tetrandum	Tetrandrous mouse-ear	Along the coast	June.
XII.	1.	Prunus padus	Bird cherry	Newton Dale and Beck Hole	May.
	3.	Geum rivale	Water avens	Grosmont	June and July.
	5.	Rosa spinosissima	Burnet rose	Cock Mill Wood	June and July.
		———— villosa		Esk Banks	July.
		———— rubella		Cross Cliff	July.
		Rubus cæsius	Dew-berry	Esk Banks	July and August
		Tormentilla reptans	Trailing tormentil	(Common)	June.

149

Class	Order	Genus. Species.	English Name.	Where found.	Time of Flowering.
XIII.	7.	Clematis vitalba	Traveller's joy	Near Whitby, (doubtful if wild)	July.
		Trollius Europaeus	Globe flower	Esk Bank	June.
		Cistus helianthemum	Dwarf cistus	On the Moor near Newton Dale	July.
XIV.	1.	Galeobdolon luteum	Yellow weasel snout	(Common)	June.
		Origanum vulgare	Common marjorum	Pickering Castle	August.
	2.	Bartsia odontites	Red bartsia	Stainsacre	June.
		Lathraea squamaria	Greater toothwort	Newbegin—Sleights	April and May.
		Scrophularia aequatica	Water fig-wort	Esk Banks	June and July.
		Scutellaria Galericulata	Water Betony	Randymere and Newton Dale	August.
XV.	1.	Lepidum latifolium	Broad-leaved pepperwort	Sandsend	August.
		Cochlearia armoricia	Horse raddish	Ruswarp	August.
		Cardamine amara	Bitter ladies' smock	Eskdaleside, by Newbegin and Groves' Hall	April.

Class.	Order.	Genus. Species.	English Name.	Where found.	Time of Flowering.
		Brassica oleracea	Sea cabbage	Cliffs at Whitby & Sleights	May.
XVI.	2.	Geranium sylvaticum	Wood crane's-bill	Mulgrave Woods	July.
		—— malvæfolium	Mallow-leaved	Near Whitby	July.
		—— cicutarium	Hemlock, do	Cliffs near Newholme	August.
	3.	Malva moschata	Musk mallow	Eskdale	August.
XVII.	1.	Fumaria capreolata	Ramping fumitory	Near Whitby	June.
		—— claviculata	White climbing, do	Arncliff Wood	March.
		Trifolium Millite	Official Millot	Newton Dale	June.
	2.	Polygala vulgari	Common milkwort	Eskdale	June and July.
	3.	Genista tinctoria	Dyer's green weed	Whitby Cliffs	June.
		—— Anglica	Needle broom	Cawthorn Camps	June.
		Lathyrus latifolius	Broad-leaved everlasting pea	Near Kettleness	June and July.
		—— sylvestris	Narrow leaved everlasting pea	Near Scarborough	
		Ulex nanus	Dwarf whin	Whitby Moors	June.
		Vicia sylvatica	Wood vetch	Cliffs, Mulgrave Woods	June.
		—— bithynica	Rough podded purple (rare)	Upgang Beck	July.

Class.	Order.	Genus. Species.	English Name.	Where found.	Time of Flowering.
XVIII.	1.	Hypericum androsemum...	Tutsan...	{ Larpool Wood, Kilton Wood, &c.	May and June.
		—— humifusum	Trailing St. John's wort...	(Common)	June.
XIX.	1.	Hieracium sylvaticum	Wood hawkweed	Iburn Dale	July.
		—— paludosum	Mountain	Iburn Dale	June and July.
		—— villosum	Alpine	Arncliff Wood	August.
		Carduus tenuiflorus	Slender flowered thistle	(Common)	July.
		—— murianus	Milk thistle,	Runswick	July.
		—— acanthoides	Welted, do.	Newton Dale	July and August
		—— eriophorus	Woolly headed, do.	Hackness	
		—— nutans	Musk, do.	Newton Dale	July.
		Cnicus heterophyllus	Melancholy do.	Newton Dale	June and July.
		Picris ochioides	Bristly oxtongue (rare)	Ruswarp Banks	July.
		Lactuca virosa	Strong scented lettuce (rare)	Mulgrave Woods	July.
	2.	Gnaphalium dioicum	Mountain cud-weed	Egton Moors	July.

Class.	Order.	Genus.	Species.	English Name.	Where found.	Time of Flowering.
			Artamasia maritima.........	Sea wormwood.........	{ The Esk Banks, near the Toll House....... }	August.
			Seneico lividus...........	Livid groundsel....	Abounds near Whitby....	August.
			Solidago virgaurea...........	Common golden rod.....	Larpool Wood..........	July and August
			Inula helenicum.........	Elecampane........	Near Growmond Bridge.	July and August
		3.	Centaurea calcitrapa	Star thistle........	Sandsend.........	August.
XX.	1.		Orchis bifolia...........	Butterfly orchis......	Egton........	July.
			—— canopsea........	Aromatic......	Banks of the Mirk Esk ..	July.
			Epipactis palustris.......	White satyrion......	Newton Dale..........	July and August
			—— nidus-avis.........	Bird's-nest ophrys	Mulgrave Woods......	August.
			—— cordata...........	Least twayblade........	Aislaby Low Moor......	July.
			Ophrys apifera...........	Bee ophrys.........	Carrmount......	July.
			—— anthropofera........	Green man ophrys......	Newbegin	July.
			—— muesifera...........	Fly, do...........	Kirkby Moorside.........	July.
			Typha latifolia...........	Great Reed mace, or Cat's tail	Near Ruswarp.........	August.
XXI.	3.		Carex pauciflora.........	Few-flowered sedge.......	Near Lilla Cross.........	August.

Class.	Order.	Genus.	Species.	English Name.	Where found.	Time of Flowering.
			—— curta	White flowered sedge	Sleights Moor	June.
			—— vulpina	Great, do.	Newton Dale.	July.
			—— axillaris	Axillary, do.	Newton Dale.	
			—— paniculata	panicled, do.	Newton Dale.	
			—— pendula	Great pendulous, do.	Mulgrave Woods, Sleights, &c.	May.
			—— fulva	Tawny, do.	Hole of Horcum	June.
			—— binervis	Green ribbed, do.	Aislaby Moor	July.
			—— vesicaria	Short-spiked bladder, do.	Randaymere	July.
			—— riparia	Common, do.	Newton Dale.	
			—— ampulbacea,	Slender beaked, do.	Newton Dale.	May.
			—— paludosa.	Marsh, do.	Newton Dale.	May.
	4.	Betula alba		Common birch	Newton Dale.	May.
XXII.	1.	Salix rosmarinifolia		Rosemary leaved willow	Saltergate.	June.
	3.	Hippophae rhamnoides		Sea buckthorn	Cliff near Upgang	May.
		Myrica gale		Sweet gale	Newton Dale.	June.

154

Class.	Order.	Genus. Species.	English Name.	Where found.	Time of Flowering.
		Humulus lupulus.........	Hop................	Arncliff Wood and Beck Hole............	July.
XXIV.	1.	Equisetum sylvaticum......	Wood horse-tail........	Goathland Dale.......	April & May.
		———— hyemale.......	Shave grass.........	Goathland Dale.......	
		Ophioglossum vulgatum.....	Adder's tongue (rare).....	Aislaby Low Moor.......	August.
		Osmunda regalis........	Flowering fern........	Beck Hole..........	June & July
		———— lunaria........	Moon wort.........	Near Swarthoue.......	July.
		Lycopodium selago......	Fir club moss........	Aislaby Low Moor......	May.
		———— alpinum........	Savin leaved., do.....	Aislaby Low Moor......	May.
		Polypodium dryopteris.....	Tender 3 branched polypody	Randaymere.........	July.
		Aspidium oreopteris.......	Heath shield fern........	Wheeldale and at Beck Hole............	July.
		Asplenium lanceolatum.....	Lanceolate spleen wort....	Mulgrave Castle........	August.
		Hymenophyllum Tun- bridgense........	Filmy leaved Fern........	Eskdale side..........	May.

155

THE ACCOUNT

THE OPENING OF THE RAILWAY.

The Railway has been opened since the preceding pages were written, and the Editor having been favored by Thomas Clark, Esq. the Treasurer, with the following account of that event, has thought that it might prove an interesting addition to his work.

THE ceremonial of opening the Whitby and Pickering Railway took place on Thursday, the 26th of May, and as no event which had hitherto occurred to the inhabitants of Whitby, had been regarded by them as of equal importance to their present and future prospects, so it was determined that this occasion should be celebrated so as to give it all the eclât of which it could possibly be made deserving.

The Directors had on the previous week announced to the Proprietors the day on which the opening was to take place, and also that tickets for places in the carriages would be issued to them only up to a certain day, and after that time to the public until the 19th instant, but not afterwards; by which means the Directors were enabled to ascertain the precise number of those who intended to be present, and provide carriages accordingly. An additional carriage was prepared for the accommodation of the strangers who might visit Whitby on this occasion. A programme of the regulations requisite to be observed was also issued; and as it was desirable that all confusion and disorderly conduct should be guarded against and repressed: it was intimated that means had been taken and would be strictly enforced to carry the regulations into effect, and to keep the rail-road clear of people—and in order to present, if possible, any accident occurring to mar the festivities of the day, policemen were engaged and stationed at certain points near the railway depôt, and also on the rail-road itself throughout the whole length of the line. Barriers were also erected protecting the approaches to the offices, and placards above the doors shewed where the first and second class passengers were to enter and exchange their tickets for cards, which were to be kept and delivered by the passengers to the guards of their respective coaches, on the parties leaving Pickering to return to Whitby. By these means all hurry and confusion were avoided on the passengers taking their places, as every individual previously to his arrival at the station knew the coach assigned to him; and also that his seat was secured from being occupied by others. We have been particular in mentioning these preparatory arrangements, and have attached a greater importance to them than they may appear to warrant; but on occasions like the present, if strict order and regularity had not been enforced, and observed alike by the passengers and officers, the best and most careful arrangements might have been nullified, the good intentions of the Directors frustrated, and the expectations of the passengers themselves disappointed.

The morning which had so long been anxiously looked for, and with no little apprehension as to the probable state of the weather---on which so very much of the effect of the day's proceedings depended---broke forth most brilliantly, with every prospect of continuance. Early in the day the bells rang a merry peal, and by half past seven o'clock crowds drew to the Angel Inn where the Directors had assembled, and where they were joined by their friends and the tradespeople of the town. Banners of various descriptions were unfurled, and some splendid flags made for the occasion were exhibited. Amongst the most conspicuous, we noticed a beautiful flag belonging to the "Agricultural Society," with appropriate devices and inscriptions, the Railway Company's flag, the Lime Company's, the Coal Company's, &c. &c.

The Whitby Brass Band preceding played their favorite and inspiring tunes, and the procession consisting of four constables, some of the railway workmen: the flag of the Whitby and Pickering Railway; Mr. Wilkinson, chief police officer; the band; Robert Campion, Esq. chairman—Thomas Fishburn, Esq. deputy chairman—and the remainder of the Directors—the Engineers and Solicitors—flags—gentlemen three abreast—the remainder of the workmen and constables, proceeded to the Railway Depot. On arriving there the procession halted, and was received with three hearty cheers.

The ladies (who on this as on all former occasions where their attendance had been solicited, had kindly acceded to the request of the Directors, and condescended to favor them with their presence, thus giving an additional eclât to a proceeding, which without them would have been deprived of its most interesting and beautiful features), had taken their places previously to the arrival of the procession, and the passengers being seated, which was announced by the ringing of a bell, the horses belonging to the Company were brought out, and attracted the attention and praises of the passengers and the numerous spectators, for their beauty and the excellence of their equipments. Each coachman and guard had a green card placed in his hat, shewing the coach to which they belonged. On the bell again ringing the horses were attached to the carriages, and immediately started off at a brisk pace, the crowds on each side of the Railway, and on the contiguous eminences, cheering the passengers as they passed along. The speed of the different coaches was regulated by flags of different colors entrusted to the guards, a white flag to "go on"—a red one to "go slow"— and a blue one to "stop"—the whole were under the control of F. Swanwick, Esq. and Mr. Harding, the Engineers of the Company. Every part of the line where the public could have access to it, or where a view of the railway could be obtained, was crowded with spectators to witness the departure of the carriages: many flags were exhibited, and the most hearty cheers were given and returned by the bystanders and passengers in the coaches.

On arriving at the first stage (the Tunnel Inn) the attention of the visitors was attracted by, and that of the proprietors of the railway pleasingly gratified at, the sight of the lime kilns now being erected near that place by the spirited and active exertions of the "Whitby and Growmond Lime Company," one of the numerous companies formed in consequence of the railway. In the course of a few weeks four large kilns will be brought into active operation. An opportunity was also afforded of seeing the iron stone collected by the Stone Company, and which is likely to be another very profitable source of traffic: and as the train proceeded, an occasion was given of witnessing a most interesting, and to many present a very novel sight. On approaching the quarries of the Whitby Stone Company at Leaserigg, the men belonging to the Company were seen stationed on the refuse stone heaps by the quarries, where they produced a very picturesque effect, and from whence they greeted the passers by with loud and hearty cheers. They also favored the Company with a sight of the manner in which the stones are brought down the steep declivity to the rail road, by means of a self-acting inclined plane. The train of coaches having been stopped, and a preconcerted signal given, a loaded waggon was seen to start from the top of the hill with a union flag waving in front; it rattled down the plane at a fearful speed, and whilst the apprehensions of the parties were excited for its safe arrival at the bottom, they were as quickly allayed by the way in which it was (imperceptibly to them) stopped at the requisite point. On the signal being again given to "go on," at a merry speed the train proceeded, and soon arrived at the inclined plane—the horses were detached and some delay necessarily took place, which afforded to the passengers an excellent opportunity for inspecting that which had been decried by those not very favourable to the undertaking, as an insurmountable obstacle to the operations of the Company, no pains having been spared to invest the "inclined plane" with a most formidable and terrific character. The ladies and the gentlemen, however, who had never seen the place before were surprised and agreeably deceived in their expectations, for on the signal being given three carriages loaded with passengers glided up the steep ascent with a pleasing, rapid, and easy pace; and both on going and returning many were heard to declare that the ascending and descending of the incline so far from being in any way disagreeable, was certainly as pleasant as any other part of the day's journey. The other carriages followed in succession, and the band during the time played several enlivening airs to the manifest delight of a large assemblage of country people collected about the top of the inclined plane and who with colours flying and firing of guns welcomed the visitors, whilst the most sincere wishes for the prosperity of the undertaking were elicited from all present.

The country through which the road passes from this point assumes a totally different character, from that which had previously been witnessed, being wild and desolate but not without some claim to admiration by all true lovers of nature. Those, however, who have no taste for scenery of this description are quickly carried through it, for on arriving where the inclination falls somewhat rapidly, the horses were detached, the coaches were connected together with coupling bars, and started at a great pace which rapidly increased, insomuch that in order to oblige and gratify the wishes of the Company they were allowed to go at the rate, in some parts, of 30 miles an hour; but this speed gradually lessened on approaching the line in Blansby and Pickering Parks, sufficient impetus however having been given to enable the coaches to run on this beautiful portion of the line, which has but very slight inclination at the rate of fourteen or fifteen miles an hour; and much amusement was occasioned at the sight of several Gentlemen who had come on horseback to witness the procession, racing away with each other at a quick pace, to overtake and beat the carriages into Pickering.

On putting to fresh horses the train proceeded to Pickering, and on coming in view of the castle a sight broke upon the passengers which attracted and at once riveted their attention, and made an impression which will not be quickly effaced. The castle of Pickering stands in all its mouldering glory a remnant of its former beauty, extent, and magnificence; and the sides of the hill which it surmounts were covered from the base to the top with a dense mass of people assembled from all the adjacent country, as well as from the towns of Scarbro', Malton, Kirby, Helmsley, and York, amounting to upwards of seven thousand strangers, who with one united voice cheered the carriages as they approached and entered the Company's depot. It is understood that from this point the effect of the carriages emerging one after another from the well-wooded Vale of Blansby Park was particularly pleasing.

It is highly satisfactory to be able to remark, that though every thing connected with the ceremony was necessarily of a perfectly novel character, that great zeal and excitement prevailed and the difficulty under such circumstances of restraining the feelings and preserving good order is proportionably great, not a single individual beyond the policemen was observed to intrude on the line, nor was the least infringement attempted on the regulations of the day; when all this is considered it may be justly remarked that the greatest praise is equally due to the public for observing, as also to Mr. Thompson the Company's agent at Pickering for acting upon, and enforcing the regulations issued by the Directors. A procession was now quickly formed, the Pickering band preceded, and other bands of music from Scarbro' and other places joined in and played whilst the procession passed up the town to Mr. Munkman's the Black Swan Inn, and a great crowd followed. The houses looking into the street through which the

159

procession passed were crowded with ladies, who seemed delighted at the view, and vied with their male friends in welcoming and congratulating their Whitby friends on the result of their meritorious efforts.

The party sat down to a most excellent dejeuner à la fourchette prepared by Mr. Munkman according to previous announcement, and for which during the preceding fortnight most formidable preparations in the way of good eatables had been made.

Every thing had up to this point exceeded the expectations of all concerned; not the slightest dissatisfaction had been expressed, and above all, not the least accident occurred to damp the hilarious feeling which was alike shared by all; after remaining until the appointed time for departure, the procession again moved from the Inn and proceeded to the railway depot, when the same regularity and order were again observed, and the carriages started off, cheered by the loud huzzas of thousands, assembled to witness their departure.

The ride back was equally as pleasant and as beautiful as the one in the morning, and on descending the inclined plane, and whilst going at a good speed the Engineers gave the passengers an opportunity of witnessing the command they possessed over the carriages, for on a preconcerted signal being given, the guards applied the breaks, "and the carriages were stopped gradually, but most effectually in the midst of their rapid and downward course; the rope was then disengaged and the "breaks" released, when those who delight in quickly passing through the air, were gratified in being carried at the rate of twenty miles an hour to within six miles of Whitby. The Company's horses were again brought into action, and did their work to the admiration of all present, taking the carriages in fine style into Whitby where they arrived almost to a minute of the time appointed, and where crowds of people thronged to meet them. Mutual congratulations now passed between the Directors and officers of the Company and their friends on the most gratifying termination of the proceedings, connected with the ceremonial opening of the railway. The utmost delight was evinced by all, and not a single voice dissented from the general expression of joy and satisfaction that a day replete with interest, from the novelty and animating nature of the circumstances attending it, and its prospective results, so intimately connected with the prosperity of the place, had passed off in a manner so completely in accordance with the most sanguine wishes of the Directors and Shareholders at large.

Railway Office, May 30, 1836

CHAPTER 6

FROM SURVEYING TO ARTISTRY : GEORGE HAYDOCK DODGSON (1811-1880)

Hugh Dodgson

The Whitby-Pickering Railway has always been noted for its scenic beauty. Before the widespread use of photography, the main means of conveying its picturesque charms was through the arts of printmaking. Prints were produced by lithography - literally "writing on stone" - or from woodcuts, etchings, or engravings. At much greater cost, paintings in watercolours or oils would provide an enduring record of a place or event. When Henry Belcher commissioned the young assistant surveyor of the line, George Haydock Dodgson, to record its appeal, the profession of watercolour artist was still in its infancy and watercolour painting was struggling for acceptance on equal terms with oils as works of art in their own right.

*George Dodgson not only helped to bring the Whitby to Pickering Railway into being, he also made it his own through the images he created. At the age of twenty-two, his pleasure in drawing and painting together with the interest and encouragement of Henry Belcher (see Ch.3) helped to convince George that his future lay in transforming the skills of surveying into artistry. The outcomes of this life-changing decision are outlined below by his direct descendant, **Hugh Dodgson,** Great-Great-Great Nephew of the artist. (Ed.)*

George Haydock Dodgson c1865
An engraving after a photograph by John Waller of Whitby

The Dodgson Family

George Haydock Dodgson, born on 16 Aug 1811 at 38 Castle Street, Liverpool, was destined to become an artist of some repute although much of his professional life would be spent in London.

The Dodgsons of Bridekirk in Cumberland were a yeoman farming family of some antiquity as the churchyards in the associated villages of Tallentire, Dovenby and Broughton testify. By marriage with other local families such as the Pearsons and Fawsetts, they owned or leased substantial land within the parish. In about 1800, one of the sons, Pearson Dodgson, then working at the Curwen estate at Cammerton Hall, moved to Liverpool with his young wife Hannah and took up residence in Castle Street. Hannah Haydock had come from a well-to-do cotton weaving family in the Blackburn area, and she and Pearson established a linen drapery business in Lord Street, Liverpool, just round the corner from their house. Over the next 25 years, they found time to produce fifteen children, some of whom joined the parental business. The eighth child was, however, an exception.

George Haydock Dodgson was educated at a small private gentlemen's academy maintained in Church Lane, Liverpool by Richard Prior, and a teacher friend of Pearson Dodgson. George's ability with a pencil and his undoubted interest in art came to notice early and it was farsighted of Richard Prior to seek the advice of the Liverpool artist, Andrew Lucas Hunt (1790-1861). Hunt, who gave George his first drawing lessons, was the father of the painter Alfred William Hunt (1830-1896) and grandfather of the notorious novelist Violet Hunt (1862-1942). Hunt Senior lived in Oxford Street, a short distance from the Church Lane School. He was so impressed with Dodgson's abilities that when George was fifteen, he recommended him to the renowned Liverpool surveyor Jonathan Bennison, who took him as an apprentice for five years. George was released on 1st July 1831 with a glowing testimonial that Bennison wrote on the reverse of the Indenture:

"The within-named George Dodgson has this day completed the Term of his Apprenticeship during which time I have always found him to conduct himself with great propriety and I believe him to have faithfully and diligently complied with all the conditions of this Indenture".[1]

From Liverpool to Whitby

Following a recommendation from Bennison, George was employed as a surveyor by George and Robert Stephenson, the celebrated railway engineers. The details of George's employment with the Stephensons are yet to be uncovered, but he was involved at an early stage in the surveying of the Whitby

163

and Pickering Railway. The historian of the Old Watercolour Society, John Lewis Roget, writing in about 1890, noted that George:

"... and three companions were set to prepare plans for the line which now runs between Pickering and Whitby. They had to be ready for delivery without fail by a certain 30 November in order to fulfil the legal requirements, Royal Assent for the railway having been received in May 1833. To complete the drawings in time the young men were obliged to work day and night, and they sat up without taking their clothes off for a whole fortnight, keeping themselves continuously awake by the aid of opium and strong black coffee." [2]

One of the Whitby residents most closely associated with the planning for, and financing of, the railway was a local solicitor and magistrate, Henry Belcher. Belcher seems to have befriended the young George and introduced him to his clerk, George Weatherill (1810-1890), who would later make a name for himself as an artist and famous Whitby son. The two Georges became life-long friends and George Haydock would return regularly in later years to stay with Weatherill and to join him in sketching forays around the Whitby area.

A miniature pen and ink drawing (1.5 x 2.0 inches) by George Weatherill of his employer, Henry Belcher, framed in Whitby in 1914. (Private Collection)

164

Original Sketch for *Entrance to the Vale of Goathland*

During his work on the railway, George Haydock made several drawings of Whitby Abbey that impressed Belcher and led to a commission to produce a series of some twenty sketches of the countryside through which the railway would pass. These drawings were subsequently engraved and used to illustrate Henry Belcher's book on the Whitby and Pickering Railway published in 1836.[3] George Weatherill acquired the originals of these drawings from Henry Belcher. Weatherill then passed them to his son Richard, who later sold them to Thomas Hacks English, a local doctor. Although their current whereabouts is unknown, one has recently been found in a copy of Belcher's book purchased at an auction in Yorkshire.

By the end of 1834, George Haydock began to show signs of ill health. As Bennison had noted in his testimonial, later supported by Roget, George was extremely conscientious and the long hours spent in far from ideal working conditions had left him with a weak chest and nervous tic. He returned home to Liverpool, resigned his position with the Stephensons and resolved to make his way as an artist.

His father, Pearson, was unimpressed with this decision but after the intervention of George's elder brother Thomas, who shared his interest in art, he became resigned to the situation. His father gave George £300 and agreed to lend him a further sum should it be needed. The careful Pearson, however, made it clear that the loan, if drawn, would attract interest at "five pounds per cent per annum but such interest to cease at my death"[4] When Pearson's will was proved in 1850, George's share of his father's estate was just under £1000, of which George had already drawn about £600.

The London Years

In 1835, George moved to London taking rooms in Lambeth before moving in 1839 to Camden. He seems to have made a particular effort to befriend architects and several of the noted engravers of the day including Joseph Lionel Williams (1815-1877), William James Linton (1812-1898), the Dalziel Brothers (1817-1906), and the Radclyffe family. In 1838, he spent several days at Stowe in the company of Williams who was sketching in the Stowe Gardens and during this time Dodgson undertook the sketches of features of the London and Birmingham Railway which were later published in Thomas Roscoe's book on the line.

In a long letter dated 27 Mar 1839 to his mother in Liverpool, George complained of being overworked and being short of money.

"I am quite well and as usual at this time of the year previous to exhibition time quite busy but I have been almost ill with anxiety. I have been fortunate and have taken a commission – a drawing of the staircase of Goldsmith's Hall (to be exhibited at the Academy) one of the most difficult subjects to treat I ever had, and I have had some posers. You cannot imagine how it has worried me, caused me more than one sleepless night as I knew my artistical reputation in some measure depended on it. I begin to find that a name is sometimes a source of uneasiness and I find that I have gained one amongst architects especially. Mentioning to several my fears that I should not be able to make a good drawing of my present subject they have generally replied that the man that did Cockerell's drawing could not make a failure. This, tho it has amazed me, has spurred me on and I have now the satisfaction to find that it is coming all right and that it will make an effective picture. But I have been obliged to have recourse to all sorts of expedients. I have used gold and silver all over it, stuck in lots of figures, rich draperies, picture frames and all manner of accessories. I think none have such alternations of pleasure and pain as an artist. I feel as thoroughly happy now as I have felt miserable for the last week. Pictures are to be sent in on Monday week. I have no time to spare and shall probably have to work all night but I feel double strength now that my picture begins to look right – it is for Hardwick the architect, a first rate man and who may be of great service to me. I have been obliged to refuse three orders – they were to be done

for the academy and I had not time. I sent two small things – they are hung in first-rate places on the line (the place for the best pictures). I find more every day the inconvenience of my present rooms and I must in the course of the summer have others....."[5]

"Cockerell's drawing" refers to a work by the architect Charles Robert Cockerell (1788-1863). In 1838, he produced a fascinating capriccio as a tribute to Sir Christopher Wren, showing a mixture of real and imaginary features of a large number of Wren's buildings gathered in a London setting. The original version was coloured by George and was exhibited at the Royal Academy that year under Cockerell's name

"Hardwick the architect" is Sir Philip Hardwick (1792-1870). Hardwick had produced designs for Robert Stephenson's London and Birmingham Railway, including Euston Station and its famous Doric Arch. Hardwick was also the architect of Goldsmith's Hall (1829-1835) but there is no mention in any other source material of the Staircase drawing. George had shown a picture at the Royal Academy in 1838 (A view of Dutton Viaduct) but nothing else until 1841. The painting of the viaduct on the Grand Junction Railway near Aston Bridge, Cheshire, is now in the collection of the National Railway Museum.

The letter continues with a catalogue of real or imagined problems; a request for his mother to look out for second-hand furniture (cheaper than in London), his need to borrow some money from his father – as had been promised and finally, a reference to an exchange of presents between George's sister Hannah and "Jenny".

It is difficult not to see this letter as an attempt to impress his mother. Her reaction is unrecorded but this extremely business-like and shrewd woman is likely to have had few illusions about dear George. Given her husband's reaction to their son's departure from safe employment with the Stephensons to become an artist, it is likely that she will have kept her counsel. But she may also have noted with satisfaction the mention, at the end of the letter, of "Jenny" for six months later, Jenny was to become her daughter-in–law.

The connections here lie through Andrew Hunt who, it is believed, provided his former pupil with some artistic introductions in London. Amongst these was the artist George Sims, then living in Lambeth. There is other, rather more tenuous evidence, that Sims had some connection with Whitby and that he may have met George Dodgson there in the 1830s. It therefore seems likely that Dodgson's choice of Lambeth, when he left Liverpool to settle in London in 1835, was to be near the Sims household.

Sims had a very beautiful daughter, Jane, known as "Jenny", and on 30 Sep 1839, she and George were married in Lambeth. George's newly found father-in-law came from an artistic family, a member of the New Society of Painters in Watercolours, and a regular exhibitor at the Royal Academy.

The National Gallery, home of the Royal Academy from 1837 to 1868

He was sufficiently impressed with his son-in-law's efforts to encourage him to apply for associate membership of the New Society. Sims never knew the outcome as he died in 1840, two years before George's application was successful.

In 1841, George showed another painting at the Annual Exhibition of the Royal Academy, then housed at the recently built National Gallery in Trafalgar Square. Dodgson's exhibit was a depiction of Rydal Water, one of the smaller lakes of Cumberland. The lake is situated in an area closely associated with the poet William Wordsworth who, by tortuous genealogy, was a relative of the artist. The year ended happily for George and Jane with the arrival of their first child, Jenny.

In the following year, there were two further notable events in the family fortunes: George was elected an associate member of the New Watercolour Society and his second child, George Pearson, was born. At about this time, Dodgson obtained some useful work for the Dalziel Brothers (fl. 1840-1890), providing them with drawings on woodblock for engraving. These works were, in the main, romantic miniatures usually based on his watercolours to be used as illustrations to volumes of poetry. The contact with the Dalziels also led to several years of work for the *Illustrated London News* and later for *The Graphic*, and for the *Cambridge Almanac*. He also undertook some lithographic work for Day and Haghe (fl. 1835 -1850) one of the more important print publishers of

168

the day. For the *Art Union of London,* George contributed several illustrations for their editions of the poetry of Byron, Milton and Goldsmith.

His Works and Career c.1843-1880

Up to this time, George's watercolours had been a mix of genre scenes, small landscapes and architectural studies, the latter including a particularly fine drawing of St Paul's from Blackfriars Bridge in London, now in the Walker Art Gallery in Liverpool. This picture, dated 1843, belonged to the artist's brother, Thomas, who presented it to the city of Liverpool in 1877.

He appears to have retained the friendship of both George and Robert Stephenson for whom he continued to produce depictions of their railway architecture until about 1850. However, from about this time, his watercolours become predominantly landscapes of areas of the countryside of which he had become particularly fond. Over the years, he returned regularly to sketch in Cumberland, North Wales (especially Snowdonia), Durham, Derbyshire (notably the romantic setting of Haddon Hall), Yorkshire (particularly Richmond and Whitby), Berkshire (the upper reaches of the Thames), South Wales (mostly the Gower Peninsula), Devon (Lynmouth) and Kent (Sevenoaks and particularly Knole Park).

George Dodgson seems never to have ventured out of England and the few paintings ostensibly of locations in Ireland and Scotland, bear legends apparently added by overenthusiastic framers or auctioneers rather than the artist. He continued to exhibit in London at the Royal Academy, The Society of British Artists (Suffolk Street), the Royal Institute of Painters in Watercolours (formerly the New Watercolour Society), the British Institute in Pall Mall, and at the Old Watercolour Society. Elsewhere his pictures appeared at the Liverpool Academy (and its successors), the Liverpool Society of Fine Arts, the Royal Manchester Institute, and in 1852 (only) the Royal Hibernian Institute in Dublin, the last-named probably as a result of his friendship with the Dublin-born artist Edwin Hayes RHA (1819-1904).

In 1844, he had been elected a full member of the New Watercolour Society but resigned in 1847 and, in company with his fellow artists and close friends, Edward Duncan (1803-1882) and Francis William Topham (1808-1877), applied for associate membership of the Old Society.

In about 1849, George was recalled to Liverpool to attend the sick bed of his father. He took the opportunity to make a sketching trip in the Lake District but the period was overshadowed by his father's death on 8 Dec 1849. He attended the funeral later that month but was back in London for Christmas with his family. It appears that some time later in 1850, George fell out with his mother. The reasons are not known but it is possible that it had something to do with Pearson's will. It must, however, be noted that Hannah had become autocratic in her old age and was given to spectacular tantrums at signs of independence amongst her many children. She was at this time living with her son William whom she had forbidden to marry his long-suffering fiancée, Margaret Houghton. By her death in 1857, George had not been in touch with his mother for some time and there is no evidence that he attended her funeral. George seems to have dropped the "Haydock" from his name because of this row and was hitherto known simply as George Dodgson, both professionally and personally.

Three years after the death of his father, Dodgson advanced to full membership of the Old Watercolour Society on 14 Jun 1852. In the Society, he joined with other members of his circle of friends and fellow artists including Edward Angelo Goodall (1819-1908), George Fripp (1813-1896) and John Joseph Jenkins (1811-1885).

Jenkins, the secretary of the Old Watercolour Society from 1853, was an inveterate collector of letters, notes, anecdotes and related records about the members of the Society. This archive, now owned by the Royal Watercolour Society, contains several references to George Dodgson, not all of them entirely accurate. It eventually formed the basis of John Louis Roget's history of the Royal Watercolour Society published in 1891. It was from this group of friends that George made a number of sketching trips – in 1840 with Jenkins to the Gower Peninsula

In 1853, Jenkins introduced George to the artist Thomas Miles Richardson Junior (1813-1890), a fellow member of the Old Watercolour Society. Richardson had become interested in the newly emergent techniques of photography and on 26 Nov 1853 wrote to Jenkins; *"Should Wednesday morning the 30th be fine, and convenient to Mrs Dodgson to accompany you to my house between the hours of 10 and 1 o'clock I shall have the greatest pleasure in making a collotype of Mrs Dodgson. I expect to have 2 or 3 other sitters on that day".*[6]

The collotype process, invented by William Henry Fox Talbot in about 1840, produced a latent negative image on sensitised paper which could then be used to produce a positive print. Sunlight was an important element of the procedure, hence the need for the day to be fine. Sadly, history does not record whether Jane's image was successfully taken that day. George was interested in the generalities of photography but does not seem to have pursued it himself.

Six months after the studio appointment for photography, George's and Jane's third child, Jessie, was born on 14 Mar 1854. She quickly became her father's favourite, inheriting some of his artistic abilities and becoming his pupil. Jessie, as a young woman of twenty-two, spent time with her father painting the autumnal scenes of Knole Park in Sevenoaks, Kent.

George Dodgson's sketching tours with his artist friends continued in 1858 with Edward Duncan in Hastings and in the same year visited Whitby staying with his old friend George Weatherill. The following year, he was sketching with George Fripp, Francis Topham and Edwin Field near Wargrave on the Thames. He was again in Whitby in 1865, this time with Jenkins, and again in 1867 to see the Weatherills.

In mid 1867, one of George's pictures "The Ferry" was exhibited at the Old Watercolour Society. Amongst the *Art Union of London* prizewinners that year was James Roberts Brown, a goldsmith working in the artist's colony building at Langham Chambers, London. He was a close friend of George Pearson Dodgson, George Haydock Dodgson's son, who encouraged Brown to buy his father's picture with the prize money. Although this did not cover the cost, Brown supplemented it with a cheque of his own, thus providing the ever-depleted Dodgson coffers with about £100. Meanwhile, George Pearson and his sister Jessie seemed to be making their own way as artists with pictures exhibited at the Society of British Artists and the Dudley Gallery

A decade later, the Dodgson family moved to St John's Wood and in 1878, George returned to the Gower Peninsula on what would prove to be his last sketching trip. In May 1880, he was taken ill with a bronchial infection that at first gave no great cause for concern. However, his condition suddenly worsened towards the end of the month and he succumbed on 4 Jun 1880 at his home. He left no will but Letters of Administration were taken out on 24 Jun 1880 with his estate being declared at less than £5000. It is perhaps an echo of the long standing family feud that although the death was registered as "George Haydock Dodgson", his widow, Jane, demanded a formal amendment to read "otherwise George Dodgson".[7] One year later, on 25 Mar 1881, the Old Watercolour Society held a retrospective for him and the auctioneers, Christie, Manson and Woods, sold his remaining pictures. Over 200 were purchased, raising nearly £1,100.

Jane left St John's Wood almost immediately after her husband's death and returned to the Lambeth area of her childhood. Jessie took a job as a china painter, probably at the nearby Doulton factory, thereby supplementing the limited family income. However, by 1885, they were living in straitened circumstances in Streatham and for the first time in Jane's life, there was no domestic servant. The eldest daughter, Jenny, died after several years of sickness in 1899 and Jane herself died in 1908. The loyal Jessie, having cared for the family in later years and having provided the only income for their support, died in sad circumstances in 1911, apparently never returning to her painting. Her brother, George Pearson Dodgson, the last member of the family, died in 1928 having been taken ill at his home in Croydon. He continued to paint and teach up to the end of his life.

The Artistic Legacy of George Haydock Dodgson

Research suggests that George Dodgson produced about 600 works between about 1830 and his death in 1880. These range from extremely detailed architectural drawings in pencil, through miniatures on woodblock for others to

171

engrave, to watercolours of his favourite areas of England and Wales. Interspersing these are some interesting charcoals, many romantic views of Haddon Hall, and some atmospheric depictions of rural and city life. He usually provided a title for pictures when he exhibited them but the name seldom appeared on the picture and many of the titles appearing in auctioneers' catalogues are, for one reason or another, spurious. In very general terms – and there are no hard and fast rules – the watercolours before 1850 are seldom signed and dated. After that, the majority are signed at the lower left often with a two-digit date, the sixes looking like zeros. The signature of G. Dodgson is seen painted but on most examples is written in precise calligraphy in black/brown ink: given the painter's trembling hand apparent in contemporary letters, it is thought that these ink signatures were, in fact, added by Jane, his wife. A very small number of watercolours bear the ink signature and date at lower right.

Roget comments; *"The work of Dodgson, though much varied in scope and sometimes rising to the importance of pictures with human interest and motive, and although always motivated by a spirit that is truly artistic, and always complete in pictorial arrangement, were as yet limited in range, in so far as they never, or rarely, extended to a distant horizon, or embraced a width of landscape such as those of Fielding and Cox, and others of his contemporaries. But Dodgson never crossed the borders of England; and moreover the delicate handling demanded by a far perspective may have been beyond his physical power. His skill in landscape composition and breadth of chiaroscuro are evinced in a number of charcoal studies, one or more of which he sent to the winter exhibitions. His manipulation in watercolour was peculiar, arising probably in some degree from the unsteadiness of his hand. He used powerful colours including vermilion and emerald green, spotting them separately upon the paper, whereon he worked when it was in a very wet state, and in some marvellous way produced a richness of broken tints without losing purity."*[8]

Realistically, George Dodgson cannot be regarded by any measure as a great painter, but his topographical studies for Henry Belcher and his architectural studies for the Stephensons provide a rare and invaluable record of the early days of the railways. The later landscapes seldom fail to please and they take their own place in many museums, art galleries and private collections as examples of a very British tradition.

References

1.George Haydock Dodgson, Indenture 1 July 1826 – family papers
2. J L Roget, *History of the Old Watercolour Society*. Longman, 1891
3. Henry Belcher, *Illustrations of the Scenery on the Line of the Whitby and Pickering Railway in the North Eastern Part of Yorkshire from Drawings by G. Dodgson*. Longman, Rees, Orme, Brown, Green, and Longman, 1836

4. The Will of Pearson Dodgson Senior, draper of Liverpool, dated 2 March 1841 – family papers

5. Letter to Mrs Dodgson, 27 Clarence St, Liverpool, dated 27 Mar 1839 – family papers

6. S Fenwick and G Smith, *The Business of Watercolour – a guide to the archives of the Royal Watercolour Society.* Ashgate, 1997

7. Letters of Administration – George Haydock Dodgson. 24 Jun 1880 – family papers.

8. Roget (1891) op cit.

Brief Biography

George Haydock Dodgson was one of the fifteen children of Pearson Dodgson, referred to in the family as "old" Pearson Dodgson. He was particularly close to two of his brothers – Thomas, who shared his love of art, and Pearson Junior who died young, leaving a widow and family. Thomas took this family into his care and left his collection of George's pictures and memorabilia to the eldest son, James Haydock. In due time this collection passed through the family to James Haydock's son, Fred Pearson and then to Fred Pearson's son James Herbert, the father of the current author.

Hugh Dodgson, after a career in the Crown Service during which he was awarded the OBE, retired to undertake a long-held ambition to research the life and works of his painter-relative, George Haydock Dodgson. It is a work in progress, currently concentrated on compiling a catalogue of the surviving paintings.

George Haydock Dodgson *Regent's Canal Dock and the Limehouse Viaduct c.1840*, exhibited at the Royal Academy in 1840. The viaduct was built by Robert Stephenson and now carries the Dockland Light Railway in East London.

CHAPTER 7

WHITBY AND PICKERING RAILWAY
THE STRANGER'S GUIDE FOR A SUMMER'S DAY
EXCURSION

Henry Belcher wrote this guide seven years after his "Scenery on the Line". It was intended to attract the many visitors of the Spa resort of Scarborough to take a day trip to Whitby by stage-coach or private carriage and then by rail. The rail journey took "an average of about two and a half hours". The fare was three shillings outside and four shillings inside. A private carriage "carried the whole distance" was set at twenty shillings.

(Ed.)

WHITBY & PICKERING RAILWAY.

THE

STRANGER'S GUIDE

FOR A

SUMMER DAY'S EXCURSION

FROM SCARBOROUGH TO PICKERING,

AND THENCE BY

THE RAILWAY TO WHITBY.

BY HENRY BELCHER, ESQ.

WITH A MAP OF THE DISTRICT AND SEVERAL ILLUSTRATIONS.

SCARBOROUGH:

S. W. THEAKSTON, 31, LONG ROOM STREET.

1843.

To

GEORGE STEPHENSON, ESQUIRE,

CIVIL ENGINEER,

IN WARM ADMIRATION OF THE EXTRAORDINARY

TALENT,

AND PERSEVERING AND ENTERPRISING SPIRIT,

WHICH HAVE FOR MANY

YEARS CHARACTERIZED HIS PROFESSIONAL

PURSUITS,

AND SO JUSTLY RENDERED HIM THE ADMIRATION

OF ALL COUNTRIES,

AND

MOST PECULIARLY THE PRIDE AND ORNAMENT

OF HIS OWN,

THE FOLLOWING PAGES ARE RESPECTFULLY

INSCRIBED, BY

THE AUTHOR

STRANGER'S GUIDE.

"Hail modem Science! Who dares now to scan
The endless powers, that thou canst give to man?
Aided by thee, o'er trackless seas he glides
Braves adverse winds, and stems opposing tides.
Earth's depths attains, her hidden wealth explores.
Applies to varied use her boundless stores;
On Iron roads (o'er levell'd hills convey'd,
Through blasted rocks or favour'd mountains made,)
By steam favour'd, pursues his rapid way,
And ends ere noon, what erst employ'd the day,
Air, water, fire, at STEPHENSON'S command,
Such magic powers unfold, beneath his master hand."
H.B.

All persons approaching Scarborough from the south will observe, that towards the north and north west the view is bounded by a range of elevated moorland, as little picturesque in outline, as it is barren and uninviting in its aspect. These bleak and heath-clad heights, however, contain within the numerous and precipitous dales that intersect them, a very great variety of scenery possessing more than ordinary attraction to the lover of the beautiful and romantic, and abounding with remnants of antiquity, not merely of monastic and baronial origin, but also of the more remote periods to which history and tradition extend. The dikes and tumuli, and other marks of the inhabitancy of the Britons, the roads and castramentations of the Romans, the magnificent ruins of Whitby Abbey, and the traces, small though they be, of the priories of Rosedale, Grosmont, Handale, and Baysdale, and the remains of the proudly seated castles of Pickering, Danby, and Mulgrave, all attest the importance of this moorland district in former ages, and add no little to its interest in the present.

These varied subjects of antiquity are not however to be seen, any more than the secluded and picturesque valleys which so peculiarly characterize the district, without being sought for. In fact so little promising are the general features of the country that when viewed from any of the higher points of observation with which it abounds, little more is to be observed than

"A weary waste expanding to the skies."

And the stranger is therefore unprepared for the rural and romantic valleys which in traversing that waste, continually and most unexpectedly break in upon his view.

The sylvan beauties of the vale of Hackness with its numerous ramifications, and which form, as it were, an introduction to the scenery of the more distant parts of that elevated tract of country, of which the heights near Hackness are but the commencement, are well known to the visitors of Scarborough, and never fail to meet with the admiration to which they are so abundantly entitled; but the scenery of the remoter parts of the moorland district is of a much more varied character.

The grand division of these moorlands into north and south is founded by the extensive valley of the river Esk, which rising near the summit of the highest part of the ridge on the south, pursues a rapid and winding course of about thirty miles, through a succession of luxuriant and richly wooded scenery and falls into the German Ocean at Whitby.

This secluded and most interesting and lovely valley is not very readily accessible either from the vales of Rye and Derwent on the south, or the plain of Cleveland on the north, except by surmounting the lofty eminences that enclose it, and travelling by roads of a description to discourage rather than to invite communication with the country to which they lead.

As regards the approach from the south, this difficulty has been removed by the formation, few years since, of a railway, which "passing in a westerly direction from Whitby, up the rich valley of the Esk, for about six miles, then turns to the south, entering through a short tunnel into the previously secluded vale of Goathland leaving which and attaining the summit level at the distance of about twelve miles from Whitby, it runs into Newton Dale and threading the romantic windings of that singularly formed chasm and the rich wood-scenery of Blandsby Park, arrives at the town of Pickering, developing throughout its course a series of highly beautiful and romantic views."

As the scenery through which this railway passes invariably calls forth the admiration of all who visit it, and as by a little contrivance and *previous arrangement* not only may that scenery, but the important and singularly situated town of Whitby, and the ruins of its far-famed Abbey, be visited in the course of a day's excursion from Scarborough, the following pages have been drawn up with a view of giving to strangers such general information as may facilitate their making the attempt. To those who may be desirous of obtaining more particulars as to the Railway and the Scenery, than we here propose entering into, we beg to observe that a book descriptive of the railway and embellished with engravings by artists of celebrity, was published a few years ago, and may be procured through the medium of the publisher of these pages.

In that book the description of the Railway is commenced with the Whitby end; but it is our intention in the present instance as we think that the object of visiting the scenery of the railway by persons from Scarborough, will be best attained by proceeding in the first instance to Pickering, to reverse the order of description.

The distance from Scarborough to Pickering is about eighteen miles, the roads being good, and the country passed through fertile and well wooded, and abounding in villages and gentlemen's seats. On reaching Pickering and driving to the railway station, the remains of the once extensive and stately castle of the Honor of Pickering, and the lower part of the valley up which the railway passes, simultaneously burst upon the view.

The Castle of Pickering, imposing and magnificent even in decay, stands on a bold eminence of limestone, and commands an extensive prospect over the luxuriant vale of Rye. The ruins, cover a considerable space of ground and are of great antiquity, the inner mound being supposed to be of British origin. The Castle was probably erected about the middle of the reign of William the Second, whose father retained Pickering in his hands after the conquest. It remained the property of the crown for many years, and was sometimes the abode, and on one occasion the prison of royalty. Richard the Second was immured here shortly before his removal to Pontefract. After various vicissitudes during the turbulent times of our Henries and our Edwards, the manor, castle, and honor of Pickering became the property of John of Gaunt in right of his wife, from whom they passed into the hands of Henry the Fourth, and by him are supposed to have been annexed to the possessions of the Duchy of Lancaster, to which they now belong.

Though the early history of the town of Pickering has never been satisfactorily ascertained, yet all the information that has been collected on the subject tends to shew that it is of very great antiquity, and was in former ages a place of much consequence.

Leaving the railway station the traveller proceeds for about a mile through a rich and open valley, passing on the left some limekilns and quarries used for the supply of the district connected with the railway in the vale of Esk, where no lime is to be found. The valley then becomes more and more confined till at last a narrow stripe of grass land on either side of the railway, alone separates its course from the steep and richly wooded banks that extend along its course for several miles, presenting at every curve, new combinations of park-like scenery. At about four and a half miles from Pickering a small well wooded valley is seen on the right, in the upper part of which Levisham Church is situated in a sequestered and sheltered spot. The whole valley thus far, and until the approach to Raindale, two miles further, gives the idea of extreme seclusion,

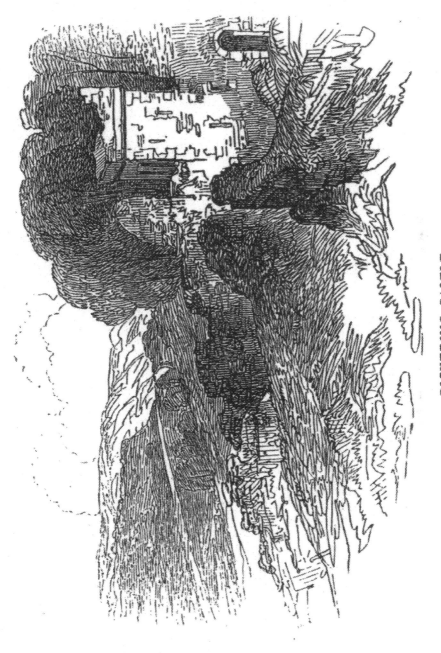

PICKERING CASTLE.

for in the whole distance alluded to, but one house is seen. The extensive plantations on the right, in this part of the vale, belong to Capt. Fothergill, of Kingthorpe, whilst those on the left are the property of the Duchy of Lancaster.

On approaching Raindale several houses are to be seen, the valley becomes less wooded, and the inclosing hills more elevated and abrupt, and symptoms of approaching a wild and rugged district begin to shew themselves. Shortly before arriving at Raindale (where a change of horses takes place,) a small dingle winds up the heights on the left, to the village of Newton, which gives a name to the valley through which the railway is continued for the next four miles. About a mile beyond Newton, to the west, and in a very commanding position, are to be found Cawthorn Camps, the most complete remains of Roman fortifications in the district, or perhaps in any part of England. The camps are four in number; the largest of then contains an area of 560 by 550 feet. The most westerly camp, though the smallest, has been superior to the others in strength and workmanship; it is nearly square and fortified by a double trench. A Roman road from the camp towards the sea at Dunsley near Whitby, is still to be traced in several parts of the country.

From Raindale mill, to the summit level, the speed of travelling is somewhat slower than before on account of the steepness of the gradients, and two horses have generally to be used.* The hills on either side assume bolder forms and a more precipitous character, and the scenery is altogether of a wilder description though not the less pleasing from the contrast. On the left is seen a neat farm house, pleasantly seated in a commanding situation, amongst thriving plantations. This, as well as several others on the hill above, has been built by George Liddell, Esq., of Hull, who has very extensive property and a residence in the neighbourhood.

A sudden turn in the railway brings the traveller into the middle division of Newton Dale,

> "Where hills with naked heads the tempest meet
> Rocks at their sides and torrents at their feet."

and of which the general features are very peculiar, the ground on each side of the railway rising rather abruptly, to a considerable elevation, above which range perpendicular masses of rock, of strikingly bold forms and picturesque appearance. On both sides of this portion of Newton Dale, as also in the parts as do also the stratifications, as to leave no doubt as to their having, in times long

*It is absolutely necessary here to observe that in setting out this railway the Engineer was confined to a certain sum, and thus compelled to contrive a line that could be formed at the least possible expense, without regard to its being the best line that even the impracticable nature of the country would admit of.

gone by, been one solid mass, which being riven asunder by some mighty convulsion of nature, has left the valley as it now appears. On the left hand in particular is a fine semicircular range of rock, called Killingnoble Scar,

"where the Hawk
High in the beetling cliff, his eyrie builds."

This scar has for ages been celebrated for a breed of Hawks which is still to be found there. In a survey of the district on behalf of the crown, in the year 1612, evidence was given "That there hath been Hawkes bred in Newton Dale, in Killingnoble Scar, which the inhabitants were charged to watch to the King's use."

The high mound of earth that fills the space between the railway and the base of this scar, appears to have been formed by an immense mass of the scar having at some remote era, been detached and precipitated into the vale. At the extreme point of the range of the cliff, to the east of Killingnoble Scar, is a perforation in the rock, called the Needle's Eye. Near the foot of the scar is a small pool of water called Newton Dale Well, to which in former times much superstitious .reverence was shewn, the waters being considered as possessed of some healing influence, and on midsummer Sunday a fair was then held here.

Beds of Ironstone of considerable thickness extend for several miles in the upper part of the cliffs, along the windings of this valley; and as some heaps of scoriæ were met with in the cuttings, when the railway was in progress, it is evident that at some remote period, Iron has been smelted here.

Sweeping round the curve below the Needle's Eye, a scene of ruggedness and sterility presents itself and continues till the summit level is gained, where there is a bog of considerable extent, but the further growth of which is probably arrested by the formation of the railway, and the various drains necessary for making the bog passable. As soon as the bog is crossed, the traveller will observe that the mountain stream that now accompanies his course has its current towards the north, and after following its windings for about a mile, the inclosures of Goathland are approached. In the valley to the right, stands a farm-house, called Abbott house, where according to local tradition stood a cell annexed to Whitby Abbey, and of which the records of that institution make mention. In the excavations of this part of the line some fragments of pottery of very ancient and rude construction were found, and at a little distance on the left is a place called the Killing pits supposed by some to have been the site of a British village. A little further to the west stands Hunt House, the shooting box of Richard Hill, Esq., of Thornton, the lessee under the Duchy of Lancaster, of the extensive manor and moors of Goathland. A road that crosses the line just above the inclined plane leads on the right to Goathland Mill in a romantic situation and where there is a waterfall of no mean attraction.

The view from the summit of the inclined plane and in the course of its descent is highly beautiful, but altogether different in its general character from that of the valley towards Pickering. The length of the inclined plane is about 1500 yards. Near the foot of it are to be seen amongst the trees to the right a few cottages of very rural appearance. This place is called Beck-Hole, and the enchanting scenery that surrounds it has been the occasion of its being sought out and visited long before it was so easy of access as is now the case. Two moorland valleys with their tributary streams here meet to form the lower vale of Goathland, and the rapid and powerful current of Goathland beck. The valley from the east is confined and rugged, but highly picturesque; and at the distance of about half a mile from Beck-Hole there is a waterfall called Thomason's Foss, that is much admired. The valley from the west has equal claims upon the admirer of nature in her wilder moods, and there too are to be found some falls of water. That called Malin Spout is in rainy seasons a considerable one, the waters of a tributary brook being precipitated from an elevation of about sixty feet.

The lovers of the picturesque should contrive to spend a little time in this sequestered and beautiful vicinity. In the summer of 1841 were discovered in the course of clearing out an acre of rough ground on the Julian Park farm, about a mile to the west of Beck-hole, and near the course of the Roman road, the foundations of an extensive range of buildings, and amongst the stones turned up were several of an ecclesiastical character; the principal one being a very elegantly formed piscina* in high preservation. As the Lords de Malolacu or Mauley had a mansion at Julian Park in the time of Henry the Third, this probably was its site. There has long been a tradition as to the existence of a religious edifice in the vicinity in former times, and the recent discovery of these relics seems to remove all doubt of such having been the case.

From Beckhole to the Tunnel Inn at Grosmont the inclination of the railway is sufficient to render the application of any tractive power unnecessary unless there be a strong opposing wind. The scenery through the whole of this lower vale of Goathland is of the most romantic character. About midway between the inclined plane and the Tunnel Inn the railway intersects the great Basaltic Dyke which entering the County of York near Yarm traverses the North riding from thence in a south easterly direction and forms a very striking feature

In the geology of the district. The stone is wrought to a considerable extent and shipped for London where it is in good repute for the repair of roads. Passing this dyke the traveller soon reaches the Tunnel, which however is only one

*This piscina and several of the other ornamental stones that were found have been removed to Egton Bridge and placed in the garden attached to the Inn there, that they may be the more readily inspected by the curious.

hundred and forty yards in length, and after emerging from its shade finds himself in the vale of Esk. The rising grounds which enclose the vale of Goathland so completely overlap each other at the northerly end where they descend into the vale of Esk as to shut out from view the communication between the two valleys.

Near the North end of the Tunnel is situated the Tunnel Inn and in its immediate vicinity a number of Cottages, a warehouse, shop, and limekilns, forming the nucleus of the village of Grosmont, so callcd from there having formerly been a priory of that name in this part of the vale of Esk. And as a further indication of an improving village a church capable of accommodating four hundred persons has recently been erected here by means of subscriptions and the produce of a Bazaar. The site (including also what may be requisite for a Parsonage House and School) was given by R. C. Elwes, Esq. the owner of the manor of Egton and of extensive estates in the vicinity. The church was opened in June, 1842, under licence, and is well attended; and it has hitherto, with little exception, been served once and occasionally twice, every Sunday, through the kind and gratuitous assistance of the neighbouring clergy; but it is hoped that the means of endowment may ere long be procured, and the blessing of a regularly appointed minister obtained for an increasing population, in a district far removed from every other church.*

The vicinity of Grosmont abounds with objects of interest. Of the Priory that once adorned this lovely valley no trace remains, the trifling ruins that had survived its destruction and pointed out its site and former extent, having been altogether removed a few years ago, and a farm-house and Offices built upon the place, with the materials, amongst which a few stones bearing marks of having belonged to a religious edifice of the olden time may be observed. The picturesque beauties, however, of this beautiful spot, still continue.

Between the north side of Grosmont Church and the river are to be seen a number of circular stone-pits supposed to have belonged to an Alum Work carried on here, at a remote period. Some heaps of scoriæ in this vicinity also show that Iron has been smelted here; but tradition is silent as to the time when either iron or alum works were in existence. The stream that flows from the vale of Goathland falls into the Esk just above Grosmont Bridge, where the scenery is particularly beautiful, the bridge itself forming a most interesting feature in the view. Crossing that bridge and turning to the left a winding road along the

*Exertions are being made to raise an endowment fund, and contributions towards this object are respectfully solicited, and will be received by the Publisher, or by Henry Belcher, Esq., of Whitby. Should these pages catch the eye of any person desirous of endowing this church and securing the presentation, it is probable that such arrangements might be accomplished.

River's banks leads to the hamlet of Egton Bridge, most delightfully situated, and near which is some of the finest scenery in the vale of Esk.

Resuming the course of the railway at the Tunnel Inn, the traveller soon finds himself in the heart of the vale of Esk, down which he is rapidly conveyed towards Whitby, crossing the river Esk, no less than eight times by means of wooden bridges, which though substantially built have a light and elegant appearance, and harmonize well with the surrounding scenery. The situation of the bridges is in every instance picturesque, and one of them of which the annexed is a representation is formed of a single bearing from bank to bank, and though of considerable span is found more firm than the bridges which have supporters.

The fine hanging woods which adorn the north side of this part of the valley, belong to Henry W. Yeoman, Esq., whose ancient mansion of Newbegin Hall is to be seen amongst the trees on the left. A little further there are to be seen, in a field adjoining the railway on the right, the ruins of a small chapel of considerable antiquity, being noticed in some of the records of Whitby Abbey, in the year 1224, as having been erected on the site of an hermitage that had then fallen into decay. Sleights Moor rising rather abruptly from the vale, on the south to a considerable elevation is an imposing feature in the scenery of this part of the vale. Near the apparent summit of this hill are some traces of a British encampment.

The village of Sleights is now to be seen crowning the hill in the middle distance in front, at the foot of which, surrounded by some noble trees, stands Esk Hall, the mansion of Samuel Campion, Esq. On the opposite side of the valley, Woodlands, the seat of H. W. Yeoman, Esq., peeps forth from the luxuriant plantations that surround it. And on the hill above is seen the village of Aislaby, with the mansions of James Wilkinson, Esq. and Mrs. Watkins, forming conspicuous objects in the view.

The railway now passes through a cutting in the lias rock, close to the river, and soon reaches the Sleights station, where the turnpike road from Whitby to York is crossed. The scenery though still beautiful, is less bold and interesting for the next two miles, but after passing the village of Ruswarp the approximation of the sea and a sea port becomes apparent and produces a complete change in the general features of the landscape. The beauty of the approach to Whitby is much enhanced if the tide happens to be near its height at the time. The graceful bends in the river, when bank full, and the richly wooded declivities which enclose them, produce a most imposing effect, and give the river a lake-like character, thus imparting to the portion of the line an interest of a most pleasing description.

BRIDGE IN ESKDALE.

A bold curve in the line introduces the traveller to the town and harbour of Whitby, with the Abbey rising above them, and filling up the distance. The broad expanse of the harbour with its boats and shipping in motion or at rest, the singular position of the town along its shores and creeping up the steeps that surround it and above all the ruins of Whitby's cloistered pile, luxuriant in decay, give to the terminus of the railway a charm that under favourable circumstances as to light and shade, can only be appreciated by being seen. But amidst the many objects that present themselves to eye, the Abbey still becomes the resting place of sight.

> Yon towering cliff, where proudly stand
> A ruin'd Abbey's sculptured walls,
> Points out to view, from sea to land,
> The site of Streonshalh's halls.

> The scenes where sainted Hilda prayed,
> Where Cædmon penn'd his heav'nly lays;
> Where holy men their zeal display'd
> And sang their choral hymns of praise.

The antiquity and importance of this once noble edifice, (alas now fast crumbling to decay,) has for ages conferred on the district a degree of celebrity that has alike attracted the notice of the historian, the poet, and the antiquary. Of its earliest history, however, but little is known, except that it was founded in the year 658, by the celebrated Abbess Hilda, and destroyed by the Danes about 200 years afterwards. Soon after the conquest it was rebuilt, and being richly endowed by the noble families of Percy and De Bruce as well as by several distinguished individuals, it flourished till the reign of Henry the Eighth, when it shared the common fate of all similar institutions.

Though built in portions at different periods, the Abbey when complete was in the form of a cross, and consisted of a nave, choir, and side aisles, and transepts with side aisles on the east side only.

In the centre stood a noble tower, 104 feet high, which on the 21st June, 1830, suddenly gave way, and now lies a shapeless mass of ruins on the very spot once sheltered by its hallowed roof. Notwithstanding the loss of the tower enough remains of this richly sculptured pile to make it deserving of the attention of the artist, the antiquary, and the man of taste and feeling. And the more minutely the ruins are examined the more beautiful and curious do they appear—and varying in general effect with every change of atmosphere, they form a never failing subject of interest and contemplation.

WEST END OF WHITBY ABBEY.

Returning from the Abbey the stranger should linger awhile in the Church yard, from whence there are some delightful views both towards the land and to the sea, and which in a communication to the Gentleman's Magazine in 1828, were thus most truly and comprehensively described; — "From the acclivity extensive prospects present themselves on every side—the tenantless monastic ruins, the wide ocean ever washing the sandy beach, with ships scudding along its bosom in the distance—the woods and castle of Mulgrave, the piers, the concave town, harbour, shipping, and curious draw-bridge, [now removed] across the river, all immediately beneath the eye—the winding and fertile valley of the Esk, through which rolls in many a serpentine curve the stream of that name, the numerous swelling hills intersecting one another, and studded with villas, hamlets, groves and homesteads, the high and lonely moors beyond, covered with dark purple heath, and which seem to frown upon the humble but smiling dales below, the tout ensemble affording panoramic views of mingled beauty and sublimity of which few have hitherto been pictured by the artist, and words must fail to convey an adequate representation."

The outer piers of Whitby Harbour have long been the objects of commendation for the boldness of their situation, and the excellence of their workmanship. The west pier in particular, and to which the approach has very lately been altered and improved, is greatly to be admired. It forms a most favourite promenade with the inhabitants and strangers. The views along the coast are seen from them to much advantage, and there is no other point from whence the town and harbour display with better effect their peculiar characteristics.

There is a Museum at Whitby, rich in specimens of the geological treasures of a district justly celebrated for the extent and variety of its fossil productions.

Though the scenery along the line of railway has in the preceding pages been principally adverted to, yet if the stranger at Whitby have time to remain there a few days he will find in the vicinity, a variety of romantic scenery, both inland and on the coast, deserving his regard. Saltwick, Robin Hood's and Runswick Bays, the creek and town of Staithes, the towering cliffs at Kettleness and Boulby, varying from 300 to 600 feet in perpendicular height, the latter presenting a complete section of the lias beds, and some of their superincumbent strata, altogether combine to render this part of the Yorkshire coast one of the most interesting portions of our sea-girt isle; whilst on the other hand the numerous valleys with their picturesque combinations of wood, rock, water, and frequent silvery and sparkling waterfalls, the magnificent rock and wood scenery of Mulgrave Park and Arncliffe, with the ruins of the ancient castle in the former, and the supposed remains of a British village overlooking the latter, with many other objects of attraction, seem to be equally as deserving of the notice of the stranger, who will not we think consider as misspent the time that may be devoted to their exploration.

The average time of making the journey by railway between Whitby and Pickering is about two hours and a half; supposing therefore a party to reach Pickering from Scarbro', by half-past 9 or 10 o'clock, they would arrive at Whitby so as to have several hours to spare for looking about them there, and be enabled to reach Pickering again sufficiently early in the evening to return to Scarboro'. Should however the direct road to Scarborough over the moors, a distance of 21 miles, be preferred, post horses may be had at Whitby, and the daily Coach also leaves Whitby for Scarboro' between five and six in the afternoon. Private carriages and horses may be conveyed on the Railway, but to present disappointment especially at the Pickering terminus it is desirable to give a day's notice of the carriage and horse trucks being required. With respect to the regular modes of conveyance on the Railway, on every day excepting Sunday the following are the arrangements at the present time.

The FARES by the Daily Coach between Whitby and Pickering are 4s. Inside, and 3s. Outside. Short Fares in the same proportion.

A special Coach may be had by any Party or single person, (by giving half-an-hour's previous notice at the Railway Office,) to any station on the Line, when 10 seats are engaged, at the rate of one penny per mile for each passenger: all over and above that number paying after the same rate.

The charge for conveying a four-wheeled carriage the whole distance, will be 20s.; and for every person conveyed in such carriage, 2s.

The Daily Coach will continue to leave Whitby at half-past 8, A. M., and Pickering, at 3, P. M.

THEAKSTON, PRINTER, SCARBOROUGH.

CHAPTER 8

EARLY VICTORIAN RAILWAY ARTISTS and ENGRAVERS

VER THE YEARS, WRITERS HAVE paid a great deal of attention to the topic of railways and a vast literature has built up. Yet, few authors have investigated the world of the artists who gave us views of the railways as their engineers and passengers first saw them. This was a world without photography. It was also a world with a fast growing number of people who wanted to see more of what was happening around them at a time of rapid change.

Personal wealth was increasing, and education was becoming more widespread. An appetite for self-help and self-improvement mushroomed across the social divides. In the first decade of railway development between 1829 and 1839, publishers launched over twenty illustrated railway books and guides. Between 1840 and 1860, artists and engravers were engaged in illustrating many of the newspapers, magazines, and books reporting railways that appeared at this time.

Making Railway Pictures

Before photography revolutionised printing during the latter half of the nineteenth century, there were three main ways for artists to make multiple copies of their work. All of these methods involved using a flat bed, block, or plate on which a drawing is made in reverse. Ink is then applied, paper placed on the inked surface, and the whole set in a hand operated press.

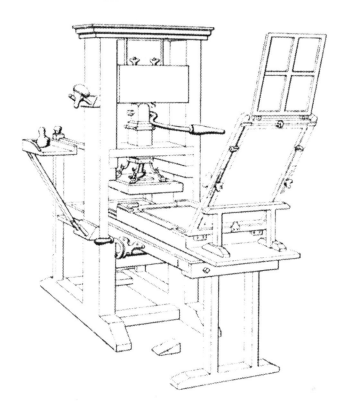

In this way, an artist could reach a wider audience than the connoisseur or patron in order to meet a growing demand for visual records of real or imagined places or events.

Prints were very considerably cheaper than an original work of art. They could be produced after the artist's death or for as long as the plates lasted. They could be conveniently sold in books or folios and did not depend upon access to galleries or the salons of the privileged few. They could be bought at stationers, circulating libraries and newsrooms, and from print sellers in shops or from barrows on the street.

Artists could supplement their income from publishers, and their customers could satisfy a growing appetite for cultural pursuits. Just as they do today, certain works of art gained celebrity status and their popularity increased through easy access to copies at a fraction of their original cost. A whole class of skilled craftsmen emerged to support a burgeoning industry.

The usual means of making prints were from steel, zinc or copper plates, wood blocks, or Bavarian or Indian limestone tablets. Artists used a variety of

191

techniques to process these basic materials to produce different qualities in their pictures. A variety of terms came into use to identify the type of print and the technique that produced it, e.g. "woodcut" – from soft wood such as cherry, sycamore or beech, cut so as to leave areas and lines in relief to take up the ink. Woodcuts had the advantage of being placed alongside lettering and printed at the same time. Examples by G H Dodgson can be found set within Belcher's text in chapter five. The chief disadvantage was the relative lack of detail and limitations on size.

"Engraving" overcame the problem of detail by carving into the end grain of harder woods such as boxwood or by cutting the surface of steel or copper plates. Examples can be found throughout the various chapters of this book and in Dodgson's individual plates in chapter five.

Engraving techniques were widely used in illustrating newspapers and magazines, most notably *Punch*. First published in 1841, it featured radical political commentary and satirical cartoons. George Hudson was a favourite target for its lampooning activities and a famous cartoon from 1849 showed him on a derailed truck hurtling down a line with the caption "Off the Rail".

In 1842, the first edition of the weekly *Illustrated London News* provided a more popular approach to presenting news, including news about the phenomenal rise of railways. This was especially significant for foreign news, by making reports more immediately accessible through their visual appeal. And to meet the demand for self-improvement, the "Society for the Diffusion of Useful Knowledge", under the pioneering editorship of Charles Knight (1781-1873), published the richly illustrated; *The Land We Live In: A Pictorial, Historical and Literary Sketch Book.* By mid-century, the popular taste for illustrated books on railways was well represented by Frederick Williams' *Our Iron Roads* (1852) from which several of the illustrations in this book are taken.

Perhaps the model embodiment of links between journalism, illustrated books, writers, railways, artists, engravers, and self-help, is Samuel Smiles (1812-1904). He was the campaigning editor for social reform at the *Leeds Times* in 1838 and seven years later became secretary for the Leeds and Thirsk Railway. Between 1854 and 1866, he served as secretary for the South Eastern Railway. These were years in which he wrote some of his most significant works including *The Life of George Stephenson* (1857) and the fully illustrated *Story of George Stephenson* (1859) as a "manual for the young".

These and other illustrated publications chiefly relied on woodcuts and engravings. An alternative method, frequently used for single prints or higher quality work, involved the technique of "etching". Here, instead of leaving lines and forms in relief, the design is drawn through blackened wax and placed in a bath of acid. The acid bites into the exposed metal leaving the remainder protected by wax. This technique creates hollowed-out, "intaglio" lines, which hold the ink during printing.

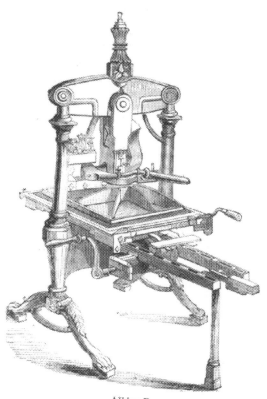

Albion Press.

Some of the earliest railway prints used etched plates to produce copies of monochrome drawings, or more usually copies of watercolours. The development of "aquatints" aimed to represent the wash effects of watercolours by covering the plate with a granular ground of porous resin. The acid bit into the metal in a web of tiny dots and with repeated immersions and the use of varnish, graded tones could be produced. The prints were later hand coloured or sold in black and white form, as required. By etching first without the powdered resin base, lines could be included in the design. Reproducing brush strokes was achieved by using a sugar solution. The image would then be covered with varnish and immersed in water. This process dissolved the sugar to leave areas of exposed metal. An aquatint ground could then be applied in the usual way to provide a richly varied effect.

The resulting prints, in the hands of gifted craftsmen under the direction of the artist or by artists themselves, were exquisitely evocative of the scenes they portrayed. Whilst lacking the uniqueness of originals, they were, and still remain, works of art in their own right.

Ackermann's Repository of Arts

Thomas Talbot Bury (1811-1877) was one of the first of these highly accomplished artists to depict railways. He was articled at the age of thirteen to Charles Pugin, a noted architectural draughtsman and father of Augustus W. N. Pugin (1812-1852), better known as the designer of the architectural details of the Houses of Parliament. At the age of fifteen, Pugin Junior designed furniture for the refurbishment of Windsor Castle. The two boys were about the same age when they became assistants in the practice of Pugin Senior. Their ways parted in 1831 when, at the age of twenty, Bury produced *"Six Coloured Views of the Liverpool and Manchester Railway* whilst his co-worker of later fame was briefly imprisoned for debt.

Ackermann's, the leading print sellers and publishers in London at the turn of the nineteenth century, first published Bury's views as a set of hand coloured aquatints in paper covers. Over the following years, in common with later railway printmakers, they were sold singly or issued in numerous editions with sales extending to France, Germany, and Spain.

Rudolf Ackermann (1764-1834) came to London from Paris around 1793 and over the next thirty years established a uniquely distinctive business that included running a drawing school, designing carriages, manufacturing watercolour paints, selling paintings, producing paper, and publishing high quality decorative prints and illustrated books. He created a centre for the interchange of ideas and influence amongst a wide variety of clients, artists, writers, and merchants, supplying their needs with sixty-nine shades of watercolour pigment. His trade in watercolour paints extended throughout Britain.

The prevailing taste for historical painting and portraits began to change in favour of topography and landscape. Aquatints were well suited to these subjects and the growing fashion for watercolours fuelled their rise to prominence. This new market created an opportunity for building a business in picture dealing that, up until then, had largely been confined to the continent.

Ackermann's prints, produced in steadily increasing numbers, were hand coloured by both adults and children living in the blocks and tenements surrounding his "Repository of Arts" in the Strand. In the short space of eight years between 1818 and 1816, it is estimated that he printed and distributed 372,000 aquatints.

His premises were a short distance from the Royal Academy, then situated in Somerset House. He opened a "Gallery of Ancient and Modern Paintings and Drawings" and charged a shilling for entry. In addition, he introduced a circulating library for prints and drawings, an idea copied in other parts of England, including Scarborough. At one time, his drawing school had eighty pupils and he employed fifteen people. His business continued to flourish until the outbreak of the Napoleonic Wars.

However, the years that followed saw a gradual return to normal business. An emerging fascination with the newly formed landscape of railways acquired both grandeur and credentials through association with Ackermann's reputation and the artists he commissioned to illustrate his publications or for whom he acted as dealer.

His ability to identify innovation and talent amongst young artists in particular, put him in the vanguard of fashion. As a result, he promoted and sold works by painters who were destined to enter the foremost rank of watercolour artists. These artists rescued this medium from "lowly tinted drawings" to build the renowned tradition of British watercolour painting. Their names are a roll call of the finest; J M W Turner, Thomas Girtin, Peter De Wint, John Varley, Samuel Prout, David Cox, John Martin, and Francis Nicholson. Three of these artists went on to create some of the most iconic of all railway images, of which more later.

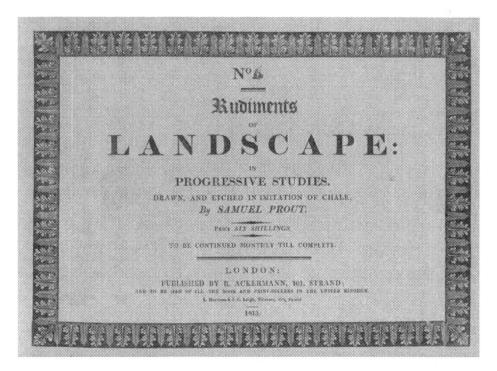

By way of contrast, a reminder of the wider social environment may be gathered from the prosecution at the Central Criminal Court in 1836 of a twenty-eight year old colour-grinder and employee of Ackermann's. He was accused of stealing a watercolour box worth thirty-five shillings and two framed works valued at five pounds. The jury recommended mercy which translated into being transported for seven years.

Some Early Railway Artists

Thomas Talbot Bury's views of the Liverpool and Manchester Railway appeared as aquatints. Several of his fellow artists adopted the more versatile medium of "lithography" - literally meaning 'writing on stone'. Ackermann had begun experimenting with this new process some time after 1817 and progressively adopted this method for many of his later publications.

The basic process uses a flat block of fine-grained limestone onto which the image is drawn or transferred. A greasy ink is applied by a crayon or brush to create an image. When water is washed over the stone and printing ink rolled across it, the water repels the ink which only adheres to the greasy surface of the image. Paper is placed on the inked stone and both are rolled through a press.

Three other artists published books of railway scenes in the same year as T T Bury's views; a series of etchings by Isaac Shaw, *Views of the Most Interesting Scenery on the Line of the Liverpool and Manchester Railway*, and lithographs by A B Clayton , *Views on the Liverpool and Manchester Railway*, and Henry Booth, *An Account of the Liverpool and Manchester Railway*, all published in 1831.

In the following years, illustrated books or locally published prints would usually accompany the opening of a line. Bury, for example, went on to record *The London and Birmingham Railroad* in 1837. It is estimated that between 1830 and 1850, approximately two thousand different railway prints were published and around two hundred appeared in book form.

Outstanding work during this period included A F Tait whose splendid lithographs of *Views of the Manchester and Leeds Railway* (1845) and of the *London and North Western Railway* (1848) were both drawn and lithographed by the artist himself.

Several other noted artists' works were enhanced by their association with specialist lithographers including Louis Haghe, (1806-1885) one of the finest lithographers of his generation. Haghe, working in partnership with William Day, produced superlative lithographs on a wide variety of mainly topographical subjects and created an appreciative following. This was partly due to his pioneering work on "tint stone" prints which enhanced multi-coloured images, and to his skill as a watercolour painter in his own right; a path he chose to follow in his later years.

Day and Haghe's reputation for high quality printing and publishing attracted some of the best authors and artists including David Roberts (1796-1864) whose views of the "Holy Land" were amongst the first directly observed images by a Western artist to become widely available. Haghe's work from Roberts' watercolours extended over a period of eight years. Soon after Roberts had concluded his eleven months sketching tour in 1839, Louis Haghe, working with W. W. Young, published *Illustrations of the Great Western and Bristol and Exeter Railways* in 1840.

Other artists such as John Wilson Carmichael (1799 -1868) benefited from their association with architects, as did both Thomas Talbot Bury and George Haydock Dodgson. Born in Newcastle, Carmichael found employment, whilst living there, from John Dobson (1787-1865), architect of many of the finest buildings in Newcastle and the North East.

Dobson and Carmichael collaborated on creating architectural perspectives of projected works, a growing trend that enlivened the more formal presentations of plans and elevations. The genius of Dobson and Carmichael working together resulted in some of the most alluring of topographical watercolours, especially of the interior of Newcastle Central Station, commissioned by George Hudson c.1845. Dobson's association with Hudson about this time also included the preparation of plans for the West Cliff Building Company at Whitby.

John Dobson advocated a special role for railway stations;

"Being quite a new class of structures erected for purposes unknown until the present age, they ought to suggest a character of their own, and fresh combinations in design…..They are, moreover, especially public works – structures constantly seen by thousands and tens of thousands of persons; and might, therefore, do much towards improving the taste of the public."

John Dobson, Presidential Address to the Northern Architectural Association. April 1859 in T Faulkner and A Gregg *John Dobson: Architect of the North East.* 2001.

Earlier in his career, Dobson submitted proposals for a railway station at Carlisle and other designs for the Newcastle and Carlisle Railway. Newcastle publishers, Currie and Bowman, commissioned Carmichael, at the suggestion of the directors of the company, to provide a commemorative volume of scenes along the line. Twenty-three engravings from drawings by Carmichael were published in book form in 1836, priced at one guinea.

The views Carmichael created are richly evocative scenes, full of atmosphere, social commentary, and vitality. Unlike many other railway prints of this period, with the exception of cartoons and caricatures, the social viewpoint was typically taken from the celebratory outlook of the promoters and investors. Given the strength of opposition to railways from some sections of early Victorian society, railway prints were to a certain extent propaganda pieces. The incidence of top hats, bonnets, shawls, corseted frocks, and crinolines is a striking feature of the passengers and onlookers depicted in several examples. By contrast, the social mix in Carmichael's case is refreshingly direct by showing third class passengers crowded on the roofs of the first class carriages.

Arguably, however, the flowering of railway printmaking is to be found in the virtuoso illustrations of John Cooke Bourne (1814-1896). His *Drawings of the London and Birmingham Railway* (1839) and *The History and Description of the Great Western Railway* (1845) are not only technically brilliant but also carry a particular authority in their portrayals of railways at work, breaking through the proscenium arch and tableau qualities of other lesser railway artists.

A reviewer for the Fine Arts in the *Gentleman's Magazine* for 1838 had this to say about Bourne's first publication;

"This work is sufficient evidence that, without leaving England, - confining ourselves, moreover, to the unpromising subject of a railway, with all its mechanical and commercial associations, ample scope is afforded to the artist for making effective and interesting pictures of scenery, buildings, and figures. A more singular combination of the pictorial and the scientific than is shown in some of the drawings before us, cannot easily be imagined"

John Bourne was twenty-two when Robert Stephenson commenced construction of the London to Birmingham line. The reviewer had only seen the first eight lithographs of a four-part series. Rudolf Ackermann was the publisher, Bourne lithographed the stones himself, and Day and Haghe printed them. In 1839, the complete series was published in one volume. This work stands as one of the very best examples of the harmony that can be achieved between the arts of printing, publishing and the world of the artist.

Henry Belcher must have agreed with this judgement, for he commissioned John Cooke Bourne to provide; *A View of Grosmont Church, School, and Whitby Railway Bridge from the Lime Kilns.* Bourne's lithograph was published 'in Aid of the Fund for Endowing Grosmont Church'. It depicts one of the first locomotives to cross the newly built stone bridge soon after Hudson had opened the extended line for steam working. The choice of publication date was an appropriately calculated one: New Year's Day, 1848.

Thomas Roscoe and George Haydock Dodgson

Soon after George Dodgson's illustrations of the Whitby and Pickering railway appeared in 1836, he was commissioned to contribute to Thomas Roscoe's two railway books; *The London and Birmingham Railway with the Home and Country Scenes on each side of the Line,* (1839) and *The Book of the Grand Junction Railway* (1839).

George Dodgson's illustrations helped to build his artistic reputation as the following steel engraved plates from "The London and Birmingham Railway" demonstrate. In all cases except one (Euston Square Entrance), the plates are signed with the name of the engraver with whom he worked.

George Dodgson's *Entrance to the London and Birmingham Railway, Birmingham.
To C R Moorsom, Esq. Capt. R.N. this plate is inscribed.* **The dedication refers to the
son of Captain Robert Moorsom (1760-1835) - afterwards Admiral Sir Robert
Moorsom KCB - who was born in Whitby. He captained** *HMS Revenge* **and
brought home the news of Nelson's victory at Trafalgar in 1805. Captain
C.R.Moorsom (1792-1861) was a director of the Company who presented his
father's pistols, used at the Battle of Trafalgar, to Whitby Museum in 1841.**

The author of *"The London and Birmingham Railway"*, Thomas Roscoe
(1791-1871), was a writer and translator on art and history who turned his
attention to travel writing during the 1830's. He begins his London and
Birmingham railway book with these words:

"When new and interesting facts regarding the progress of *steam-science* -
for it has now assumed a nomenclature of its own – continue to excite popular
wonder and admiration, - when a voyage across the Atlantic is thought little
more important than a trip in one of our pleasure yachts, it would be strange,
indeed, were the completion of the most extensive and magnificent Railroad in
Great Britain to produce no feelings of national exultation, or be allowed to go
unduly celebrated."

He continues,

"The effect can only be adequately realized by *ocular* observation; and its vast capabilities seem, as it were, to be revealed to the eye, as its grand successive trains – filled with a world of business and pleasure – come sweeping majestically by........Another attribute, no less attractive, of this wonderful power is that, hand in hand with profit and instruction, the most distant scenes are brought within our view. The beautiful, the picturesque, and the sublime, - afar in the deep recesses of the lake and mountain splendours of our islands, or of foreign lands, - will no longer be described as a marvel and a dream; they will become obvious to all - the inheritance of the most plodding and industrious, as of those who lord it over the soil."

G H Dodgson, ***Entrance to The London and Birmingham Railway Station, Euston Square London, To R Creed Esq this Plate is inscribed.*** **Richard Creed was the Secretary of the Company.**

G H Dodgson, *The Wolverton Viaduct near Stony Stratford* Engraved, D Wilson.

G H Dodgson, *The Hill Above Box Hill Moor Towards Berkhamstead* is an example of a plate also sold separately. In an edition of Roscoe's book, it is entitled "View on the London and Birmingham Railway, Looking from the Hill above Box Moor Station towards Berkhamstead, *To George Carr Glyn this plate is inscribed*". G C Glyn (1797-1873) known as the "railway banker" provided finance for over one hundred railway companies. He became chairman of the London and Birmingham Railway in 1837, shortly before this plate was engraved by W Radclyffe.

G H Dodgson, *Berkhamstead Station*. Engraved by W Radclyffe.

G H Dodgson, *Viaduct Over The River Colne Near Watford*. Engraved, W Radclyffe.

202

Roscoe's publisher and Dodgson's patron, was Charles Tilt (1797-1861). After early experience in the book trades, Tilt set up his own print selling and publishing business from premises in Fleet Street, London in 1826. Over the next fourteen years, he commissioned some of the leading young artists and engravers to illustrate his publications including, Turner, Cox, Bentley, Duncan, and Cruikshank.

His business was highly successful and Tilt soon accumulated considerable wealth. His junior employee, David Bogue (1807-1856) gradually took over the business from around 1843, continuing the tradition of illustrated railway guides by publishing John Cooke Bourne's "Great Western Railway" in 1845.

George Dodgson, in common with many other artists, found that building a career and artistic reputation was a long and arduous process. Apart from skill and talent, success depended on place, patronage, and enterprise. In addition to attracting the admiration of fellow artists and collectors, he also had to overcome some common prejudices.

One such prejudice appears in the memoirs of the Dalziel Brothers. This firm, from whom Dodgson gained many commissions, was at the forefront of wood engraving in Victorian England. The brothers recall that Dodgson had formed a sketching club with several fellow members of the Old Watercolour Society. Whilst sketching in a field on the banks of the Upper Thames, a farmer accosted them:

"What be you lot o' lazy devils a-doing in my field?
- Sketching, sir, sketching!
Is that fit work for men? When the young ladies from Miss Gray's boarding school come down to 'sketch' I say let 'em; if that pleases them, it don't hurt me, an there be no harm; but when I see a lot of great hulking men like you fellows about such nonsense it makes me fair angry! Why, damn it, you might be doing a lot o' good work o' some sort! I would rather break stones by the roadside for a shilling a day than fool away my time like you be doing. You ought to be ashamed o' yourselves, you ought."

The confrontation continued as the party explained they made their living by painting pictures. Dodgson was asked what he would get for the one he was doing;

"Perhaps as much as ten shillings or maybe twenty if I can find a friend who fancies it
- Thee be a damned liar as well as a lazy lout!
Then with a look of contempt, the tiller of the soil stumped away"

From: *The Brothers Dalziel; A Record 1840-1890* first published 1901. (The resulting watercolour is now in a private collection,)

Denbigh Hall Bridge

The Cavalry shown is a detachment of the Buckingham Yeomanry Cavalry that evolved to become The Royal Buckinghamshire Hussars. Formed in 1794 at the time of the Revolutionary and Napoleonic Wars, its Colonel was Richard Plantagenet, 2nd Duke of Buckingham and Chandos (1797-1861) who provided the highly ornate uniforms. The design originated from the elaborate uniforms of the Hungarian Cavalry of the 15th century. We might suppose that the white horse led by a figure in undress uniform would be the personal mount of the Duke. The symbolism of the riderless horse might also refer to the death of the 1st Duke who died in the year this drawing was made. The 2nd Duke of Buckingham and Chandos was the owner of the nearby Stowe House Estate, one of the most important historic buildings in Britain. In 1845, he hosted a three-day visit of Queen Victoria and Prince Albert who conferred the title of Royal Buckinghamshire Regiment of Yeomanry Cavalry. George Haydock Dodgson sketched in the famous Stowe Gardens with several engraver friends in 1838.

George Dodgson's contacts with the world of engraving began early in his career and very probably provided him with the necessary introductions to break into the London art scene. He worked with seven noteworthy engravers who made the plates from his drawings to illustrate Belcher's book.

They were all young men, roughly of the same age, several of whom, like Dodgson, also became watercolourists. For example, Robert Brandard (1805-62) engraved plates for many leading artists including J M W Turner, (e.g. *Rain, Steam and Speed* in 1859-1861), Clarkson Stanfield, David Roberts, and John Martin and exhibited at the Royal Academy from 1831 to 1858. Charles Cousen (1813?-1889), best known for his work for the *Art Journal,* also occasionally exhibited paintings at the Society for British Artists. Ebeneezer Challis (fl. 1831-63) illustrated many books and engraved paintings after Thomas Allom, James Duffield Harding, and David Roberts amongst others. Challis engraved plates for Dodgson again in 1840 and in his later years, turned exclusively to painting and exhibiting at the Royal Academy and Suffolk Street Galleries.

Finally, J T Willmore (1800-63) engraved plates for four of Dodgson's illustrations to the "Scenery of the Line" - "Entrance to the Vale of Goathland", "Thomason Foss", Entrance to Newton Date, North End", and "Newton Dale Scarrs". He also engraved the illustrations for several of Roscoe's travel books, over thirty plates after Turner, and many other early Victorian artists. Willmore was elected to the Royal Academy as Associate Engraver in 1843.

Dodgson's association with William Radclyffe (1783-1855) was another source of encouragement and support. They worked together on Roscoe's railway books when Radclyffe established an engraving business in Birmingham where Tilt and Roscoe's "London and Birmingham was printed. Another artist encouraged by Radclyffe was David Cox (1783 -1859), originally from Birmingham, who later rose to become one of the foremost watercolour painters of his age. Radclyffe's skills as a landscape engraver were highly regarded and at one time, J T Willmore was one of his pupils.

William Radclyffe was much appreciated for the leadership he gave to the city's engravers and for the role he played in the formation of what is now the

Royal Society of Birmingham Artists. Dodgson was fortunate in meeting so skilled and generous a mentor in making the move from being a surveyor to becoming an artist.

The Avon Viaduct, engraved by William Radclyffe (1783-1855) from a drawing by his youngest son, Charles Walter Radclyffe (1817-1903) afterwards a landscape painter exhibiting at the Royal Academy between 1849 and 1881.

Artists and Draughtsmen

Recalling the career of George Dodgson may serve to remind us that his role as a young man was to apply his graphic skills to surveying. His move into artistry was in fact rooted in technical drawing and the world of the draughtsmen of his day. The engravers with whom he worked were largely draughtsmen. Many of the best were artists too. There is an interesting territory to be explored between fine drawing and fine art. Dobson's collaboration with Carmichael was of this sort, probing the boundaries between architectural drawing and works of art.

Not all railway images, of course, were directed towards collectors and connoisseurs. This is not to say that railway images for engineers and surveyors would lack skill or discriminating judgement. Quite the reverse, as these images demonstrate;

206

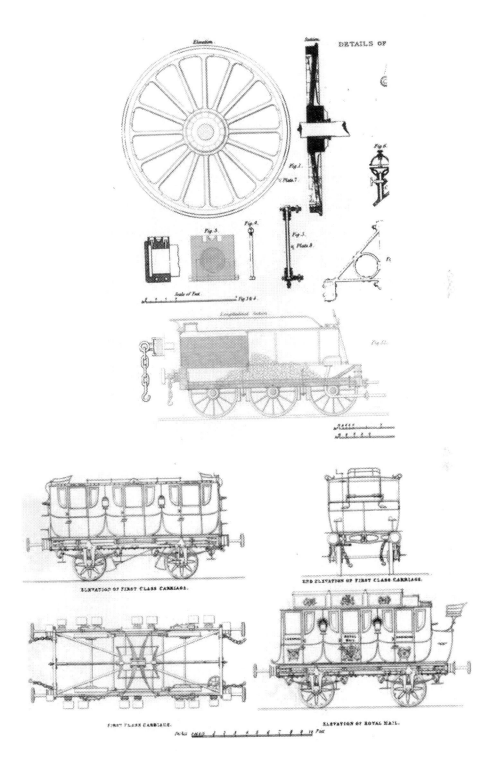

DETAILS OF

Elevation.
Section.

Fig. 1.
Plate 7.

Fig. 6.

Fig. 3.
Fig. 4.

Fig. 5.
Plate 8.

Scale of Feet
Fig. 3 & 4.

Longitudinal Section.
Fig. 2.

ELEVATION OF FIRST CLASS CARRIAGE.

END ELEVATION OF FIRST CLASS CARRIAGE.

FIRST CLASS CARRIAGE.

ELEVATION OF ROYAL MAIL.

Scale
Feet

207

FIRST CLASS CARRIAGE

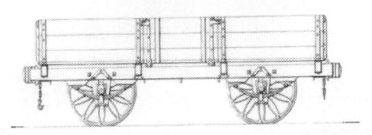

TRUCK

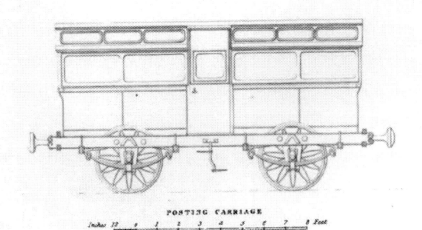

POSTING CARRIAGE

Inches 12   0   1   2   3   4   5   6   7   8 Feet

Fred Humble. del.

Railway Cartoons and Caricatures

An appetite for parody and visual puns paralleled the growing interest in railways amongst publishers, artists, and engravers. With the launch of the satirical magazine *Punch* in 1842, a long tradition of British caricature from Hogarth (1697-1764), Gillray (1757-1815), Rowlandson (1756-1827) –whose publisher was Rudolf Ackermann – and George Cruikshank (1792-1878), extended to reach a wider audience, assisted by a new crop of humorists to provide wit and entertainment.

Such illustrations were invariably wood engravings, and they ranged over a wide variety of subjects and styles. Three examples may serve to indicate this range.

A vignette from the opening chapter of Roscoe's "London and Birmingham Railway" shows a cherubic figure driving a steam-powered contraption. Although it appears to puff its way across a celestial landscape, it is constructed from apparently banal and everyday objects such as a pram and a teapot – a possible reference to the story of James Watt's (1736-1819) boyhood experiments with a steaming kettle. Two charioteer-cupids ride in attendance with spears, alluding perhaps to their intention to defend its progress or infatuate others with this mode of travel. The visual pun refers back to "putti", often seen in 16th century paintings. Such visual devices had a variety of meanings, generally of paradise, playfulness, innocence, delight, love, or leisure.

This tailpiece from Chapter IV of "The London and Birmingham Railway" is a much more brutal image, signalling the death knell of the stage-coach industry. A postillion rider to the left clutches his bugle whilst overcome with grief. To the right, a coach driver inconsolably hands over his badge of office - the coach whip. In the centre, the skeletal spectre of death firmly displays the triumphal evidence of many such surrenders. On the ground, a discarded horse collar and nosebag completes the picture of ruin whilst in the background, a locomotive steams effortlessly across a majestic viaduct, impervious to the howls of protest from a lone objector.

A third example of railway engravings providing caricature and satire appeared in the *Illustrated London News*. The images (over page) from the *Illustrated London News* (1847) caricatures the hierarchy of class divisions in Victorian society as passengers are shown travelling by rail to Epsom Races.

In a similar vein, it is possible to trace a hidden hierarchy in the images of railways between 1830 and 1850; from the third class multiple black and white woodcut prints on paper of varying quality, to the second class hand coloured aquatints or tint stone lithographs in limited editions on hand made paper, to some first class watercolours of railway scenes by artists of the highest calibre, including David Cox's "The Night Train" painted in 1849.

And the ultimate destination of this hierarchy of Victorian railway art? Arguably, it was the respectability gained for railway images achieved by a move away from paper to canvas and from landscape to social commentary. These developments reflected wider social changes in outlook and tastes so that by mid-century, the aristocracy of painters in oils had finally taken up the themes of the early railway artists and engravers.

First Class

Second Class

Third Class

Beyond The Beautiful, The Picturesque, and The Sublime.

An instructive example of the effects of norms and values on works of art is shown in Abraham Solomon's (1823-1862) *First Class-The Meeting, "And at first meeting loved"*, and *Second Class-The Parting, "Thus part we rich in sorrow, Parting poor"*. These oil paintings are companion pieces and are both narrative scenes of the interior of railway carriages. When first exhibited at the Royal Academy in 1854, they caused uproar. Such was the rumpus that Solomon felt obliged to paint a revised version of the "The Meeting" in the following year.

The original scene shows a young man apparently flirting with an attractive young woman seated somewhat ambiguously alongside. An old man, presumed to be her father, sleeps in the corner bathed in evening sunlight. A fishing rod rests in the opposite corner. This combination of symbolism, subject matter, and vivid use of colour provoked impassioned debate. Described as "an adventure in a railway carriage", one critic urged; "As a picture, it is executed with great knowledge and power, but it is, we think, to be regretted that so much facility should be lavished on so bald-or vulgar-a subject".

Solomon, doubtless concerned about future income, felt compelled to paint a second version. This time, the old man separates the "youth and maiden" and leaning forward in a somewhat didactic pose, engages in conversation with what now appears as a young officer, seated more obviously cornerwise, with his sword to the right and braided hat to the left. The young woman now occupies the furthest corner with fingers gently meeting the nails of each raised hand to form an evocative bridge. Her gaze, demurely directed under softly drooping eyelids, makes ambiguous contact with the young man. In this triangle, a boquet of red roses replaces a fishing rod.

Another striking example arises from the sumptuous and enigmatic qualities of *Travelling Companions,* painted by Augustus Leopold Egg in 1862. It shows two identically dressed young women sitting opposite each other, depicted in luxuriant grey silk dresses, one asleep – the other reading, with the blue waters of a coastal scene viewed through the window of a gently swaying railway carriage. Are they sisters or companions, mirror images of the same person, or references to the pleasures of railway travelling?

In the same year, after eighteen months' work, W P Frith completed his classic portrayal of *The Railway Station*. It shows a series of incidents amongst a crowd of passengers and others-some identifiable as portraits- on the platform of Paddington station. An indication of the popularity of this type of painting may be judged from the fact that Frith was persuaded not to exhibit it at the Royal Academy, but to sell it for exhibition as a single work in a London gallery. Visitors paid to view it and were offered an opportunity of buying an engraving of the scene.

Over twenty one thousand visitors came to see the painting. It was exhibited a second time a year later and then sent on tour around Britain and abroad. An estimate of the total proceeds from this enterprise indicates a sum of not less than £60,000, of which Frith received a fraction. The business of railway art was booming.

But perhaps the most dramatic oil painting of a railway scene is *Railway, Steam, and Speed – The Great Western Railway* painted during the 'Railway Mania' years by J M W Turner (1775-1851). He completed it some seven years before his death and was exhibited at the Royal Academy in 1844. The scene is of a locomotive on a river bridge, roaring out of swirling yellow, grey, and blue mists, its bright metal gleaming through the murky, rain-lashed track. A hare bolts along the rails in front, trapped on either side by the darkened parapets of the bridge. A lone figure ploughs a field in the distance below. This work remained unsold, yet it heralded in the decades that lay ahead the emergence of a new school of "Impressionist" painters as portrayed in the expressive canvases of Claude Monet's railway scenes.

The second iconic use of railway imagery was created by the Northumberland-born artist, John Martin (1789-1854). His skills ranged over engraving and painting in both watercolours and oils and by the age of twenty-three was exhibiting at the Royal Academy. One of his early patrons was Rudolf Ackermann who published his first print. Martin then went on to publish many other engravings and etchings over his lifetime. However, it is for his historical and biblical oil paintings that Martin is best known, especially his three vast canvases based on a text from the Book of Revelations; *The Great Day of His Wrath, The Plains of Heaven* and *The Last Judgement.* He completed each of these works shortly before he died in 1854.

The last of the three is an apocalyptic vision of the end of the world. A vast chasm dominates the centre of the composition into which immense mountains, vast cities, molten lava, and bodies flow. This anarchic scene, overhung by ashen clouds riven by lightning, is bathed in a lurid crimson light, dramatised by stark black and purple shadows. To the left are the righteous who are to be saved. To the right are the sinners sucked into a wild vortex from which there is no escape. The relevance of this panorama for our present purposes is that the damned are seen tumbling into the bottomless pit, carried in a train of third class carriages.

CHAPTER 9

Dr. GRANVILLE ON THE MEDICAL BENEFITS OF RAILWAY TRAVELLING (1841)

Introduction

Dr Augustus Bozzi Granville practised as a doctor in London for twenty-three years before embarking on his tour of "Spas and Principal Bathing Places" in 1839. His background as a foreigner lends added interest to his general observations on railway travelling that he claims, "had never before.....been treated..(from).. a medical point of view".

He was born in Milan in 1783 and at the age of nineteen qualified in medicine at the University of Pavia. Napoleon had invaded Italy and in order to avoid conscription, Granville escaped via Venice to Corfu. Befriended by an English diplomat, he took a post as a physician at the British Embassy in Constantinople (Istanbul). After recovering from bubonic plague and serving as a surgeon to the Turkish fleet, he went on to become a surgeon on a British ship.

During his years in the Royal Navy, he was shipwrecked and served for a time in the West Indies. By 1812, he had married and retired from the Navy at the age of twenty-nine. On a brief visit to Manchester, he was introduced to the Literary and Philosophical Society and afterwards opened his medical practice in London. Able to speak several languages including Spanish, Italian and English , he was engaged by the Foreign Office to travel to Italy where he was arrested as a spy. Following his release, he returned to resume his practice in London until his retirement in 1863. Dr A B Granville died in March 1872.

(Ed.)

THE

SPAS OF ENGLAND,

AND

PRINCIPAL SEA-BATHING PLACES.

BY

A. B. GRANVILLE, M.D., F.R.S.

AUTHOR OF "THE SPAS OF GERMANY," "ST. PETERSBURG," &c.

NORTHERN SPAS.

SCARBOROUGH.

LONDON:
HENRY COLBURN, PUBLISHER,
GREAT MARLBOROUGH STREET.
1841.

CHAPTER II.

RAILWAY TRAVELLING.

Quick Travelling makes Short Books—PRINCE GEORGE, Arthur Young, and the Railway—Is the latter a blessing, or the reverse to Travelling Invalids? Important Question for a Doctor to solve—Supposed grievances and positive Advantages—Author's Experience—Qualifications and Exceptions—THE LONDON AND BIRMINGHAM RAIL-CONCERN—Its Bustle and Bullyism enough to kill a Nervous Patient—Contrasted with other Lines of Rail-road—Difference between PROMISES and DEEDs—Imposition and Rapacity—Necessity for a Parliamentary Interference—The London and Birmingham, and the Grand Junction Contrasted—Other Sins of the London and Birmingham Line—Promise kept.

Of the many unexpected results consequent upon the enormous change in the internal communications of the country, brought about by railway travelling, there is one in particular at which writers, as well as readers, of books of travels, ought equally to rejoice. Railway travelling has left the former no excuse for dilly-dallying at the very outset of a journey, on a long, tedious, and uninteresting road, to regale their readers with some exquisite bit of novel information, touching the number of milestones and turnpike-gates; and it has taken from them the power of filling up the first twenty pages of a book with preliminary *verbiage* about what nobody cares for: it has, in fine, compelled them to plunge immediately *in medias res*—that is, to come to the purport and burden of their song at once, and leave all preparatory notes, of difficulties to be overcome, and fatigues to be undergone, out of the question. This is no trifling boon to the reader, who thus finds his curiosity likely to be speedily gratified without previous tantalization.

Nothing is so tedious as the narrative of preliminary steps in a book of travels. The *locomotive,* thanks to the philosopher of Soho, has at one stroke of a piston, swept all such prolixities away. When Prince George of Denmark undertook to visit Petworth, the royal traveller was engaged for nine hours in toiling down to his destination (a distance of about fifty miles); and the account given by contemporary chroniclers of the measures taken to ensure safety and expedition on that occasion, together with the narrative of the mishaps on the journey, is as irksome to read as the journey itself must have proved to the royal traveller. Now behold the difference which a little more than a century has brought about in these matters! Look at the wonders of a *locomotive* as compared to a state-carriage!

Another royal prince, on his way to this country, to become what George of Denmark was at the time, quits the station-post of a Belgium rail-road at the extremity of a line of one hundred miles, to reach the sea that separates him from his queen; and in half the time of his royal predecessor, accomplishes more than double the distance without a single event the telling of which could occupy more than a line in the narrative of his journey.

Arthur Young was a great traveller in his day, and wrote almost as many books as he had journeyed miles. But look at his narratives! One-half of the time of his reader is taken up with the perusal of entire pages of anathemas against roads and road-makers, and in lamentations at his own slow progress.

"I know not in the whole range of language," he exclaims in one of his tours to the North of England, "terms sufficiently expressive to describe this *infernal* road," &c. &c. and further on he adds, "Let me most seriously caution all travellers who may propose to travel this terrible country, to avoid it as they would the *devil*—for a thousand to one but they break their necks or their limbs by overthrows or breakings down."

And where do my readers think that such dismal adventures were portended to the traveller in honest Arthur's time, namely, just seventy years ago? Why, between Preston and Wigan, a nearly direct line of about seventeen miles in length, which I actually rolled over twice last summer, in less time than one occupies in sipping his breakfast—that is to say, in twenty-eight minutes each way!

How delightful it must be to all who feel the *pruritus peregrinandi* to know that from the identical place whence an active traveller dated his lamentations of old against the almost insurmountable difficulties of journeying to his destination, lines of communication, of equal velocity to the one I have just referred to, are shooting out in a northerly direction, one of which will reach Lancaster before the expiration of 1840, thereby affording the means of transport in ten short hours from London, to within twenty miles of the pure atmosphere of *Winander Meer,* and the other lakes in the north. To a person of delicate health and susceptible nerves, such a journey, with comparatively little or no fatigue, and less of adventure, must be a real blessing.

But is it so, in sober earnestness, with regard to all invalids or susceptible persons who may attempt or be recommended to avail themselves of these propulsory modes of travelling? What is the formed opinion of medical men on such a point? Have we sufficiently studied the operation of railway travelling on our patients, or even only upon such people as are prone, liable to, or threatened with disease? What, if a person is endowed with such exquisite sensibility of the nervous system, that the clumsy slamming of a door by a careless footman at home, or the tumbling down of a set of fireirons, at once produce a start, a commotion, and a headache for the day? Can such a person trust himself to railway travelling? And if a lady be thrown into a fever and a state of agitation at the sight of mere ordinary bustle— at the incessant grinding of a carriage ploughing a gravelled road—or at the rapid passage of objects before her, — is such an individual fit to travel by railway? Should, in fine, a person of either sex, subject to what is commonly denominated fulness of blood in the head, risk a rapid journey in one of the locomotives of the Western or the South Western trains, to rattle on at the rate of thirty miles an hour?

These are important questions for a physician to treat; especially if, in undertaking a work wherein traveling may form a prominent subject of recommendation, he is likely to point out the convenience and facilities of the new and striking mode of transport, which forms the subject of the present chapter. Such are precisely the reasons which gave rise to the chapter itself, and but for which some of my readers might think it out of place in a work on "The Spas of England!"

I am not aware that the question has been fully considered or discussed in medical works. Incidentally there have been opinions mentioned as emanating from medical authorities, which are, however, as yet unsupported by sufficient experience and undoubted facts, Some one or two awkward or unfortunate events that have occurred on a rail-road, to travellers supposed to have been in infirm health, have been explained in an off-hand manner, and upon very feeble evidence, as the effect of railway travelling on such constitutions—nay, some of my brethren have gone so far as to analyze with mathematical and nosological precision the different degrees of mischief, which the various incidents, inseparable from railway travelling, are likely to produce.

It has been alleged, that the being wafted through the air at the rate of twenty or thirty miles an hour, must affect delicate lungs and asthmatic people; that to such as are of a sanguineous constitution, and labour under fulness of blood in the head, the movement of rail-trains will produce apoplexy; that the sudden plunging into the darkness of a tunnel, and the emerging out of it as suddenly, cannot fail to make work for the oculists; and finally, it has never been doubted, but that the air in such tunnels is of a vitiated kind and must give rise to the worst effects; while that at the bottom of deep cuttings or excavations, being necessarily damp, will occasion catarrhs, and multiply agues!

Such is the list of alleged grievances said to have been started by medical men, against railway travelling.

I have availed myself of that mode of conveyance as often as possible upon all rail-roads, good, bad, or indifferent, in all directions and in all classes of' carriages; from the superb mail chariot with its spring cushions and well-stuffed back and sides, to the open platform in which passengers of the humblest description, as on the Manchester and Leeds s, are penned-in like sheep. I have tried a journey of nine hours consecutively in one of the close carriages, and again, in the second or open class of vehicles. In the course of all these goings and comings, I have studied not only myself but my neighbours, and purposely entered into conversation with them as to the effect of railway travelling, on themselves and their friends or acquaintances.

It is in this manner alone, that positive information on such topics can be obtained. Well, the result of all my observations is, that there is not much of truth in the alleged medical grievances against railway travelling, and that, *per se,* such a mode of conveyance is not more likely to do mischief to people's health than any other hitherto adopted.

I am bound, however, to qualify this declaratory opinion by stating, that constituted as rail roads are at present, without proper and responsible control, or uniform legislative regulation; and varying, as almost all of them do, in their mode of construction, management, and condition, so that while one is smooth, joltless, and almost noiseless, another is the very antipodes of all these; it is not impossible that some easily affrighted dame, some highly nervous old gentleman, or a readily excitable person prone to fulness, may suffer from railway travelling or from some of its concomitants.

But these are the exceptions and not the rule. I admit, that if the first of those morbidly disposed individuals, on presenting herself at the station of the London and Birmingham line in Euston-square, in order to procure a ticket for any one of the classes of carriages on the rail-road, is made to go through the necessary process in the most hurried manner possible, and without the smallest chance of gathering a syllable of information, or a civil answer to a question, from one of the spruce clerks busily employed in slicing and distributing pink, blue, and yellow slips, for pounds, shillings, and pence, which keep flowing in from every quarter: I admit, that if, at the beckoning of a policeman, the same easily affrighted lady be squeezed through a funnel-like passage, as if she were forcing her way with the rabble at half-price into the pit of old Drury, in order that, she may afterwards find her way, *tant bien que mal*, to the platform from whence she is to embark on her venture: I admit, that if, having once reached the platform, dragging her own portmanteau and *sac-de-nuit*, she finds the former suddenly snatched from her by some lusty porter, and thrown upon a new-fangled pair of scales at the bidding of a young fop, who at the same time peremptorily demands some additional ten or twelve shillings, for an alleged excess of weight in her luggage: I admit, that if, marvelling at so exorbitant a demand while questioning its justice, the first signal-bell for the passengers to take their seats is heard to sound, and the servants of the Company, running to and fro, hardly offer to relieve her of her burden, or place her and it in the carriage she is to occupy, but leave her to do all that in the best way she can: I admit, that if, while perplexed as to what she ought next to do, she hears the last signal-bell ring, and a second policeman addresses her with " Now, ma'am; you'll be too late … in with you, ma'am, quick, quick, or you'll be left behind;" lifting her at the same time from the platform on to the step of the nearest carriage (probably not the one she ought to take for her destination), and the train all the while moving forward: I admit at once, that if all these things are to take place, if an easily affrighted dame is to be thus jostled, hurried, and bullied, then the railway journey which is to follow is likely to prove of serious injury to her.

But reverse the picture: see the same person going through the quiet, easy, civil, and reasonable proceedings which accompany railway travelling on any other line, the South Western for example, and our easily affrighted lady will find no inconvenience whatever, but on the contrary every comfort from that mode of conveyance

The rail-road, from London to Birmingham, is in fact an ill-managed concern. Present yourself in any garb you please to the counter of their offices, assume the most affable or beseeching tone of inquiry you can, still you will either get no answer at all, or one which you would hardly give to your own menial servant. The difference in that respect between the two ends of the line, the London and the Liverpool lines, is quite striking; as compared to London, all the officers and servants at the Liverpool terminus are perfection, and their arrangements incomparably superior.

The rapacity, too, of the persons managing the concern has no end. I have before me their soft-lipped, alluring prospectus of 1833. Not only was *safety* amid *expedition* promised, but *economy* also. The latter was illustrated by comparison to the then inside fares of stage-coaches, of which the charge for the first class of carriages on the was to be less than the half. This forbearance did not last long. The price was soon raised to the full amount of the inside of an ordinary

219

Stockton &; and within the last few months, with as much reason for any further increase in the fares of the principal classes of carriages as there was for any addition before,—namely none, but the good will and pleasure of the directors, and the despotic uncontrollable power granted to them by a loosely and vaguely defined act of Parliament,—they have raised the principal carriage fare by an additional half-a-crown, and have visited with a still heavier demand the traveller who prefers the second class of carriages, by increasing his fare five shillings more, that is, double the increase upon the first class carriages, by way of penalty, it must be supposed, for presuming to prefer the second to the first class of vehicles!

This is hardly honest towards the public; and done too in the face of many successive favourable reports from the Board of Directors, upon the progressive gains of the Company, and the declaration of high dividends.

Where is this eagerness after lucre, unvisited by any usury laws, to stop, if Parliament does not interfere in behalf of the public, which the legislature has hitherto left unprotected, and at the mercy of any set of monopolizers?

It is really worth while, as we are on the subject of rail-road travelling, and as I am disposed on the whole to recommend the use of it to certain classes of invalids, not only as a convenient but as a salutary mode of transport from one place to another—it is worth while, I say, to reduce to a few formulæ of numbers the iniquity of this mode of proceeding on the part of the London and Birmingham Railway Company. For this purpose we have only to contrast what is done in regard to charges upon the two extreme lines, between London and Liverpool, which meet at Birmingham as a centre.

The distance between the last-mentioned city and Liverpool by railway is ninety-seven miles and a quarter. The charge for the first class carriages is and has invariably been one guinea. That it is a remunerating charge, we may conclude, first, from its never having been raised; and, secondly, from the recent declaration of a very high dividend to the shareholders. Between London and Birmingham the distance by railway is 112 miles (so laid down in all their maps and sections); the charge, therefore, if that of one guinea for ninety-seven miles and a half be an equitable and remunerating charge, ought to be twenty-four shillings and fourpence. But it is, in reality, thirty-two shillings and sixpence; *ergo* there is, in this case, a positive extortion of eight shillings and a fraction above what is *equitable.*

Such an extortion, however, becomes even more glaring when we take into consideration the London and Birmingham fare for the second class of carriages, which, as before stated, has been lately raised without notice or reason to twenty-five shillings. On the Grand Junction the distance of 97¼ miles is charged 14s. 8d. for that class of carriages. The proportionate charge, therefore, for the same class of carriages on the London line should be 16s. 3d. Instead of which it is £1. 5s; *ergo,* there is here an excess of nearly nine shillings above what is just and equitable! And the legislature, in granting acts for this new mode of conveying passengers, never provided against the possibility of such extortions being practised on the public!

But these are not the only sins against the London and Birmingham management. Their behaviour with regard to the charge for luggage is even more reprehensible. In all their printed documents it was stated that all excess of weight of luggage above 100lb. would be charged one penny per pound. Even to this day it is so printed on some of the luggage tickets. It is the charge still demanded on the Junction or Liverpool line, and I may add on many other lines; though several of them make no charge whatever for luggage. But one penny is not so good as double that sum: so thought some able financier at the board, on some unlucky day for the public;—and his compeers assenting, the printed *one* is forthwith changed into a written *two* on the luggage ticket.

In that guise the charge stands on my own ticket of the 18th of July; 1839, now before me (8 P.M. o'clock train), by which an excess of luggage weighing 72 lb. above what is allowed, and which, according to the declaration of the chairman of their board to a committee of the House of Commons, made two or three months before, would have been charged six shillings, now cost me twelve! What Chancellor of the Exchequer would, by the stroke of a clerk's pen, Venture upon doubling the amount of any tax on the public, in the truly off-hand manner of these executives?

The said luggage consisted of a leathern portmanteau *only.* It was rather bulky to be sure; still it was but a portmanteau, and I could carry it with one hand. I ventured, almost tremblingly, to put in one word of remonstrance against the unexpected transmutation of one into two, which I saw juggled before me by the clerk's quill, and also against the amazing ponderosity discovered in a *clin d'oeil* in my portmanteau, which had been thrown carelessly on a newfangled weighing machine that left no leisure or means to verify its operation; but I was instantly abused.

As I am not of the most pacific temper in such sudden emergencies, I, too, raised my voice and plucked up courage to demand for myself; and others (who by this time had entered the office with similar protestations), some explanation. But lo! I might as well have tried to out-whistle the steam which just then was rushing with a violent hissing noise out of our locomotive. "Pay, or your luggage *shan't* go!" I did pay, and told them they should hear from me,—and thus I keep my promise.

CHAPTER III.

RAILWAY TRAVELLING CONCLUDED.

ABUSES Abroad and Abuses at Home—Reform necessary—Every other Species of Conveyance under Legislative Control except Rail-road—DANGERS and Inconveniences of Rail Travelling—Author's Experience—FIRST START—Darwin's Prophecy—Progress—Impediments—Accidents—Delays—RESULT—Sum total of the Benefit to Mankind, and Invalids in particular, from Railways.

I dare say that when these pages see the light, some one will stand up to defend the Company in the proceedings described in the last chapter. But then I know, that the whole voice of the public is with me on the subject. Some reviewers, too, will be retained, to show up the Author for introducing questions of this nature in a work professing to treat of mineral waters.

When on a former occasion, treating of the mineral waters of Germany, I exposed the impositions practised at the frontiers and custom-houses of some of the continental places on those who travelled to and from the several spas, no one found fault with my proceedings, but rather applauded the act. Is it only when abuses are met with in foreign countries by a traveller, that their exposure is proper? And if the same individual travels at home upon a like errand, and discovers equal, if not worse abuses, does he not render the same service to the public by exposing them likewise?

That a corrective reform must take place of all such abuses connected with rail-road travelling, and at the hands, too, of that very legislature which allowed the creation of many fruitful sources of these abuses,—every thing around us seems to indicate; and that reform cannot come too soon. Rail-roads, to be a blessing to this country, must be placed under wholesome and distinct parliamentary regulations, and watched over by authorities *wholly independent* of the speculative part of the undertaking. Not the pecuniary part of that undertaking alone, should be regulated and put under control, with a view to the protection of the public; but the safety of the latter also should be considered—a point of the most vital importance, for which, as yet, no provision whatever, of an official character, has been made or thought of.

If a smack, or the smallest bark, is to be licensed to trade from London to any port of Great Britain, certain precise and definite regulations to ensure its safety and that of the crew are strictly enforced, by a Trinity board or some such authority. Some of these vessels, placed under the command and management of a master, may be manned, perhaps, by three seamen and a cabin boy only. Yet that master has certain strict orders to observe, for the protection of the four lives temporarily placed under his care.

The legislature has in such cases, and from time almost immemorial, interposed to save human life. Among the many public carriages that convey a dozen passengers to and from the various cities of England, not one is permitted to ply without strict rules being laid down, established by acts of Parliament, by which its management and progress on the king's highways are strictly defined; so that the limbs of the traveller therein and thereon, may be, as far as possible, protected. In this second case again has the legislature interposed to save life.

But how differently stands the case with the new mode of railway travelling authorized by the very same legislature! Why, instead of three or thirteen, three hundred, or three thousand lives have often been committed in one day, on the several railways of England, to the sole direction of one man, an engineer, so called, or engineman, whose skill, prudence, sobriety, alertness, presence of mind, strength of nerves, promptitude in action, and knowledge of the Leviathan power he has to control, have never been preliminarily examined or ascertained; neither have they been acquired by regular scientific training or education! And yet on the failure of all or any of these requisites, in a man having the momentary charge of so many human lives, may the whole or most of those lives be suddenly extinguished, or as many limbs maimed and disfigured.

I would advise those who have feeble nerves, and especially travellers of the weaker sex, when once embarked in one of the well-stuffed coaches of the Great Western, or of any other rail-road, after having surveyed the superb display of closed and open vehicles arranged on rails under a splendid colonnade, in one almost interminable line, teeming with live beings,—not to suffer their thoughts revert for an instant to the consideration of how and by what mighty power, and under whose sagacious and provident direction, all these creatures, beaming with life and spirits, are to be transported to their remote destinations. Such a reflection, at such a moment, would deter them from the prosecution of their journey, or make them miserable throughout it if they proceeded. It is in such cases as these that I admit the possibility of railway travelling being likely to prove detrimental to health.

To glance at all the possible dangers to which the traveller on a rail-road is at present liable, from the mere want of a uniform and intelligible legislative enactment to regulate that new and prodigious invention, which seems destined to annihilate space,—is a task to be shrunk from, were it not thrust upon us by the very nature of the subject and intention of the present chapter. In fact, no other mode of travelling is encompassed by so many dangers.

In the course of the professional tour which the following pages are meant to describe, the author purposely availed himself of every species of conveyance along a circuitous route of nearly three thousand miles, ranging through almost every county in England; in order that he might be prepared to give his best advice, founded on personal experience, to those who are likely (as in the case of the Spas of Germany) to apply for that advice, respecting the most eligible mineral spring to be resorted to, or the most desirable mode of conveyance thither to be adopted.

Railway travelling formed the larger proportion of the various modes adopted by the author. Carriages drawn or pushed by locomotive as well as by stationary engines; carriages sliding down an inclined or dragged up an ascending plane; carriages moved along by a trotting horse on iron rails; all these were employed in turn. The inside and outside of mail and stage-coaches were also put in requisition, and so were postchaises, gigs, and errand-carts. Finally, a saddle-horse, a canal-boat, and a coasting-steamer, were not forgotten. All these means of conveyance were purposely had recourse to by way of experiment; but none suggests to the mind so large a category of perils almost inherent in it (so long as it shall remain in its present state) as that one marvellous species of conveyance on which we have been descanting.

We will imagine that we are about to start on a rail-road, from the terminus or first station. A long line of carriages charged with their live lumber awaits the signal. Hitherto the huge locomotive, which had been brought out of the engine-house like an impatient warhorse, and placed at the head of the line,—had only given tokens of its presence to the passengers by the continuous hissing of its steaming breath issuing through a narrow opening. But now the bell has sounded—the carriage-doors are all secured—the farewell and the good-by have been given to the travellers by the friends who remain behind and who retreat back on the platform— "All's right," cries the inspector at the end of five minutes. The monster-engine, roused by fresh fuel and loosened by the swarthy engineer, first changes the hissing into a hoarse yet shrill whistle, throwing up a shower of misty water into the air like a huge Leviathan of the Greenland seas; and then panting loudly, and in measured beatings, sets off on its rapid journey, dragging along with it (chained to each other) the fifty vehicles to which it has been harnessed, "and outstripping," as a recent writer has said, "the fleetest race-horse and antelope in its speed."

How clearly did the illustrious Darwin, in his Cruscean distich, predict this wonderful consummation of man's industry, many years before it had even been dreamt of by the world!

Soon shall thine arm, unconquered steam, afar
Drag the slow barge and drive the rapid car.

Once launched on its errand, the train is at the mercy of one man's skill and carefulness; and all that are committed to it have suddenly and voluntarily changed their individual chances of the worldly perils likely to affect their existence. The train in its rapid course has come into collision with another, or with a ballast train which did not get out of the line into the siding at its proper time or it has overtaken a long train of goods which had set off before, but had been detained In each of such *rencontres* the effects have been tremendous.

Presently the train has found the moving rails, or switches, which are to direct its course, turned the wrong way, by the neglect of a policeman deputed to set them properly and the engine, with the string of carriages, by being suddenly thrown off the straight line upon a sharp curve, have been fatally overturned. Such switches, upon a lofty embankment, turned the wrong way, have precipitated the whole train down its sloping sides.

In some places the train of one railway and that of another have to cross each other on a level at certain angles; as in the case of the Great North of England and Clarence Rail-roads, for example:—who can contemplate the effect of a collision, should the two trains meet by miscalculation of time or accident? Yet such a collision has taken place on the Darlington and Stockton railways.

Farther on the train is to change the line, in order to enter upon another at right angles. The time appointed for this is arranged, so that no other train may be at the point of confluence of the two roads at the same time; but some accidental occurrence has baffled this pre-arrangement, and two trains have reached, from two different lines, the point of confluence at the same moment of time, and the contact has been terrific and fatal. Newton station can testify to that fact.

Similar, though not equally dangerous rencounters, the trains may fall into, from the rail-road crossing in places, and on the same level, ordinary highways.

Presently the train reaches an embankment, the soil of which, loosened by the effect of heavy and continued rains, and incapable of supporting any weight, is unsteady and gives way, just as the rumbling engine advances over it, and is suddenly imbedded in the quaking mass of earth.

In another part of the line, a long train of carriages has entered a very deep cutting, the banks of which are not sufficiently inclined away from the rail-road. Incessant rains for two or three days have loosened the earth of these banks, which the vibration caused by the train has afterwards shaken down, overturning the engine and half burying several of the carriages. The Grand Junction can bear witness to the possibility of both these occurrences, and November 1839 is not too far remote a period for recollection.

Lastly, a bridge or a viaduct has broken down at the very instant of the string of vehicles passing over it, and some of them have been precipitated into the chasm. The Greenwich, the Birmingham, and the St. Germain's rail-road in France, have, each in turn, furnished an example of this species of danger, inherent in rail-road travelling.

Next to such danger come inconveniences ever inseparable from a mode of travelling of this description. Of these, that of delay on the road is, perhaps, the most lamentable; in as much as the causes of it have hitherto been as frequent as they have proved disastrous. At one time it is a stray cow or a sheep lying athwart the rail, which the engine's scuper tosses into the air, being itself checked in its progress by that act.

At another time, a deaf railway-labourer is knocked down, or a drunken policeman falls just as the engine approaches him, and the rapid machine passes over their bodies, being thrown out of the line at the same moment.

A supply of water to feed the boiler is required; the train reaches the pump at one of the stations, but the pump is frozen or refuses to work. The stoker, who ought to be like Argus, ever vigilant, falls asleep now and then; the fire goes out; and the locomotive, which was to have conveyed the night-mail at twenty-five miles per hour, is standing stock-still.

Here and there the rails will be covered with snow, or be excessively wet; and the wheels refuse to *bite,* wasting their power in useless girations. All these *contretemps* will cause delay, though not so much so as when, upon some unlucky occasion, a grand explosion takes place, and all power of locomotion is suddenly annihilated.

These inconveniences and dangers are not imaginary or merely possible; they have actually all occurred upon some one rail-road or another; they have all been recorded in the public journals, and been admitted in evidence before a parliamentary committee; neither will they be averted until superior arrangements shall be made, and a general supervision of all the rail-roads be established, through the agency of a general Board

The immense advantages, however, of this stupendous invention still remain; and although, as in the case of almost every one of the more surprising discoveries of man, practically applied by his ingenuity to the curtailment of labour, the increase of wealth, and the multiplication of luxuries,—the result has been obtained at the expense of new dangers, with an increased liability to the loss of life; nevertheless, the great, the enormous sum of benefit that must accrue to mankind from the establishment of a means of conveyance which seems to level all topographical distinctions, and not only brings distant cities, but remote countries nearer to each other, and annihilates time and distance,.—is not to be questioned, and becomes every day more manifest.

Railway travelling is a fruitful theme of many important reflections, besides those which I have deemed sufficiently akin to the general objects of my present work to introduce into this and the preceding chapter. Its reference to political results—to agricultural considerations—to statistical conclusions—and to the possible amelioration of the condition of the people, form so many points of interest, which it is not my province to touch upon in this place, yet to some of which I may perchance have to allude in the course of this work, with certain illustrations drawn from personal experience. At all events they are points well worthy of the consideration of statesmen, as involving questions of the first importance,—whether in regard to the immediate interests of enterprising persons, and the convenience and intercourse of the community at large, or in reference to the safety and protection of human life.

CHAPTER 10

POSTSCRIPT

STATION SIGNAL, WITH COTTAGE.

"The Whitby and Pickering Railway belongs not to the class that may be literally said to "annihilate both time and space", locomotive engines not being employed thereon, its inclination being unfavourable to the propelling power of that valuable machine, the visitors will nevertheless have no reason to regret the absence of a rapidity that most assuredly and very considerably diminish the interest of this delightful ride, the Railway passing as it does through a country unrivalled for the beauty and diversified nature of the scenery in one month in the summer of 1836, nearly 5,000 persons were conveyed upon it, an immense number, taking into consideration its vast distance from the metropolis, the places whence it starts and where it terminates."

Mogg's "Pocket Itinerary" 1837.

Retrospect

In this extract from his pocket guide, Edward Mogg (1804-1848), inveterate traveller, publisher, engraver and mapmaker, provides us with his observations on the original railway soon after it opened in 1836. In its horse-drawn days, the Whitby and Pickering railway lasted some twelve years; just a small part of its long history, progressing now towards its bi-centenary.

Through the various chapters of the present book, some reminders of how and why the railway came into being have been assembled from the first effects of George Stephenson's inventions reverberating from Stockton and Darlington, to the visionary influence of George Hudson at Whitby, Pickering, York and Scarborough.

The artistry of George Dodgson and the railway artists of his generation, remind us of other worlds, liberating our imagination from the purely practical towards the enduring appeal of the romantic, the picturesque, and the overcoming of nature through art and technology. These are just some of the elements that have ensured that this line, unlike many others, has survived.

Henry Belcher's book, based upon George Dodgson's illustrations, provides a gateway into the families and fortunes of the people who tried, and in some cases failed, to survive their ambitions. Robert Campion's bank crashed in 1841 with debts amounting to more than half the cost of the railway, Hudson was sent to jail whilst seeking election as MP for Whitby, and the Railway Company itself proved not to be profitable - 'profitable' that is from the standpoint of its shareholders.

Viewed in a wider perspective, the total regenerative effects, both then and now, greatly outweigh the investment made. In the first fifty years, the resulting growth of stone quarries, the jet industry, and lime production was a considerable development. For thirty years from the introduction of steam working on the line, the ironstone processing at Grosmont supported three blast furnaces, employed up to 400 workers, and transformed an area hitherto remote and unused. Meanwhile, the town of Whitby grew rapidly as a holiday destination and Pickering enjoyed greatly improved access to the main centres of population.

The King is Dead - Long Live the King!

George Hudson's legacy in the years following the purchase of the line by the York and North Midland Railway, is shown in the revised train timetable for1848. Three return services operated daily during the summer months from York to Whitby, except Sundays, when one train made the journey leaving York at 7.0 a.m., arriving at Whitby at 10.0 a.m. with eleven stops en route. The single fare for first, second and third class passengers was twelve shillings, nine shillings and sixpence, and seven shillings respectively. (An agricultural labourer would be receiving around nine shillings a week and the annual wage for skilled workers in engineering, printing, shipbuilding, building would be around £60.)

After Hudson's resignation from the York and North Midland, fierce competition between the three main railways operating in the north east was rationalised by the creation of the North Eastern Railway Company in 1854. The resulting amalgamation brought some 700 miles of track under a single management with headquarters at York. By this time, stage-coach services had long since disappeared.

The increasing monopoly exercised by the North Eastern curtailed or absorbed competing Companies including a planned railway along the coast from Scarborough to Whitby, first proposed in 1863. It was to take another twenty-two years before this line opened in 1885. Whitby and Pickering were then served by many lines in Ryedale and the adjacent Vale of Mowbray, creating a rich mix of possibilities for travel by rail from all points of the compass.

In 1908, the original line from Grosmont to Beck Hole at the foot of the incline plane re-opened for summer excursions. This service used "autocars" comprising a tank engine and clerestory carriages coupled to allow for forward or reverse working. This arrangement meant that engines coming to the end of their normal life could be re-used for this much lighter duty. The outbreak of war in 1914 led to the closure of this service and the partial removal of track between Levisham and Pickering for use in France as part of the "war effort".

At the end of World War 1, the changed economic climate brought new challenges for the post-war years. In 1923, the North Eastern Railway became a part of a grouping of railways under the newly formed London and North Eastern Railway. The Second World War brought about yet more sweeping changes when the railway system was nationalized.

The emergence of a corporate culture, partly in response to growing competition from road transport and an ever-deepening deficit, led to the emergence of "British Rail" and the controversial "Beeching Report"; *The Re-Shaping of British Railways*. The 1960's proved as radical and turbulent for the railways as the frenzy and mania of the 1840's.

The Beeching plan proposed the closure of all existing railways to Whitby. The only survivor was the line from Whitby to Middlesbrough, part of which used a section of the original Whitby and Pickering railway to Grosmont. The axe fell in 1965 and the Whitby to York line closed.

A New Beginning

After a spirited opposition to the closure plans, a number of determined people, whose imagination and enterprise echoed the founders of the line, made it possible to form a charitable trust. The North York Moors Historical Railway

Trust then set about the very considerable challenge of re-opening the line;

"Picture the line when the North Yorkshire Moors Railway signed the first contract with British Rail: it had been disused for some three years, weeds grew everywhere, one of the tracks had already gone for scrap, and the stations and buildings were in disrepair. Just two steel rails running into the distance with no locomotives or coaches to run on them....There was very little money, but gradually the picture began to change. Paint soon brightened up the stations, and as people began to hear about the railway, so they turned up to help. Not just local people, and not all rail enthusiasts, but folk of all ages from Tyneside, and Teeside, York and the South, singly and in groups."

Extract from the Commemorative Booklet for the Official Opening of the North Yorkshire Moors Railway on May 1st 1974.

Today, the North Yorkshire Moors Railway is a thriving concern, a multiple award winner, and a key tourist attraction conveying over 300,000 passengers annually.

Kept within the invaluable archive and library of the Whitby Literary and Philosophical Society in Pannett Park, Whitby - the body that might reasonably claim to be the founder of the Whitby and Pickering Railway - is a bound album of photographs. G. W. J. Potter, who wrote the classic text on the history of the line, put it together in the early decades of the last century. His history, published in 1906, was followed in 1914 by another classic; W. W. Tomlinson's, *The North Eastern Railway: It's Rise and Development.* Historians of the line owe a considerable debt to their pioneering work.

Potter's album of photographs, captions and comments ends with the words: "Work loved in life leave to posterity" - a fitting tribute to the numerous people who have created the remarkable Whitby and Pickering railway and in countless ways have made its presence felt, valued, and cherished.

SOURCES AND FURTHER READING

Chapter One: **By Rail from Whitby to Pickering**...............**pages 1-21**

Barker, R. *Whitby North Yorkshire: An Extraordinary Town.* Pickering: Blackthorn Press, 2007.

Beales, D. *From Castlereagh to Gladstone 1815-1885.* New York and London: W.W. Norton & Company, 1969.

Bebb, P. *Life in Regency Whitby 1811-1820.* York: William Sessions Ltd, 2000

Briggs, A. *England in the Age of Improvement, 1783-1867.* London: The Folio Society, 2000.

Briggs, A. *Victorian Cities.* London: Penguin Books, 1990.

Browne, H.B. *Chapters of Whitby History 1823-1946:The Story of the Whitby Literary and Philosophical Society and of Whitby Museum.* Hull and London: A. Brown & Sons Ltd, 1946.

Butlin, R.A., (ed) *Historical Atlas of North Yorkshire.* Otley: Westbury, 2004.

Chadwick, 0. *The Victorian Church 1829-1859.* London: SCM Press, 1997.

Davies, H. *George Stephenson: A Biographical Study of the Father of Railways.* London: Weidenfeld and Nicolson, 1975.

Fletcher, J. S. *The Making of Modern Yorkshire 1750-1914.* London: George Allen & Unwin Ltd, 1918.

Harrison, J. F. C. *The Early Victorians 1832-1851.* London: Weidenfeld and Nicolson, 1971.

Hartley, W. C. E. *Banking in Yorkshire.* Lancaster: Dalesman Books, 1975.

Home, G. *The Evolution of an English Town.* London: J.M.Dent & Co., 1905.

House of Commons Research Paper 99/20. *Inflation: The Value of the Pound.* www.parliament.uk/commons/lib/research

Jeffrey, P. S. *Whitby Lore and Legend.* 3rd ed. Whitby: Horne & Son Ltd, 1971.

Joy, D. *Whitby & Pickering Railway.* 3rd ed. Lancaster: Dalesman Books, 1973.
        North Yorkshire Moors Railway. Lancaster: Dalesman Books, 1987.

Kendall, H. P. *The Streets of Whitby and their Associations.* Middlesbrough: The Vision Press, 1988.

Mingay, G. E. *Rural Life in Victorian England.* Stroud: Sutton Publishing Ltd, 1998.

North Yorkshire Moors National Park. *Historical Railway Trail.* York: H.Morley & Sons Ltd, n.d.

Robbins, M. *George and Robert Stephenson.* London: Her Majesty's Stationery Office, 1981.

Rushton, J. *The History of Ryedale, North Yorkshire.* Pickering: Blackthorn Press, 2003.

Stamp, C. *Scoresby.* Whitby: Caedmon of Whitby, 2007.

Simmons. J., and Biddle, G. *British Railway History from 1603 to the 1990's.* Oxford and New York: Oxford University Press, 1997.

Weatherill, R. *The Ancient Port of Whitby and its Shipping.* Whitby: Horne & Son, 1908.

White, A. *A History of Whitby.* 2nd ed. Chichester: Phillimore & Co. Ltd, 2004.

Wilson, A. N. *The Victorians.* London: Hutchinson, 2002.

Young, G. *Picture of Whitby and its Environs.* Whitby: R. Rogers, 1824.

Chapter Two: **Thoughts on a Railway from Whitby into the Interior.**

A Townsman. *Thoughts on a Railway from Whitby into the Interior. Whitby: R Rodgers, 1831.*

Chapter Three: **Politics and Personalities**

Arnold, A. J., and McCartney, S. *George Hudson: The Rise and Fall of the Railway King,* London and New York: Hambledon and London, 2004.

Bailey, B. *George Hudson: The Rise and Fall of the Railway King.* Stroud: Alan Sutton Publishing Ltd, 1995.

Biddle, G. *The Railway Surveyors.* London: Ian Allen Ltd, 1990.

Binns, J. *The History of Scarborough, North Yorkshire.* Pickering: Blackthorn Press, 2001.

Dickens, C. *The Letters of Charles Dickens.* 2 vols, 2nd ed. London:Chapman Hall, 1880

Forster, J. *The Life of Charles Dickens.* London: Cecil Palmer, 1928.

Lidster, J. R. *Scarborough Railway Station from Steam Age to Diesel Era.* Nelson: Hendon Publishing Co. Ltd, 1995.

Morris, M. C. F. *Yorkshire Folk-Talk and Characteristics of Those Who Speak in the North and East Ridings.* London and New York: Henry Ford and John Simpson, 1892.

Nock, O. S. *The Railway Engineers,* London: B. T. Batsford, 1955.

Patterson, R. *George Weatherill-his Life and his Family.* Privately Printed, 1998.

Peacock, A. J. *George Hudson 1800-1871: The Railway King.* 2 vols. York: A J Peacock, 1988.

Reussner, G. 150 Years Ago-The Story of the Whitby & Pickering Railway. *Moors Line, Magazine of the North York Moors Historical Railway Trust.* Various issues 1983-1990.

Rivett, L., and Matthew, J. *A Yorkshire Genius: A Brief Study of the Life, Work and Achievements of Sir George Cayley.* York: Yorkshire Air Museum, 2003.

Rolt, L. T. C. *George and Robert Stephenson: The Railway Revolution.* London: Longman, 1960.

Smiles, S. *The Lives of George and Robert Stephenson.* London: Folio Society, 1975. Reprint of first edition, 1857.

Smiles, S. *The Story of the Life of George Stephenson, Railway Engineer.* London: John Murray. 1859.

Stamp, C. *George Hudson and Whitby.* Whitby: Caedmon of Whitby, 2005.

Thompson, F. M. L. *Chartered Surveyors: The Growth of a Profession.* London: Routledge and Kegan Paul, 1968.

Whitworth, A., ed. *Churches of the Whitby District.* Culva House Publications, 2004.

Wray, I. *Charles Dickens: The Malton Connection.* Privately Printed, n.d.

Chapter Four: Building the Line..pages 57-86

Body, G. *Great Railway Battles: Dramatic Conflicts of the Early Railway Years.* Peterborough: Silver Link Publishing Ltd, 1994.

Chapman, S. *Grosmont and its Mines.* Cleveland Ironstone Series: Peter Tuffs, 2002

Dickens, C. *Dombey and Son.* London: Penguin Classics, 2002. Reprint of first edition 1848.

Fawcett, B. *A History of the York-Scarborough Railway.* Beverley: Hutton Press Ltd, 1995.

Howat, P. *The Railways of Ryedale and the Vale of Mowbray.* Nelson: Hendon Publishing Company, 1988.

McGowan, C. *The Rainhill Trials: The Greatest Contest of Industrial Britain and the Birth of Commercial Rail.* London: Little Brown, 2004.

Lidster, J R. *The Scarborough & Whitby Railway.* Nelson: Hendon Publishing Company, 1977.

Potter, G. W. J. *A History of the Whitby and Pickering Railway.* 2nd ed. London: The Locomotive Publishing Co. Ltd, 1906.

Simmons, J. ed. *The Men Who Built Railways.* London: Thomas Telford Ltd, 1983. Reprint of F R Conder, Personal Recollections of English Engineers. London: Hodder and Stoughton, 1868.

Whishaw, F. *The Railways of Great Britain Practically Described and Illustrated.* London: John Weale, 1842.

Tomlinson, W. W. *The North Eastern Railway: Its Rise and Development..* Newcastle-upon-Tyne: Andrew Reid & Company Ltd., London: Longmans, Green & Company, 1914.

Williams, F.S. *Our Iron Roads: Their History, Construction and Social Influences.* London: Ingram, Cooke, and Co., 1852.

***Chapter Five:* Scenery of the Whitby and Pickering Railway.**

Belcher, H. *Illustrations of the Scenery of the Line of the Whitby and Pickering Railway, in the North Eastern Part of Yorkshire.* London: Longman, Rees, Orme, Brown, Green, and Longman, 1836

***Chapter Six:* From Surveying to Artistry: George Haydock Dodgson**

Belcher, H. *Illustrations of the Scenery on the Line of the Whitby and Pickering Railway in the North Eastern Part of Yorkshire from Drawings by G. Dodgson* London; Longman, Rees, Orme, Brown, Green, and Longman, 1836.

Roget, J. L. *History of the Old Watercolour Society.* 2 vols. London: Longman, 1891.

Fenwick, S., and Smith, G. *The Business of Watercolour – a guide to the archives of the Royal Watercolour Society.* Aldershot: Ashgate Publishing Ltd, 1997.

***Chapter Seven:* The Stranger's Guide for a Summer's Day Excursion.**

Belcher, H. *The Stranger's Guide for a Summer's Day Excursion from Scarborough to Pickering and Thence by The Railway to Whitby.* Scarborough: S.W. Theakston, 1843.

Chapter Eight: **Early Victorian Railway Artists and Engravers.**
....**pages 190-213**

Bills, M., and Knight, V. *William Powell Frith: Painting the Victorian Age.* New Haven and London: Yale University Press, 2006

Child, D. *Painters in the Northern Counties of England and Wales.* Leeds: University of Leeds School of Education, 1994.

Dalziel, G., and Dalziel, E. *The Brothers Dalziel: A Record 1840-1890.* London: B. T. Batsford, 1978.

Darby, M. *Early Railway Prints from the Collection of Mr and Mrs M G Powell.* London: Her Majesty's Stationery Office, 1974.

Donald, D. *What is a Popular Print?* University of Manchester: The Whitworth Art Gallery, 2000.

Dyson, A. *Pictures to Print: The nineteenth-century engraving trade.* London: Farrand Press, 1984.

Engen, R.K. *Dictionary of Victorian Engravers, Print Publishers and Their Works.* Cambridge: Chadwyck-Healey, 1979

Griffiths, A. *Prints and Printmaking: An Introduction to the History and Techniques.* London: The British Museum Press, 2004.

Faulkner, T., and Greg, A. *John Dobson: Architect of the North East.* Newcastle: Tyne and Wear Museums, 2001.

Ford, J. *Ackermann 1783-1983: The Business of Art.* London: Ackermann, 1983.

Gascoigne, B. *How to Identify Prints.* 2nd edition. London: Thames & Hudson, 2004.

Hamilton Ellis, C. *Railway Art.* London: Ash & Grant, 1977.

Hunnisett, B. *A Dictionary of British Steel Engravers.* Leigh-On-Sea: F. Lewis Publishers Ltd, 1980.

Harland, J. *George Weatherill 1810-1890.* Whitby: The Pannett Gallery, n.d.

Johnstone, C. *John Martin* London: Academy Editions, 1974

Lowe, I. *Two Paintings by Abraham Solomon,* Bulletin 9-10 (V:1-2), National Gallery of Canada, 1967

Maidment, B. E. *Reading Popular Prints 1790-1870.* 2nd ed. Manchester: Manchester University Press, 2001.

Mallalieu, H. L. *The Dictionary of Watercolour Artists up to 1920.* 2 vols. Woodbridge: Antique Collectors Club, 2002.

Rees, G. *Early Railway Prints: A Social History of the Railways from 1825 to 1850.* Oxford: Phaidon Press Ltd, 1980.

Roscoe, T. *The London and Birmingham Railway with The Home and Country Scenes on Each Side of the Line.* London and Birmingham: c.1839.

Simmons, J. *The Victorian Railway.* London: Thames and Hudson, 1991.

Villar, D. *John Wilson Carmichael: 1799-1868.* Portsmouth: Carmichael and Sweet Ltd, 1995.
Wilkes, L. *John Dobson: Architect & Landscape Gardener.* London: Oriel Press, 1980.

Chapter Nine: Dr. Granville on the Medical Benefits of Railway Travelling...**pages 214-226**

Granville, A. B., (ed G. Martin). *Spas of England and Principal Bathing Places: Northern Spas.* Bath: Adams & Dart, 1971. Reprint of first edition, 1841.

Pictorial Sources

Clitheroe, G., ed. *Pickering: Images of England.* Stroud: Tempus Publishing Ltd, 1999.
Humble, A. F., ed. *Prints of Old Whitby.* Whitby: Whitby Literary and Philosophical Society, 1990.
Sythes, D.G. ed. *Whitby: The Second Selection.* Stroud: Tempus Publishing Ltd, 2005.
Waters, C. *Whitby: A Pictorial History.* Chichester: Phillimore & Co. Ltd, 1992.
Whitworth, A. *Whitby in Times Past.* Whitby: Culva House Publications, 2005.

Web Sites

www.genuki.org.uk
www.googlebooks.com
www.gutenberg.org/catalog
www.historicaldirectories.org
www.intute.ac.uk
www.measuringworth.com
www.nationalarchives.gov.uk
www.northyorks.gov.uk/libraries
www.oxforddnb.com
www.projects.ex.ac.uk/RDavies/arian/current/howmuch/html
www.victorianweb.org
www.whitbymuseum.org,uk

INDEX

Potter, G. W. J. 65,230

Quakers 10,26,30,49

Radclyffe family 166,201,202, 205,206
railway coaches 38,39,40,62-66, 72-73,87,91,140,141,156-159,189, 223,230
    carriages 8,20,24,25,52,62,64,69-73, 91,140,156-160,174,189,194,197, 212,213,216,218-225,229
Railway Mania 17,75,80,213,229
Rainhill Trials 40,41,68
Reform Bill 17,32,52,76,84
Richardson, T 30
Richardson, T. M. 170
Roget, J. L. 164,165,170,172,173
Royal Academy 166-169,173, 194,205,206,212,213
Royal Buckinghamshire Hussars, 204

Scarborough iii,iv,vii,5,8,10,11, 17-19,24,30,31,55,76-78,80,83, 85,134,143,174,176-178,189, 194,228-229
Scoresby, W Jr. 11,42,43,74
Sims, G 167-168
Smiles, S 41,49,68,192
Smithson, C 55
Society of British Artists 169,171,205
stage-coaches 8,32,73,219,223
Stephenson, G vi,2,18,26,28,31, 32,34,35-46,58-60,64,66-76, 85,87,89,137,163,165,169,175, 192,228

Stephenson, R vi,1,34,46-49, 54-56,60,64,66,77-81,84,163,167, 169,173,198

Stockton & Darlington Railway 2,17,26,27,30,35,38-41,44,47,48,82
Storey, T 35,58-60
surveying 23,35,47,57-60,67, 71,76,85,87,132-134,138, 161,163,181,206,223
Sussex, Duke of 73-74
Sutcliffe, F. M. 11
Swanwick, F 40,46,59-60, 66,71,76,137,158

The Times 17,82
Thompson, H. S. 81-82
Tomlinson, W. W. 230
Tories 30,77
Trench, Sir F. W. 31
Tunnel Inn 62,73,87,91,111-112, 114,138-139,141,158,182-184
turnpike 4,8,11,102,104,184,216

Victoria, Queen 72,74,204

wagon-way 26,35,38,58
Wardell, W 65-66
Weatherill, G iii,11,29,62,72-73, 85,164-165,170-171
Weatherill, R 29,43,62-63
West Cliff Development 7,11,77,80-82,98,197
whales and whaling vi,6,11,16, 29,42-43
Whigs 30
Whishaw, F 62,73
Whitby & Pickering Railway vi,vii,1,2,11-12,17,18,27,30-31,34, 39,49,50,55,57,60-62,64-65,67,71-74,76,77,82-85,87ff,157,165, 174ff,227-230

Whitby Literary and Philosophical Society vii,2,6,11-13,27,29, 34,40,56,71,74,76,84-85,230
Whitby Repository 3,4